The Lord GOD Hath Spoken

A Guide to Bibliology

Dr. Thomas M. Strouse

REVISED AND EXPANDED 2015, 2018, 2023

REPRINTED 2001

REVISED AND EXPANDED 1998

REPRINTED 2023

With Permission of Dr. Thomas Strouse by

The Old Paths Publications.com
www.theoldpathspublications.com
TOP@theoldpathspublications.com
ISBN 979-8-9877195-8-9

DEDICATION

B. MYRON CEDARHOLM

The one who first introduced me to the truth of
The superiority of the *Textus Receptus*.

ACKNOWLEDGEMENTS

I wish to express my appreciation to my pastor, Dr. Rod Bell, for allowing me to pursue this project. Much encouragement was offered by some of my pastor friends, but especially by Pastor Roger Luiken, for whom I am thankful. I must express gratitude to my computer experts, Mr. and Mrs. Jeff Feil and Mr. Randy Tichnell, who helped me with the technical wherewithal. Also, I want to thank Mr. David West for the advice in helping me put this little volume in print. Mr. Adrian Robbe has been a constant encouragement in helping to promote this endeavor. Moreover, I am indebted to the many friends and family members who have helped fund the publication of this book. Finally, I am thankful and appreciative for my wife Jan, the mother of our children—Brent, Aaron, Kristen, Kayla, Mark, Kerith, Joshua, Karis, Luke, Keren, Katie, Kiera, Ryan and Tyler—for her support and patience and love.

Dr. Thomas M. Strouse

TABLE OF CONTENTS

Chapters

Appendices

Book Reviews

PREFACE

The herdman of Tekoa queried, saying, *"The lion hath roared, who will not fear? The Lord GOD[1] hath spoken, who can but prophesy?"* (Amos 3:8). Amos prophesied! Amos prophesied even though he was a farmer and not a prophet from the liberal school of prophets in Bethel (Amos 7:14). God has preserved His spoken Word. Yet where are believers who will take up the challenge and believe and preach the Word like Amos of old? God's Words are under attack. Satan and his ministers have eviscerated the authority and message of the very Words of God. It is time for the Lord to raise up some preachers and believers like Amos who will stand for the Bible.

There are several factors which prompted me to undertake the project of writing this book. Let me list these factors and then respond to them. 1) Since the authority and message of the Bible is under constant attack, many men seem to have great reserve about entering the ministry of the Word. 2) It is a well worn statement that fundamentalists do not read books (certainly not footnotes in books) and that we do not write books. 3) Over the years some of my seminary and Bible college students have challenged me to put my course syllabi into book form for publishing. I would like to respond to these factors by producing a book which defends the authority and message of the Bible for both fundamental Baptist laymen and seminary students to comprehend and to utilize.

---

[1]The name for deity is literally *'adonay Jehovah* (אֲדֹנָי יְהוִֹה).

7

Another factor has prompted me to write. 4) Recently there has been a spate of books published which directly attack fundamentalism and the Bible. For instance, one states,

> *We maintain that, in general, the greater the degree to which fundamentalists unquestioningly accept the doctrine of Biblical inerrancy, the greater the risk to their fullest understanding and appreciation of the Bible. By treating the Bible as inerrant, fundamentalists may become increasingly unable to conceive how human limitations in wisdom and knowledge could have influenced the Bible.*[2]

Again, an Anglican bishop wants to rescue the Bible from "an anti-intellectual approach to Christianity on the part of literal-minded, conservative Christians."[3]

These factors then have prompted me to write a book which hopefully will be a guide into the discipline of Bibliology. This will be an attempt to present a fundamentalist, Baptist approach to the doctrine of Scripture. I will not attempt to interface with all the contemporary scholars who have written on Bibliology, hence limiting my use of footnotes. I will follow my Bibliology syllabus outline, from which I have taught many seminarians over the years, producing the following chapter divisions: Preface; Chapter One: Introduction; Chapter Two: Revelation; Chapter Three:

---

[2]R. L. Evans and I. M. Berent, *Fundamentalism: Hazards and Heartbreaks* (La Salle, IL: Open Court, 1988), p. xix.

[3]J. S. Spong, *Rescuing the Bible from Fundamentalism* (NY: HarperCollins Publ., 1991), p. 9.

Inspiration; Chapter Four: Inerrancy; Chapter Five: Canonicity; Chapter Six: Illumination; Chapter Seven: Interpretation; Chapter Eight: Perfections; Chapter Nine: Summary/Conclusion.

I will use the Authorized Version and *Textus Receptus* (Beza's 1598 edition) as the text for the study of Scripture. After all, the King James Version is the Bible of Fundamentalism. Even the liberal James Barr cogently and correctly states,

> *Until quite recently conservative evangelicals were extremely closely tied to the Authorized (King James) Version. The symbolic and practical importance of this tie with a particular and traditional English version is difficult to exaggerate...for the fundamentalist society as a whole the Authorized Version functioned as the direct and immediate expression or transcript of divine revelation.*[4]

It is my desire that the readers will be strengthened in their faith regarding the Bible. May the following Latin quote be the motto of the readers: *Scriptura sacra locuta, res decisa est.* "Holy Scripture has spoken, the issue is decided."

Dr. Thomas M. Strouse
Virginia Beach, VA
1992

---

[4]James Barr, *Fundamentalism* (Philadelphia: The Westminster Press, 1978), pp. 209-210.

NOTE TO REVISED EDITION

Two significant changes have occurred since I wrote the original manuscript in 1992 for *The Lord GOD Hath Spoken: A Guide to Bibliology*—one public and one personal. The conservative Christian public, including Neo-Evangelicals, Fundamentalists, and independent Baptists, had not dealt seriously with the doctrine of biblical preservation until a decade later. Second, the author made a personal decision to leave organized Fundamentalism in which he was saved, baptized, and taught.

The first change relates to the history of the doctrine of perfect word preservation in biblical churches. Since the general reception of the King James Version (KJV) as the English Bible in the middle of the seventeenth century, conservative Christians have considered it as the "authorized" version and final authority for doctrine and practice. Not until 1901 and the introduction of the American Standard Version (ASV) was there any serious alternative to the KJV. Nevertheless, the Lord's assemblies maintained that the original Scriptures were inspired and that the KJV was the translational equivalent in the English language. Questions concerning the preservation of Scripture were not germane even when the liberal Revised Standard Version (RSV) appeared in 1952. Conservative churches were content with the doctrine of the inspiration of the original Scriptures and with the accuracy of the KJV, and did not have a need to develop or defend the doctrine of the perfect words preservation.

However, in the 1970's two translations came on the scene and competed for conservative approval and acceptance.

The first printed was the Old and New Testaments of the New American Standard Version (NASV) in 1971. This translation became a favorite among Neo-Evangelicals and the Fundamentalist academic institution Bob Jones University. Following close behind on her heels was the NT of the New International Version (NIV) printed in 1973. This quickly became the queen of the Dynamic Equivalence (paraphrase) versions with increased popularity, temporarily superseding even the venerable King James Version (KJV). Now, Christians within conservative Christianity had choices about translations and needed to establish the "true" word of God translation. The KJV no longer "won" by default, but had serious competition forcing Fundamentalists and others to decide what was the "inspired," "preserved," word of God in the English language.

These developments brought several reactions within Fundamentalism, all of which focused initially on the doctrine of inspiration. 1) Bob Jones University maintained that inspiration dealt with the "originals" and that the KJV and NASV as translations were equally the word of God. 2) Pastor Peter Ruckman countered with the novel "inspired" KJV view, stating that the inspired KJV words (*sic*) were superior to the original Hebrew, Aramaic and Greek words, and consequently provided "advanced revelation." 3) Dr. Donald Waite argued that the manuscript evidence of the Textus Receptus supported the superiority of the KJV (while denying its "inspiration") as the word of God in the English language. None of these views dealt sufficiently with the doctrine of preservation, however. These three views impacted conservative Christianity in America and the western world, and through missionary outreach affected translation work worldwide.

The first book of its kind, Kent Brandenburg, ed. *Thou Shalt Keep Them: A Biblical Theology of the Perfect Preservation of Scripture* (El Sobrante, CA: Pillar & Ground Publ.), 2003, brought the many debates about what translation is inspired and where is the word of God, to a head.   The bibliological battle transferred from the doctrine of inspiration to the doctrine of preservation.   Certainly, the doctrine of inspiration has biblical support throughout (II Tim. 3:16 *et al*), but the doctrine of preservation is replete throughout the Bible, and largely ignored.   *Thou Shalt Keep Them* has forced serious Bible scholars to recognize, receive, and believe what the Scripture says not only about inspiration, but also about the Lord's promises of the perfect preservation of His words (Ps. 12:6-7; Mt. 24:35).

Since 1992 the second change was personal.   The writer has left organized "Fundamentalism" and rejects the use of "Fundamentalist" to portray an apt description of the Bible believer. "Fundamentalism" as a movement was American and Protestant, and fostered the notion that many teachings in Scripture are "non-essential."   Since "Fundamentalism" and "Fundamentalist" are unbiblical terms, it forces the question of appropriateness since historically and theologically so much unscriptural baggage is tied to the terms.   To change the meaning of either is akin to the practice of Neo-orthodoxy (new meanings for established words).   The writer has employed the terms "Fundamentalism" and "Fundamentalist" in the present essays either while he was in the movement or as he was coming out of the movement. The research for and arguments of the contents within this revised edition are appropriate bibliological challenges for those within conservative Christianity, whether Neo-evangelical, Fundamentalist, or independent Baptist. Nevertheless, the writer is simply a Bible believer.

Some of the apologetic defenses for the Hebrew Masoretic Text and the Greek Received Text[5] behind the King James Version received repetition to enable the serious student of Scripture to recognize the emphasis for and full explanation about them.   Also, I placed biblical emphasis on the exclusive role of the Lord's assemblies as the divinely-given institution to recognize, receive, protect, and propagate the preserved inspired words of Scripture (I Tim. 3:15).

Prayerfully, this revised edition of *The Lord GOD Hath Spoken* will help the present and future generations of seminarians, preachers, pastors, and church members to be edified in the Scriptures, which Scriptures teach the perfect preservation of the inspired words of our precious Saviour, the Lord Jesus Christ.

Dr. Thomas M. Strouse
2015

---

[5]Frederick H. A. Scrivener, *Scrivener's Annotated Greek New Testament: Being the Exact Greek Textus Receptus that Underlies the King James Bible.* Collingswood, NJ: Dean Burgon Society Press, 1999.

CHAPTER ONE

Introduction to Bibliology

The Definition of Bibliology

The term 'Bibliology' comes from two Greek words meaning the 'study' or 'doctrine' (λόγος [*logos*]) of 'Scripture' (βίβλος [*Biblos*]). Bibliology then is the study of the doctrine of Scripture. The following is the author's definition for Bibliology: "The doctrine which follows a Scripturally-based scheme or order of doctrinal development and which purports to incorporate into its system all the truth about the Judeo-Christian Scriptures."

The Importance of Bibliology

As Christology, or the doctrine about Christ, is central to Biblical studies, so Bibliology, or the doctrine of Scripture, is foundational to Biblical studies. If one does not have a solid foundation in Bibliology, then all of the other doctrines, such as Theology Proper, Soteriology, Ecclesiology and Eschatology will crumble.

Bibliology is important because the Bible says that it is important. The Bible declares that the Bible is God's pure word, *"Every word of God is pure: he is a shield unto them that put their trust in him"* (Prov. 30:5). Again, the Bible says that it is the Breath of God, *"All Scripture is given by inspiration of God, and is profitable..."* (II Tim. 3:16).

Bibliology is important because Jesus Christ says that it

is important. He says that the words of Scripture cannot be disregarded, *"and the Scripture cannot be broken"* (Jn. 10:35). He says that Scripture is the final authority for man, *"It is written...It is written again...It is written"* (Mt. 4:4, 7, 10). He says that the Scriptures testify of Himself, *"they are they which testify of me"* (Jn. 5:39). He says that the Scriptures are the basis for the final judgment of man, *"the word that I have spoken, the same shall judge him in the last day"* (Jn. 12:48). He says that the Scriptures show their fulfillment in Christ, *"that all things must be fulfilled, which were written in the law of Moses, and in the prophets, and in the psalms, concerning me"* (Lk. 24:44). He says that the Scriptures are an instrument of sanctification, *"Sanctify them through thy truth, thy word is truth"* (Jn. 17:17). He says that the Scriptures are important because they bring a blessing on those who hear and keep the Scriptures, *"Yea rather, blessed are they that hear the word of God, and keep it"* (Lk. 11:28). He says that the Scriptures will stand forever, *"But the word of the Lord endureth forever"* (I Pet. 1:25).

Bibliology is important because Baptists say that it is important. The New Hampshire Confession of 1833 states,

We believe that the Holy Bible was written by men divinely inspired, and is a perfect treasure of heavenly instruction; that it has God for its author, salvation for its end, and truth, without any mixture of error, for its matter; that it reveals the principles by which God will judge us; and therefore is, and shall remain to the end of the world, the true centre of Christian union, and the supreme standard by which all human conduct, creeds, and opinions should be tried.[6]

The Baptist theologian J. B. Jeter says,

> *Let us, then, reverently receive the Scriptures as an authentic and perfect revelation from God, interpret them by the laws which common sense and careful study supply, and live according to their directions, and we shall not fail to secure a blessed immortality.*[7]

Bibliology is important because famous theological leaders say it is important. John Calvin observes,

> *If true religion is to beam upon us, our principle must be, that it is necessary to begin with heavenly teaching, and that it is impossible for any man to obtain even the minutest portion of right and sound doctrine without being a disciple of Scripture.*[8]

Martin Luther declares,

> *Unless I am convicted by Scripture and plain reason—I do not accept the authority of popes and*

---

[6] W. L. Lumpkin, *Baptist Confessions of Faith* (Valley Forge: Judson Press, 1969), pp. 361-362.

[7] C. A. Jenkens, *Baptist Doctrines* (Watertown, WI: Baptist Heritage Press, 1989 reprint), p. 69.

[8] John Calvin, *Institutes of the Christian Religion*, Vol. I, Beveridge translation (Grand Rapids: Wm. B. Eerdmans Publ. Co., 1975), p. 66.

councils, for they have contradicted each other—my conscience is captive to the Word of God. I cannot and I will not recant anything, for to go against conscience is neither right nor safe. God help me. Amen. Here I stand, I cannot do otherwise.[9]

The study of Scripture is important because of what it says about itself, because of what Christ says about it and because of what Baptists and others say about it. Bibliology is important because it is the study of what God has revealed about Himself, about man and about salvation.

The Names and Symbols for the Bible

Names

The Bible gives itself some names and symbols so that man will recognize its authority and character. Of the several names the Bible gives itself, the first is 'Bible.' βίβλος is the word behind 'book' in Mt. 1:1, *"The book of the generation of Jesus Christ..."* In Lk. 4:17, βίβλος is the book of Isaiah, *"And there was delivered unto him the book of the prophet Esaias..."* The Bible refers to itself as the New Testament (NT) and the Old Testament (OT) in II Cor. 3:6 and 14, and Heb. 9:15. The Bible refers to itself as the Law and Prophets, two of the three divisions of the OT. In Mt. 5:17, Christ says *"Think not that I am come to destroy the law, or the prophets: I am not come to destroy but to fulfill."* Again, He states,

---

[9]Roland Bainton, *Here I Stand* (New York: Abingdon Press, 1950), p. 185.

"that all things must be fulfilled, which were written in the law of Moses, and in the prophets, and in the psalms, concerning me" (Lk. 24:44; cf. Mt. 12:5; 22:40).

The Bible calls itself the Scripture or Scriptures in numerous places. For instance, Christ cites the OT passage of Psm. 118:22-23 in Mk. 12:10, saying, *"And have ye not read this Scripture; The stone which the builders rejected is become the head of the corner: this was the Lord's doing, and it is marvellous in our eyes?"* In I Tim. 3:16, Paul refers to all the Bible as a whole, stating *"All Scripture is given by inspiration of God..."* Peter places Paul's Epistle to the Jews (Hebrews) on the same plane as *"the other Scriptures"* (II Pet. 3:16). Several other passages which refer to the Scriptures are Mt. 22:29, Lk. 4:21, Jn. 5:39, and 7:38. Four times the Bible refers to itself as *"the oracles"* (τὰ λόγια) of God. For instance, Paul acknowledges that the Jews had the Word of God by stating *"Much every way: chiefly, because that unto them were committed the oracles of God"* (Rom. 3:2; cf. Acts 7:38, Heb. 5:12, I Pet. 4:11).

The Bible also calls itself the Word of God. In Mk. 7:13 Christ differentiates between man's tradition and God's Word saying, *"Making the word of God of none effect through your tradition."* Paul demands the necessity of hearing God's Word for salvation, stating *"So then faith cometh by hearing, and hearing by the word of God"* (Rom. 10:17). Again, in Hebrews 4:12, the author gives qualities about the Bible, stating *"For the word of God is quick, and powerful, and sharper..."* (cf. I Thes. 2:13).

The Bible then refers to itself as the Bible, the Old and New Testament, the Law and the Prophets, the Scripture, the

Oracles of God, and the Word of God. These names teach the divine authority and specific verbal expression (in words) of the Bible.

Symbols

The Bible utilizes a multifaceted array of symbols for itself. The Lord gives these symbols to help show the character and nature of the Bible.

The Bible uses the symbol of the seed to demonstrate the nature of life-giving and power for growth that the Bible has. Peter recognizes this life-giving nature of the Bible when he states *"Being born again, not of corruptible seed, but of incorruptible, by the word of God, which liveth and abideth for ever"* (I Pet. 1:23; cf. also Mt. 13:1 ff.). The Bible uses the symbol of the Mirror to designate its reflective nature. James confirms this symbol by stating, *"For if any be a hearer of the word, and not a doer, he is like unto a man beholding his natural face in a glass* (mirror)*"* (Jam. 1:23).[10]

Another symbol for the Bible is Water. Water cleanses and refreshes, as does the Bible. Paul states in Eph. 5:25-27, *"Husbands, love your wives, even as Christ also loved the church, and gave himself for it; that he might sanctify and cleanse it with the washing of water by the word..."* The Bible is likened to a Lamp in several places. For instance, in Psm. 119:105, the Psalmist affirms that *"Thy word is a lamp unto my feet, and a light unto my path"* and *"For the commandment is a lamp; and the law is light; and reproofs of instruction are the way of life"* (Prov. 6:23).

---

[10]This symbol of the mirror is used for the developing canon of Scripture in I Cor. 13:8.

The Sword is a symbol for the Bible. As an offensive piece of Roman armor, a sword cuts and pierces its object of attack. Likewise, the Bible cuts and pierces the heart of man, as Heb. 4:12 states, *"For the word of God is quick, and powerful, and sharper than any two-edge sword, piercing even to the dividing asunder of soul and spirit, and of the joints and marrow, and is a discerner of the thoughts and intents of the heart."* Again, Paul commands, *"And take the helmet of salvation, and the sword of the Spirit, which is the word of God"* (Eph. 6:17). Incidentally, the word for *'word'* is ῥῆμα ([*rhema*), which refers to the spoken word of Scripture, such as Christ used when He was tempted (Mt. 4, 7, 10). For the believer, the spoken or memorized portion of Scripture is his *'sword.'*

The Bible is likened unto several foods. One such food is Honey. Psm. 19:10 states, *"More to be desired are they than gold, yea, than much fine gold: sweeter also than honey and the honeycomb."* Another food symbolizing the Bible is Milk. Peter utilizes this symbol averring, *"As newborn babes, desire the sincere milk of the word, that ye may grow thereby"* (I Pet. 2:2). Meat is another symbol for the Bible. Paul admonishes the Corinthians, stating, *"And I, brethren, could not speak unto you as unto spiritual, but as unto carnal, even as unto babes in Christ. I have fed you with milk and not with meat..."* (I Cor. 3:1-2; cf. Heb. 5:12-14). The Bible is symbolized by both Fire and a Hammer. The Prophet Jeremiah declares, *"Is not my word like as a fire? Saith the Lord; and like a hammer that breaketh the rock in pieces?"* (Jer. 23:29). These two symbols stress the purification and edification (building) natures of the Bible, respectively.

The names for the Bible help the reader to understand the authority and message of the Scriptures as the symbols help the reader to understand the character and nature of the Word of God.

The Structure of the Bible

The Old Testament

The Old Testament is comprised of three major parts, the Law (תּוֹרָה [*Torah*]), the Prophets (נְבִיאִים [*Neviy'iym*]) and the Writings (כְּתֻבִים [*Kethuviym*]). These three divisions are known as the *Tanak* (*Tenach*), an acrostic based on the first letters of these three divisions. Five books are listed in the תּוֹרָה. These are Genesis, Exodus, Leviticus, Numbers, and Deuteronomy. The נביאים have these nineteen books: Joshua, Judges, Samuel, Kings, Isaiah, Jeremiah, Ezekiel, Hosea, Joel, Amos, Obadiah, Jonah, Micah, Nahum, Habakkuk, Zephaniah, Haggai, Zechariah, and Malachi. The כתבים contain these twelve: Psalms, Proverbs, Job, Canticles, Ruth, Lamentations, Ecclesiastes, Esther, Daniel, Ezra, Nehemiah, and Chronicles. Of course, these 36 books are the 39 books of the Christian OT because Samuel, Kings, and Chronicles are not divided in the *Tanak.*

The New Testament

The New Testament has a three-fold division as well as the OT. The NT divides in the Historical, the Epistolary, and the Prophetical. The Historical division contains the Four

Gospels (Matthew, Mark, Luke and John) and Acts. The Epistolary contain the Epistles of Paul, Peter, John, James and Jude or 21 Epistles. The Book of Revelation is in the Prophetical division.

Together the Bible contains 39 OT books and 27 NT books for a total of 66 books. These numerous books written by numerous and varied human authors over about 1600 years are God's Word inscripturated. The Bible contains the Lord's total and final revelation for mankind. From this varied presentation of God's revelation man may receive a glimpse of the greatness of God.

The Language of the Bible

The Lord employed three human languages, of which He is the author (Gen. 11), to inscripturate His revelation. He used Hebrew and Aramaic for the OT and Greek for the NT.

The Language of the OT

God used the pre-Flood language of Shem (Semitic) for the OT. Hebrew and its cognate Aramaic were the languages through which Jehovah wanted His truth known to the world. That Hebrew was the language of the Garden of Eden until the Flood is evident because of its proper nouns and puns (i.e., *"Eve,"* Gen. 3:20 with 3:15), which would be meaningless with some other language. The Lord used Semitic prophets to write to Semitic people about the Semitic nation's relationship with the Semitic God, using the Semitic language.

Aramaic was the language of the Syrians and later the native language of Jesus of Nazareth. It is found in all three divisions of the OT, starting with Gen. 31:47 (תּוֹרָה), including Jer. 10:11 (נְבִיאִים) and Ezr. 4:7-6:1, 7:12-26, and Dan. 2:4-7:28 (כְּתֻבִים).

Hebrew is the language of the majority of the OT. Two characteristics of Hebrew are its tri-consonantal roots for word frames and its perfect (completed action) and imperfect (uncompleted action) verbs. It is alive with numerous figures of speech such as the simile, metaphor, paranomasia, irony, etc. The OT writers utilized anthropomorphic expressions to describe inanimate objects as well as to describe Jehovah. It is a personal language suitable for its many biographies. The verbs and nouns have broad meanings which allow some imagination for the reader. Its poetic sections present the finest poetic literature in the world. The LORD inspired and preserved the consonants and vowels, the smallest jots and tittles (Mt. 5:18; Lk. 16:17) to form inspired words (Ex. 34:27; Jer. 36:2), as well as preserving the inspired Hebrew accents for musical notation, enabling saints to sing the OT (Dt. 31:19, 22, 30). The Author of Scripture used this heavenly language of Hebrew (Acts 26:14) to sing creation into existence (Gen. 1:3), being materialized from the energized vibrations of His words (Heb. 11:3).

The Language of the NT

The Lord used the common language of the first century Greco-Roman world, κοινός (*koinos* 'common') Greek,[11] to inscripturate the final revelation about Himself.

---

[11]Greek and all other languages are confounded Hebrew (Gen. 11:1-9).

Greek was the commercial language of the Mediterranean world, and in many cases a secondary language for a bi-lingual generation. Although many Semitisms are translated in the Greek NT, it is a very precise language conducive for theological expression. Dana describes the value of the Greek language for an instrument to reveal divine truth. He comments,

> *Koine Greek is without doubt the most richly and accurately expressive language which human history has known. Its possibilities of subtle distinction in the expression of thought are vast, and the writers of the New Testament were remarkably adept at using the finer capacities of the language. It is certainly no exaggeration to maintain that the Greek New Testament is the most richly expressive text in all literature, and this fact is in no small measure due to the character of the language in which it is written.*[12]

Just as Hebrew and Aramaic were conducive to biographical narrative for Jewish people, so Greek was conducive to theological expression for cosmopolitan people. Greek employs the definite article, exact prepositions, and a precise case system for nouns to express precisely and accurately revelation about God. God had His purposes to utilize the 'broad' languages of Hebrew and Aramaic to a specific people (Jews) and the 'precise' language of Greek to a general people (the world of Gentiles) so that He could

---

[12] H. E. Dana, *The New Testament World* (Nashville: Broadman Press, 1937), p. 180.

effectively transmit all the truth He wanted known.

The Text and Translation of the Bible

When dealing with the Bible, the Bible student needs to know about not only the translation of the Bible, but also its underlying texts. The Hebrew text of the OT of the KJV is the Masoretic Text (MT) and the Greek text of the NT of the KJV is the Received Text (TR).

The Text of the KJV

The Masoretic Text of the OT derives its name from the Masoretic Scribes (AD 6-10th centuries) who perpetuated vowel pointings in the tri-consonantal *apographa*.[13] Their efforts helped standardize the OT Hebrew text from which the ancient, medieval, and Reformation versions were translated. Wurthwein declares,

> *The greatest importance for the history of the text, however, was their [Masoretes] contribution to the universal acceptance of an authoritative, established text which must have appeared to be an innovation to many at the time despite its continuity with an earlier form of the text.*[14]

---

[13]*Apographa* is the Greek word meaning "from the Scripture," and it is used to refer to the copies of Scripture. *Autographa* means "Scripture itself" and refers to the original autographs.

[14]E. Wurthwein, *The Text of the Old Testament* (Grand Rapids: Wm. B. Eerdmans Publ. Co., 1981), p. 20.

That the Masoretic Text of the Hebrew OT is the standard, received and traditional text of the OT should be apparent. It has been the basis for the OT through the centuries. Edward Hills carefully and correctly delineates the history of the preservation of the OT text. He observes,

> *By Ezra and his successors, under the guidance of the Holy Spirit, all the OT books were gathered together into one OT canon, and their texts were purged of errors and preserved until the days of our Lord's earthly ministry...These Masoretes took extraordinary pains to transmit without error the OT text which they had received from their predecessors...Thus it was that Hebrew OT text, divinely inspired and providentially preserved, was restored to the Church [sic], to the circle of true believers.*[15]

The Received Text of the Greek NT derives its name from the 1633 Greek edition of the Elziver brothers. It was declared the *textum...nunc ab omnibus receptum,* "the text now received by all." It is known as the *Textus Receptus* (TR) and it is in contrast with the Critical Text (CT) of liberalism and the Majority Text (MajT) of neo-evangelicalism. Both the CT and MajT are inundated with problems. Although both are belabored with methodological problems, the CT is laden with a major philosophical difficulty; its Greek text records at least three factual errors which in turn undermines the doctrine of

---

[15]E. F. Hills, *The King James Version Defended!* (Des Moines: The Christian Research Press, 1973), p. 93.

inerrancy.

The first error is a historical error. In Mt. 1:7, 10, the CT opts for an erroneous reading which substitutes for the two kings of Asa and Amon in Christ's kingly lineage the psalmist Asaph and the prophet Amos. Metzger speaks for the United Bible Societies' Greek New Testament (UBSGNT) committee, initially emphasizing their apostasy. He unashamedly declares,

> *Since, however, the evangelist may have derived material for the genealogy, not from the Old Testament directly, but from subsequent genealogical lists, in which the erroneous spelling occurred, the Committee saw no reason to adopt what appears to be a scribal emendation [Asa and Amon].*[16]

The second error is a scientific error. In Lk. 23:45, the CT uses the variant ἐκλιπόντος (*eklipontos*) "was eclipsed," instead of the TR reading ἐσκοτίσθη (*eskotisthe*) *"was darkened."* It would have been a scientific impossibility for the sun to have been eclipsed during the Passover since the moon was full.

The third error contradicts Christ. In Jn. 7:8, the Lord Jesus states that He is not going to the feast and then He goes to the feast. The CT uses the negative οὐκ (*ouk*) "not," instead of the TR reading οὔπω (*oupo*) *"not yet."* Jesus obviously was stating that He was "not yet" going to the feast.

---

[16]B. M. Metzger, *A Textual Commentary on the Greek New Testament* (London: United Bible Societies, 1975), p. 1.

These three errors, a historical error, a scientific error and a Christ-contradicting error, demonstrate that the textual critics of this Greek edition have a very low view of inspiration and inerrancy, and they also prove that they cannot be trusted with God's inerrant Word.

On the positive side, the TR is superior textually to the CT and MajT. It is the text of the Greek-speaking Byzantine world. This Byzantine text was the basis for Erasmus' 1516 Greek edition as he attempted to give the common man a Greek edition of the Word of God. Scores of Greek manuscripts flooded Europe when the Moslems invaded Constantinople in 1453. Erasmus, the textual critic *par excellence*, used representatives from these Byzantine manuscripts to form his edition. Of the 5500 plus Greek manuscripts for the NT, over ninety percent of them are in consentient agreement with each other. It is from these 90% or so manuscripts that textual scholars in the "TR Tradition" (Byzantine Text) based their TR editions. The remaining manuscripts represent the minority text of the CT and not only disagree with the 90% of manuscripts, but they also disagree with one another quite frequently.

The TR is superior historically to the CT and MajT. The TR represents the text of the ancient Greek-speaking world. It circulated in the geographical areas to which and from where the *autographa* were written. The TR is represented by the 2nd century Syriac Peshitta, in the 3rd century patristics, by the Byzantine Text (4th to 16th centuries), by the Reformers and in the AV. The TR was the standard, accepted, received and traditional text until the arrival of Higher Criticism (17th-19th centuries). The CT is the direct, resultant text of Higher Criticism and the MajT is the indirect, resultant text of it. Higher Criticism's approach to the Bible was evolutionary. Rationalistic scholars applied the evolutionary mindset to the transmission of the text, teaching that the shorter CT evolved into the longer, more complete Byzantine Text. One should observe this evolutionary philosophy in statements such as Gordon Fee's,

> *Most of the readings peculiar to this text [Byzantine] are generally recognized to be of a secondary nature. A great number of them smooth out grammar; remove ambiguity in word order; add nouns, pronouns, and prepositional phrases; and harmonize one passage with another. Its many conflate readings...also reflect this secondary process.*[17]

The TR is superior Christologically to the CT and MajT. Gnostic heretics tampered with many Christological passages during the first three centuries. The Gnostics denied the incarnation of God and/or denied that Jesus was the Christ. These heresies are known historically and theologically as *Docetism* and *Adoptionism*, respectively. The Apostle John refuted both of these ancient heresies. In I Jn. 4:3, John warns *"And every spirit that confesseth not that Jesus Christ is come in the flesh is not of God,"* refuting Docetism. Again, he warns *"Who is a liar but he that denieth that Jesus is the Christ?"* refuting Adoptionism. Hence, many of the variant

---

[17] R. K. Harrison, editor, *Biblical Criticism: Historical, Literary and Textual* (Grand Rapids: Zondervan Publ. House, 1979), p. 137.

readings represented by the CT attempt to deny the doctrines of the incarnation of God and the identification of Jesus as the Christ. For instance, the KJV retains the truth of the incarnation in I Tim. 3:16 and I Jn. 4:3, whereas the CT removes this truth.

Also, the KJV retains the truth of the incarnation and doctrine of the Trinity in I Jn. 5:7-8, which states *"in heaven, the Father, the Word, and the Holy Ghost: and these three are one. And there are three that bear witness in earth."* The CT and the MajT remove this passage from Scripture, disregarding several facts. 1) If this passage is retained, there is no grammatical difficulty; if it is removed, then John is guilty of a major grammatical problem. 2) Several ancient church fathers refer to this passage, especially Cyprian, who obviously had the passage before his own eyes. 3) The Holy Spirit has preserved it in Christendom's two best known versions, the Vulgate and the AV, in spite of continuing effort by liberal and heretical scholarship to remove it.

Adoptionism was the teaching that Jesus was not the Christ. This heresy runs rampant throughout the CT as indicated by the constant and deliberate removal of the full title of the Lord Jesus Christ. The Gnostics did not want to acknowledge that Jesus of Nazareth was the Lord God or the Christ. This denial is expected in the Gnostic-bred variants which are manifested in the CT and its subsequent modern versions. For instance, Fowler records some 221 times the CT omits the full title of the Lord Jesus Christ, along with some 213 times of omission by the RSV and some 210 times of omission by the NASV.[18]

The student of the Bible must recognize that the Bible's underlying texts are extremely important. For those who can use the original languages of the Bible, the Hebrew and Greek texts become the final authority in interpretation and in practice. It behooves the student, the pastor and the theologian to know what the original text *is* (TR or CT or MajT) before attempting to know what it *says*. The student of the Word should use the Masoretic Text of the Hebrew OT because it is the standardized and traditional text of the OT, and the student should use the Received Text of the Greek NT because it is superior to the CT and MajT textually, historically, and Christologically.

The Translation of the Bible

Not only is the text of the Bible important, but so is the translation of the Bible. Since the Masoretic and Received Texts are superior, it follows that their resultant translation is superior, the KJV.

The Importance of the KJV

The KJV has been the Bible for English-speaking Christendom for most of the 380 years of its existence. The KJV along with Shakespeare's works have established and standardized the English language. Expressions from the AV permeate the English language. Fundamentalists have identified with the KJV because of its textual and theological

---

[18]E. W. Fowler, *Evaluating Versions of the New Testament* (Watertown, WI: Maranatha Baptist Press, 1981), p. 51.

integrity, because of its beauty and strength of expression, and because of its protection from liberalism. Barr makes an interesting observation, stating,

> *The virtual use of only one English version, and it one originating within very traditional early 17th century Christianity, thus indirectly but very powerfully supported the alienation of the fundamentalist public from, and its opposition to, the positions, interests and methods from which all biblical criticism grew and on which it depended.*[19]

Again, a conservative commentator states the reason for his employment of the KJV, saying he uses "the Authorized Version of the Bible (KJV) since this is still regarded as the text of fundamentalism." [20] The KJV is the Bible of fundamentalism and it seems apparent then, that fundamentalists should use the KJV.

The Value of the KJV as a Translation

Two criteria arise with regard to the value of a translation of the Bible. 1) How reliable are its original language texts? 2) How reliable is it as an accurate translation? The first criterion is established by the KJV because it is based on the Hebrew and Greek texts closest to the *autographa*. The second criterion is established as well, because the KJV is a word for word, "Static Equivalency"

---

[19] J. Barr, *Fundamentalism*, p. 211.

[20] R. G. Gromacki, *New Testament Survey* (Grand Rapids: Baker Book House, 1974), p. xii.

translation. In other words, it translates the original words with the corresponding English words, as well as translating the cultural backdrop of the Greco-Roman world. It is *not* an example of "Dynamic Equivalency," as are many of the modern versions (i.e., NIV).

Dynamic Equivalency is the theory that the translator must consider not only the difference between the language of the prophets and their modern readers, but also the difference in the conditioning of the cultural patterns of the two periods. This modern translation theory, originated and propagated by the liberal Eugene Nida, attempts to re-phrase the Bible in the culture of the receiving audience, instead of retaining the Greco-Roman culture. The TEV (Today's English Version) is the classic example of the Dynamic Equivalency theory in English. But any attempt to eliminate the religious, political, geographical, and cultural backdrop of the Bible for translation purposes, effectively changes the divine message. For instance, Cloud records an example of this folly,

> *The Apostle John said, "Behold the Lamb of God, which taketh away the sin of the world." Charles Kraft and other anthropologists tell us that if you go into a culture where lamb is vulgar and the pig is sacred, you cannot say, "Behold the Lamb of God, which taketh away the sin of the world" because that would be invoking a wrong meaning to the people. So, Jesus becomes "Behold the Pig of God, which taketh away the sin of the world."[21]*

---

[21]D. W. Cloud, *Dynamic Equivalency: Death Knell of Pure Scripture* (Oak Harbor, WA: Way of Life Literature, 1990), p. 13.

There are several major problems with the theory of Dynamic Equivalency. 1) Dynamic Equivalency denies a Biblical view of inspiration. 2) Dynamic Equivalency confuses man's spiritual blindness with cultural ignorance. 3) Dynamic Equivalency undermines the role of the pastor and the local church to apply the Bible to the congregation. 4) Dynamic Equivalency fails to communicate eternal truth.

The KJV is an excellent translation based on reliable OT and NT texts. In contrast, modern versions fall short of the two criteria for an excellent translation because they are based on the inferior CT (RSV, ASV, NASV, NIV, NEB, etc.) or because they follow the theory of Dynamic Equivalency (TEV and many modern missionary translations).

The KJV as the Word of God

The KJV is the Word of God in the English language. It has no errors in it because it carefully reflects the original language texts closest to the autographa. The AV, like all translations, has 'language limitations,' but these are *not* errors. Language Limitations occur when the nuances of the original word do not correspond exactly with the nuances of the translated word. Several examples of Language Limitations in the KJV are the words "love," "know," "baptism," and "church."[22] Nevertheless, the KJV is the Word of God, the Breath of God, the Bible, in the English language.

Fundamental Baptist missionaries should be familiar with not only Cloud's book but also with J. Van Bruggen's *The Future of the Bible* (NY: Thomas Nelson Inc., Publ., 1978), pp. 67-96.

[22]The *lack of corresponding nuances* or shades of meaning, or the *lack of precision* in translated words do not constitute errors.

Consequently, since the AV is the Word of God in English, and since its Hebrew MT and its Greek TR are the preserved inspired words of the *autographa*, believers should use the KJV. It is the author's opinion that the AV should be used for personal devotions and for Bible memorization. After all, if the believer attempts to re-memorize Scripture according to the modern versions' rendering, the believer would merely be memorizing the concept of the passage, thus encouraging the fallacious theory of 'conceptual inspiration,' or that only the concepts of Scripture are inspired and not the very words. It is the author's opinion that believers should use the AV in public worship to avoid confusion and disharmony. It is the author's studied opinion that the Masoretic Text, the Received Text and the AV should be used in all missionary translation endeavors.

Summary

The doctrine of Scripture, or Bibliology, is important because it is the source for all other theology. The 66 books of the Masoretic Text of the OT and the Received Text of the NT as represented in the KJV are God's divine revelation about Himself for mankind. It behooves the fundamentalist Christian, and the fundamentalist Baptist, to recognize that the AV is the Word of God in the English language, and to believe it and to practice it.

CHAPTER TWO

Revelation of Scripture

Introduction to Divine Revelation

Man's finiteness causes a conundrum for him. How can a finite being know about an infinite Being? How can man know about his Creator, his creation,[23] his destiny and his redemption? Obviously, man needs divine revelation from the infinite God of the heavens and earth to know the essential truths of the creation. The Lord has provided a means by which He may be known by man. He has provided man with both General (Universal, Natural) Revelation and with Special (Particular, Supernatural) Revelation.

---

[23]In the coeval embroglio of creation versus evolution, some deny the scientific accuracy in the revelation of the creation passages of Gen. 1-3. Pinnock's inane comment reflects this denial of accurate revelation. He states, "The fact that God made the sun, moon, and stars on the fourth day, not on the first, ought to tell us that this is not a scientific statement (Gen. 1:14-19). This one detail in the narrative suggests that concordism is not going to work well and that the agenda of the writer must have been something other than one of describing actual physical processes." Clark Pinnock, "The Evangelical Struggle to Understand the Creation Texts," *The Best in Theology*, Vol. Four, ed. J. I. Packer (Carol Stream, IL: Christianity Today, Inc., 1990), p. 43.

General Revelation

The Definition of General Revelation

The definition of General Revelation may be "God's communication to all mankind at all times in all places." It is His revelation which He gives to all men. It is general in the sense that it is available to all mankind.

The Modes of General Revelation

The LORD has several modes for General Revelation. These modes are the Course of History, the Creation from God, and the Conscience of Man.

The Course of History demonstrates certain workings or trends in God's revelation. For instance, the history of the Nation of Israel shows God's hand on this small but prosperous group of people. Although this nation has been persecuted through the ages, its importance and significance countenances the blessing of God. Passages such as Gen. 12:1 ff. and Rom. 11:25-26 bear out the fact that God is working in and through the Jewish people in history.

The Creation of God shows that the Lord has revealed knowledge about Himself in the physical heavens and earth. Certain Scriptures teach this truth which is corroborated in nature. For instance, Psm. 19:1-3 teaches that creation gives an ongoing testimony of God's glory. Creation cries out day and night to all people of all languages about the Glory of God. In Rom. 1:20, Paul states, *"For the invisible things of him from the creation of the world are clearly seen, being understood by the things that are made, even his eternal power and Godhead; so that they are without excuse."* Creation demonstrates

God's eternal power to mankind. All one needs to do is observe the innumerable stars at night or the tremendous energy of the sun at day to recognize God's eternal power. Also, creation depicts that the One behind the cosmos is a personal deity (Godhead).[24] Pagan man may understand from nature then, that God is both powerful and personal.

Another verse which teaches that the Lord has revealed Himself through creation is Acts 14:17, which states *"Nevertheless he left not himself without witness, in that he did good, and gave us rain from heaven, and fruitful seasons, filling our hearts with food and gladness."* Creation witnesses to the character of God that He is good because of the benevolent physical blessings He bestows on all men. Then, in Acts 17:22 ff., Scripture teaches that creation gives common knowledge about God to the pagans, which truth is also taught in Special Revelation, the Word of God. For instance, the Greek philosophers knew that the creator was a life-giving spirit, according to Acts 17:24 and 25.

The Conscience of Man testifies to all men about the moral and ethical codes of God. All men have a conscience, the Greek word συνείδησις meaning literally "co-knowledge."[25] God has placed the conscience in man so

---

[24]θειότης (*theiotes*) is found only in Rom. 1:20 in the NT and it refers to the personal divinity of a god or king in secular literature. Paul's point is that God's personal divinity may be perceived in nature. *Vide* H. Kleinknecht, "Theos," *Theological Dictionary of the New Testament*, eds. G. Kittle and G. Friedrich (Grand Rapids: Wm. B. Eerdmans Publ. Co., 1985), p. 331.

[25]Conscience is the Latin translation of the Greek συνείδησις (*suneidesis*). All men have this co-knowledge of God's ethical

that he basically will know what is right and wrong. Rom. 2:15 says, *"Which shew the work of the law written in their hearts, their conscience also bearing witness..."* The Gentiles, as well as the Jews, have the impress of the Law upon their hearts. The moral code of the Mosaic Law is etched upon the heart of every man. Just as the Mosaic Law convicted the Jews of sin and pointed to Christ, so the conscience of man convicts of a falling short of God's glory and shows the need to look to the God of Creation. The conscience is probably alluded to in Jn. 1:9, which states that Christ lights everyman who enters the world.

The Lord God has given man creation as a testimony of external truth about the Person and Work of God. He has given man conscience as a testimony of internal truth about the ethical standards of the God of Creation. Through the Creation from God and the Conscience of Man, mankind may know somewhat about the LORD's person and requirements. Through the Course of History, mankind may know somewhat of the trends of God's working. The Lord has given limited revelation about Himself through General Revelation. Is this sufficient revelation for man to be redeemed?

The Efficacy of General Revelation

The Lord has given knowledge about Himself to all men through the modes of the Course of History, the Creation from God, and the Conscience of Man. Man, therefore, knows that God is interested in the affairs of man and has preserved the nation of Israel from the revelation taught in the

---

system, even though the conscience may be seared (I Tim. 4:2) or defiled (Tit. 1:15).

Course of History. Man knows that an eternal, personal deity exists by the revelation taught in the Creation of God. Man knows that he falls short of God's ethical standard taught in the Conscience of Man. Is this sufficient revelation for man to be redeemed? Can man act solely upon the knowledge of God from general revelation and be saved?

The Apostle Paul answers the question in the **negative**. Paul clearly states that no pagan man of the first century sought after God; *"There is none that understandeth, there is none that seeketh after God"* (Rom. 3:11). Paul emphasizes that all the pagans of the first century *"have sinned, and come short of the glory of God"* (Rom. 3:23). Paul affirms that all men must have the knowledge of the Gospel of Christ found in Special Revelation (the Scripture) to be saved. He states,

> *For whosoever shall call upon the name of the Lord shall be saved. How then shall they call on him in whom they have not believed? and how shall they believe in him of whom they have not heard? and how shall they hear without a preacher? And how shall they preach, except they be sent... So then faith cometh by hearing and hearing by the word of God* (Rom. 10:13-17).

Furthermore, Paul adds that the revelation from the Creation of God (Rom. 1:20), from the Conscience of Man (Rom. 2:15), and even from the Commandments of Moses (Gal. 3:11), merely condemn man and in no way saves him. As far as Paul is concerned, the efficacy of general revelation is sufficient to give knowledge about God but it is not sufficient to give redemption for man. The heathen are condemned and lost and hell-bound without the Special Revelation of the saving work of Jesus Christ.[26]

This all leads to the essence of Paul's heartbeat—*missions*. If pagan man needs special revelation to be saved, how will he receive it? Paul answers by stating *"How beautiful are the feet of them that preach the gospel of peace and bring glad tidings of good things!"* (Rom. 10:15).

The fact that Paul states man is without excuse (Rom. 1:20 and 2:1) indicates that God holds man responsible for general revelation. As previously mentioned, the pagan is responsible to God for general revelation (Rom. 1 and 2). The pagan is responsible as well for special revelation. John states,

> *He that believeth on him is not condemned: but he that believeth not is condemned already, because he hath not believed in the name of the only begotten Son of God. And this is the condemnation, that light is come into the world, and men loved darkness rather than light, because their deeds were evil* (Jn. 3:18-19).

---

[26]Paul's position on the fate of the heathen is in contrast with liberals such as Hunter, who fallaciously states "In two passages Peter hints that the scope of redemption is not limited to this life [I Pet. 3:18 ff. and 4:6]...Whatever we make of these dark passages, they embody a conviction, which we may well share, that, wherever men are, Christ has power to save." A. M. Hunter, *Introducing New Testament Theology* (Philadelphia: The Westminster Press, 1957), p. 116.

The Christian as well is responsible to God to make available to pagans the special revelation of the Gospel of Christ in missionary work.

Special Revelation

The Definition of Special Revelation

The definition of Special Revelation may be "God's manifestation of knowledge about Himself to specific men at specific times enabling men to enter into a specific, redemptive relationship with God through Jesus Christ."

The Modes of Special Revelation

There are several modes through which the Lord has given man special revelation about Himself. He has revealed Himself through Historical Events, through Communication from God, through Christophanies, through the Incarnation of Christ, and through the Scripture.

The Historical Events recorded in Scripture are revelation about God. For instance, the creation of the heavens and earth revealed God's mighty acts, according to Psalm 136:4-9. The psalmist invokes thanksgiving to the Lord for making the heavens, the earth and the light-bearers (sun and moon) which display God's mercy. The Exodus from Egypt revealed Jehovah's righteous acts, according to Micah 6:4-5; *"For I brought thee up out of the land of Egypt, and redeemed thee out of the house of servants...that ye may know the righteousness of the Lord."* The Conquest of Canaan revealed the Lord's omnipotence. Rahab recognized Jehovah's power, stating *"I know that the Lord hath given you the land...for the Lord your God, he is God in heaven above, and in earth beneath"* (Josh. 2:9-11). The judgment of God on Israel through the Babylonian Captivity revealed God's holiness, according to Ezk. 25:7. He said *"I will stretch out mine hand upon thee, and will deliver thee for a spoil to the heathen."* The most important Historical Event was the Resurrection of Christ, which revealed God's completed redemptive plan for man. Paul states, *"And that he was buried, and that he rose again the third day according to the scriptures; and that he was seen..."* (I Cor. 15:4-5). The Lord's revelation about Himself was history, according to numerous Scripture passages.

Another mode of Special Revelation is that of Communication from God. The Lord communicated to man both indirectly or mediately and directly or immediately. For instance, God used the 'lot' to indirectly communicate with man. An historical example of the use of the lot occurred in Judg. 20:9 when an invading army was chosen by lot. The principle of the lot is described in Prov. 16:33; *"The lot is cast into the lap; but the whole disposing thereof is of the Lord."* The Lord also used the אוּרִים (*'Uryim* [*'lights'*]) and תֻּמִּים *Thummiym* [*'perfections'*]) to communicate His will to the Israelites. The אוּרִים and תֻּמִּים, as indirect communication, apparently were on the breastplate of the High Priest to somehow signify Jehovah's will in important matters (Ex. 28:30). Presumably, in Ezra's day there was no high priest with the אוּרִים and תֻּמִּים to guide post-exilic Israel with regard to hard questions (Ezra 2:63).

The Lord also used direct communication to give revelation to man. This direct communication was in the form of Dreams, Visions, Angels, and Prophets. The Lord used Dreams to give direct communication to Abimelech about the marital status of Sarah (Gen. 20:3). Jehovah communicated to Jacob in a dream about His will for Jacob to leave Laban (Gen. 33:11, 13). The Lord communicated to believers in the NT era with Dreams. For instance, God showed Joseph the truth of the Virgin Birth in a Dream (Mt. 1:20), and He showed Paul His geographical will in a night vision (Acts 16:9).

The prophets learned about special revelation through Visions. For instance, the Lord gave Ezekiel *"visions of God"* in Ezk. 1:1 ff. Although difficult for modern man to understand, God demonstrated to Ezekiel truth about the person and purpose of God. The prophet Amos *"saw"* the words of Jehovah in a vision and later inscripturated them (Amos 1:1 ff.). Other prophets had visions from the Lord for the purpose of understanding His will in specific situations (e.g., Isaiah and Habakkuk).

Angels were another medium through which God gave direct communication. He used the Angels to give special revelation to the prophets. For instance, Gabriel *"informed"* Daniel about *"Seventy weeks are determined upon thy people and upon thy holy city"* (Dan. 9:20-27). The Angels communicated to shepherds about the incarnation of God (Lk. 2:8-13) and they glorified the Lord; *"Glory to God in the highest, and on earth peace, good will toward men"* (v. 14). The Angels were also instrumental in communicating the Law to man. Three times the NT indicates that the Angels were God's instrument in communicating revelation to man, as Acts 7:53 states, *"Who have received the law by the disposition of angels"* (cf. also Gal. 3:19 and Heb. 2:2).

A final medium through which God gave direct communication to man was the Prophets. The classic passage teaching this truth is II Pet. 1:21, *"For the prophecy came not in old time by the will of man: but holy men of God spake as they were moved by the Holy Ghost."* God used the prophets from Abel to Malachi to reveal and to inscripturate His truth. He used prophets to communicate NT mysteries as well, according to Eph. 3:5; *"Which in other ages was not made known unto the sons of men, as it is now revealed unto his holy apostles and prophets by the Spirit."*

A third mode of Special Revelation the Lord used was through Christophanies. These manifestations of the pre-incarnate Christ were in the person of the Angel of the Lord. The Angel of the Lord revealed truth to Hagar, stating *"I will multiply thy seed exceedingly...shalt bear a son...his name Ishmael...and he will be a wild man"* (Gen. 16:12).[27] Again, the Angel of the Lord *"appeared unto him [Moses] in a flame of fire out of the midst of a bush"* (Ex. 3:2). The Angel of the Lord identified Himself as God and the Lord, as He revealed Jehovah's plan for Moses. Another example of the Angel of the Lord is His appearance to Zechariah (Zech. 1:12 ff.). In this passage, this Christophany communicated with the Lord and then with Zechariah as the Lord about Israel's deliverance.

God gave Special Revelation through the Incarnation of Christ. Christ was the final major avenue of Special Revelation to mankind. Paul is explicit when he states, *"God, who at sundry times and in divers manners spake in time past*

---

[27]Ishmael is the father of the Arabic people, which embraced the Islamic faith founded by Mohammed in A.D. 622.

unto the fathers by the prophets, hath in these last days spoken unto us by his Son..." (Heb. 1:1-2). Furthermore, Christ was the epitome of the Father. Christ revealed the Father's nature; *"He that hath seen me hath seen the father"* (Jn. 14:9). Christ revealed the Father's power; *"for no man can do these miracles that thou doest, except God be with him"* (Jn. 3:2). Christ revealed the Father's wisdom; *"Never man spake like this man"* (Jn. 7:46). Christ revealed the Glory of God; *"And the Word was made flesh, and dwelt among us, (and we beheld his glory, the glory as of the only begotten of the Father,) full of grace and truth"* (Jn. 1:14). And Christ revealed the love of God; *"But God commendeth his love toward us, in that, while we were yet sinners, Christ died for us"* (Rom. 5:8). Not only were the life and words of Christ the Special Revelation of God, but also the words inscripturated by His prophets in the OT and NT Scriptures.

The Scriptures are the final mode through which God communicated His message. The Scriptures give characteristics of the Lord's communication to man. The Special Revelation of God is Perfect. Jn. 17:17 bears out this fact; *"Sanctify them through thy truth, thy Word is truth."* As Truth, the Scripture has no imperfections in it. The Scriptures are perfect in that they are complete. The Apostle John gives a strong caveat in his colophon to the Book of Revelation and to the Bible.[28]

The Special Revelation of the Lord is also Progressive.

---

[28]The Bible writers treated the Scriptures as a whole, and so this colophon applies not only to the Book of Revelation, but to all 66 books of the Bible, warning against anyone adding to or detracting from the words of the Bible (Rev. 22:18,19).

Not all revelation was given at any one time, but the Lord often gave the message in a progressive manner. Heb. 1:1-2 is a passage that teaches that God's revelation was progressive, culminating in Christ. Likewise, the Lord's promise of the coming of the Holy Spirit demonstrates that truth would be given in a progressive fashion (Jn. 16:13).

The Lord's Special Revelation is Purposeful. The Purpose of Special Revelation is to give the antidote to Gnostic error—the truth. Paul states, *"All Scripture is given by inspiration of God and is profitable for doctrine, for reproof, for correction, for instruction in righteousness..."* (II Tim. 3:16).[29]

The Special Revelation of the Lord is Propositional. His revelation is not merely conceptual truth, but it is propositional truth. In other words, the Lord has given proposition truth to man in the form of verbal, propositional statements. For instance, nouns (a singular rather than a plural noun) make up this propositional truth as presented by Paul in Gal. 3:16, stating, *"Now to Abraham and his seed were the promises made. He saith not, and to seeds, as of many: but as of one, And to thy seed, which is Christ."* Verbs[30] are

---

[29]The purpose of the Bible is to teach the doctrine of God and the duty of man. The passage does not teach that every Bible passage is applicable for Christian service (i.e., the genealogies in I Chr. 1-9).

[30]In Mt. 16:18, the verb οἰκοδομήσω (*oikodomeso* [*"I will build"*]) has caused great and fierce ecclesiological battles, primary because the focus by most expositors is on the tense of the verb rather than on the action of the verb. The tense is clearly a simple future; the action is on building, building-up, edifying. Christ did not say "I

propositional truth as well. In Heb. 3:7, the Apostle utilizes the present tense verb rather than the past tense verb. He states, *"Wherefore (as the Holy Ghost saith, Today, if ye will hear his voice,"* to indicate that the Holy Ghost's message is more than an ancient one to Jews 1500 years prior, but that it is a present message of warning to the first century audience.

Propositional truth is conveyed by articles. The TR rendering of I Pet. 2:10 protects dispensational distinctions. Peter says about his Jewish Christian audience, *"Which in time past were not a people, but are now the people of God: which had not obtained mercy, but now have obtained mercy."* C. C. Ryrie cogently observes,

> *While there are parallels in these verses between Israel and the Church [sic], nowhere are they equated. Indeed, the absence of the article before 'people' guards the distinction, for it is said that Christians are a people of God, not the new Israel of God.*[31]

Grammatical expressions are propositional truth. In Jn. 10:34, Christ employs the expression *"Ye are gods"* to teach the Jews Messianic theology. He argues that just as the psalmist in Psm. 82:6 calls OT spiritual leaders *"gods,"* so may the Messiah call Himself the Son of God (v. 36).

The Special Revelation of God is Personal. It is a personal message from a Person to persons. It is the personal

---

will *start"* my church, but He said "I will *edify"* my church.

[31]Charles C. Ryrie, *Biblical Theology of the New Testament* (Chicago: Moody Press, 1973), p. 276.

wording from God. Over 3000 times the OT prophets proclaim *"thus saith the Lord,"* emphasizing that their message is the personal wording of the Lord. NT books such as the Book of Revelation are the personal words of Christ. Christ spoke through the Apostle John saying *"The Revelation of Jesus Christ, which God gave unto him, to shew unto his servants things which must shortly come to pass; and he sent and signified it by his angel unto his servant John"* (Rev. 1:1).

The Special Revelation of God is Permanent. According to the psalmist in Psm. 119:89, *"For ever, O Lord, thy word is settled in heaven."* God's Word is eternal, and it will be the basis for the judgment of man. Christ declared that His words would be preserved until and utilized for man's judgment; *"He that rejecteth me, and receiveth not my words, hath one that judgeth him: the word that I have spoken, the same shall judge him in the last day"* (Jn. 12:48).[32]

Summary

The Lord has revealed Himself to mankind through General Revelation and through Special Revelation. Although General Revelation depicts God's personal divinity and power, it is not sufficient revelation for man's redemption, but it is sufficient for man's condemnation. On the other hand, God has given His Special Revelation to certain men for their redemption and mission purposes. The Word of God, the

---

[32] *"My Words"* translates τὰ ῥήματά μου (*ta remata mou*), which refers to Christ's individual words; *"the Word"* translates ὁ λόγος (*ho logos*), which refers to all of the words that the Lord has spoken, i.e., the whole Bible.

Scriptures, is God's ultimate revelation for the purpose of reconciling man to God through the redemptive work of Jesus Christ.

CHAPTER THREE

Inspiration of Scripture

Introduction

Many questions arise today about what is inspiration and what is inspired. Care is required so that one does not make theological understatements or overstatements concerning this vital subject of inspiration.

The Definition of Inspiration

Inspiration may be defined as "the process whereby the Holy Spirit influenced the writers of Scripture to record accurately His Words, the product being the inspired Word of God."[33] Inspiration is a process which occurred over a period of 1600 years, or from 1500 B.C. to A.D. 100. The product of inspiration is the *autographa* (autographs).

---

[33] A. Strong's emphasis is on the Holy Spirit's influence instead of the process and product of inspiration. He states that "inspiration is that influence of the Spirit of God upon the minds of the Scripture writers which made their writings the record of a progressive divine revelation, sufficient, when taken together and interpreted by the same Spirit who inspired them, to lead every honest inquirer to Christ and to Salvation." A. H. Strong, *Systematic Theology* (Valley Forge, PA: Judson Press, 1907), p. 196.

The Proof of Inspiration

How may inspiration be proved? The inspiration of the Bible is proved by the statements of the Bible claiming inspiration. Is this circular reasoning?

Circular Reasoning?

Any theological system must establish its own authority. If a theological system utilizes an authority outside of itself, it would be inconsistent. If Christianity utilized the Koran as its final authority, then it follows that the teachings of the Koran supersede the teachings of Christianity,[34] and the Islam faith is the true religion and not Christianity. However, the Moslems count the Koran as their final authority and Christianity counts the Bible as the final authority. All theological systems must claim their respective writings as their final authority to avoid this inconsistency. Therefore, theological systems employ circular reasoning to establish their final authority. Circular reasoning is acceptable as long as the internal testimony is credible. The Bible's internal testimony consists of the Character of God and the Claims of the Bible.

The Character of God

The God of the Judeo-Christian Scriptures is a holy and loving God (Isa. 6:2 and Jn. 3:16). This holy and loving God has made a means to reconcile sinful mankind to Himself.

---

[34] The Church of Jesus Christ of the Latter Day Saints (Mormons) claims to use both the Bible and the Book of Mormon as their authorities. Yet the Book of Mormon is the final authority for Mormonism, and consequently, it is not a Christian denomination.

Paul states, *"But God commendeth his love toward us, in that, while we were yet sinners, Christ died for us"* (Rom. 5:8). Furthermore, in His holiness and love, God has revealed His means of reconciliation to man. According to I Cor. 1 and 2, man's wisdom would never produce a system of reconciliation and redemption; so God in His 'foolishness' accomplished and revealed His plan of redemption. Again, Paul says *"To wit, that God was in Christ, reconciling the world unto himself, not imputing their trespasses unto them; and hath committed unto us the word of reconciliation"* (II Cor. 5:19). The word of reconciliation is God's revelation, which He has inspired and preserved. The Character of God is the basis for the Claims of the Bible.

The Claims of the Bible

The Bible makes General Claims and Specific Claims about its inspiration. First of all, there are several General Claims the Bible makes about being God's Word. On numerous occasions, the OT prophets claimed to speak for Jehovah, sometimes endangering their own lives. For instance, Jeremiah put his life on the line many times as he proclaimed God's revelation. He states,

> *Therefore now amend your ways and your doings, and obey the voice of the Lord your God; and the Lord will repent him of the evil that he hath pronounced against you. As for me, behold, I am in your hand: do with me as seemeth good and meet unto you. But know ye for certain, that if ye put me to death, ye shall surely bring innocent blood upon*

yourselves... (Jer. 26:13-15).

Occasionally, one book of the Bible would claim that another book of the Bible was God's revelation. For instance, Joshua recognized that the Mosaic Torah was Jehovah's authoritative revelation, stating *"that thou mayest observe to do according to all the law, which Moses my servant commanded thee..."* (Jos. 1:7). Zerubbabel recognized that offerings must be based on the authority of what was *"written in the law of Moses"* (Ezra 3:2). Daniel recognized the divine authority of Jeremiah's truth of Jer. 25:12 when he stated, *"In the first year of his reign I Daniel understood by books the number of the years, whereof the word of the Lord came to Jeremiah the prophet, that he would accomplish seventy years in the desolations of Jerusalem"* (Dan. 9:2). Again, Zechariah accepted the authority of the revelation of the Lord *"by the former prophets"* (Zech. 7:12). In numerous places in the NT, the NT writers accepted the OT Scriptures as God's authoritative revelation, such as Acts 1:16 ff. Peter recognized that Paul's writings were Scripture. He states, *"Even as our beloved brother Paul also according to the wisdom given unto him hath written unto you as also in all his epistles...also the other scriptures"* (II Pet. 3:15,16).

Another General Claim is that the OT prophets claimed the ultimate fulfillment of their prophecies. The classic example of this is Isaiah's claim: *"Seek ye out of the book of the Lord, and read: no one of these shall fail, none shall want her mate: for my mouth it hath commanded, and his spirit it hath gathered them"* (Isa. 34:16).

There are several Specific Claims of the Bible

involving particular passages.   These claims are made by Paul, Peter, Satan, and Christ.

Paul's claim for inspiration of the Scripture in II Tim. 3:15-17 requires careful examination by the Bible exegete. The Apostle's statement follows:

> *And that from a child thou hast known the holy scriptures which are able to make thee wise unto salvation through faith which is in Christ Jesus.   All scripture is given by inspiration of God, and is profitable for doctrine, for reproof, for correction, for instruction in righteousness: That the man of God may be perfect, thoroughly furnished unto all good works.*

The words *'holy scriptures'* translate ἱερὰ γράμματα (*hiera grammata*), literally 'sacred' or 'temple writings.'   Paul was ascertaining to Timothy the efficacy of the copies of the OT in the Temple in Jerusalem.   As *apographa*, or copies, they had the ability to save since they were the Word of God.   But the word *'scripture'* translates γραφὴ (*graphe*),[35] refers to the *autographa*, that is, all of the canonical scripture.

Paul obviously used a different word to differentiate

---

[35]Γραφὴ is used about fifty times in the NT in a technical sense to mean the Holy Scripture (as in Rom. 1:2).   Sometimes γραφὴ refers to an individual passage (Acts 1:16) or to all parts of Scripture (Lk. 24:45).   Scripture represents the person of God in places such as Gal. 3:8, which states, *"And the Scripture, foreseeing that God would justify the heathen through faith, preached before the gospel before unto Abraham, saying, In thee shall all nations be blessed."*

between the *apographa* and the *autographa*, especially with regard to the scope of inspiration. The precise meaning of *'all'* (πᾶσα)[36] is with regard to the 'whole' of Scripture rather than to the 'individual' Scriptures, because of its technical association with γραφὴ. Paul's point is that the whole of Scripture, rather than part ('every Scripture')[37] of it, is profitable to refute Gnosticism. The word behind *"is given by inspiration of God"* is θεόπνευστος (*theopneustos*), meaning literally "is God-breathed."[38] Paul's claim then is that only and all of the *autographa* is inspired by God, or is God breathed. The process of inspiration extends to *only* the *autographa*, and to *all* of the *autographa*.

Peter's claim for inspiration is the message of II Pet. 1:21 and II Pet. 3:15-16. In the first passage, Peter declares, *"For the prophecy came not in old time by the will of man: but holy men of God spake as they were moved by the Holy Ghost."* The word *'spake'* (ἐλάλησαν [*elalesan*]) indicates that God used human language to communicate to man. The

------

[36]Although πᾶσα is anarthrous and could be translated 'every,' its exceptional use is preferred, as in Acts 2:36, "all the house of Israel."

[37]The New English Bible (NEB) is certainly wrongheaded, stating "Every inspired scripture..." This translation puts doubt on some Scripture, as if some verses or passages were *not* inspired. Whereas, in contrast, the AV does not place doubt on Scripture, but it treats the whole of Scripture as equally inspired.

[38] The passive verbal form and the attributive position of θεόπνευστος make the AV rendering of it very accurate. *Vide* H. W. House, "Biblical Inspiration in II Tim. 3:16," *Bibliotheca Sacra*, 137 (Jan.-Mar., 1980), pp. 54-63.

words *'were moved by'* translates φερόμενοι [*pheromenoi*]), indicating that the Holy Spirit moved along the writers as the wind moves along ships, as Luke uses this verbal in Acts 27:15,17. Peter's claim is that the Holy Spirit guided the human writers in the use of the words they spoke and eventually inscripturated. In his second passage, Peter affirms that Paul's writings to the Jews were *autographa*, and that they were under attack by the heretics.

Satan's claim for the authority of the inscripturated truth is manifested by his statement to Christ, *"for it is written, He shall give his angels charge concerning thee: and in their hands they shall bear thee up, lest at any time thou dash thy foot against a stone"* (Mt. 4:6). In his claim, Satan recognized that Psm. 91:11-12 was Scripture, because he used the same formula for introducing Scripture as Christ did Γέγραπται (*gegraptai* [*"it is written"*]), and he recognized that it was the highest possible authority for the Son of God. In his utilization of this OT passage, the Devil accepted the inspiration of Scripture, the inerrancy of Scripture, and the preservation of Scripture.[39]

---

[39]Although Satan recognizes the source for truth, he has duped and deceived his ministers about the ultimate source for truth, the divine revelation of Scripture. Apostates such as Paul Tillich demonstrate Satan's deception in their own theology. Tillich denies that truth is found exclusively in the Bible, stating instead the following: "They [Fundamentalists] confuse eternal truth with a temporal expression of this truth. This is evident in European theological orthodoxy...When fundamentalism is combined with an anti-theological bias, as it is, for instance, in its biblicistic type, the theological truth of yesterday is defended as an unchangeable

Christ's claim was that all of the written OT must be fulfilled, and fulfilled in Him, the Messiah (Lk. 24:44). He affirms that the three divisions of the OT were written about Him. Also, Christ states that *"Till heaven and earth pass, one jot or one tittle shall in no wise pass from the law, till all be fulfilled"* (Mt. 5:18). He declares that all of the written OT would be fulfilled during the course of the present heavens and earth. His emphasis on the *'one jot'* (ἰῶτα ἑν [*iota hen*]) and *'one tittle'* (μία κεραία [*mia keraia*])[40] indicates the Lord's focus on the written special revelation of Scripture. In Jn. 14:26, the Lord asserted that the Holy Spirit would remind the Apostles of the words that Christ said, presumably as they inscripturated truth in the NT Scripture (compare also Jn. 16:13).

The Bible is inspired because the Bible says it is inspired. This circular reasoning is acceptable because it is

---

message against the theological truth of today and tomorrow...It elevates something finite and transitory to infinite and eternal validity. In this respect fundamentalism has demonic traits. It destroys the humble honesty of the search for truth, it splits the conscience of its thoughtful adherents, and it makes them fanatical because they are forced to suppress elements of truth of which they are dimly aware." Paul Tillich, *Systematic Theology* (Digswell Place, England: James Nisbet and Co., Ltd., 1968), p. 3.

[40]The ἰῶτα is the smallest consonant (') of the Hebrew alphabet, and the κεραία is the dot (.), the smallest vowel in Hebrew. Although both are minute, they are significant; similarly, the smallest consonants and vowels comprising the Hebrew words in which the OT prophecy was written are important, and the fulfillment of the OT will be accomplished to the very word. See Appendix D, *Lk. 16:17, One Tittle.*

based on the Claims of the Bible, including the claims of Paul, Peter, Satan, and Christ, which in turn are verified because of the Character of God, which character includes God's holiness and love.

False Theories of the Means of Inspiration

The Intuition Theory

This is the view of Liberals who teach that the Biblical writers had a natural endowment and were religious geniuses who produced highly elevated religious literature.

The Existential Theory

This is the view of the Neo-orthodox theologians who teach that the myths and tales of the Bible become the Word of God when God speaks through them to the reader at that existential moment of truth.

The Dictation Theory

This is the view allegedly held by some fundamentalists who teach that God set aside the personalities of the writers and merely used them as passive penmen, or even as robots.

False Theories of the Extent of Inspiration

The Conceptual Inspiration Theory

This is the view of some Liberals and of some Neo-Evangelicals who teach that God only inspired the concepts of divine revelation and not the words expressing the concepts.   Therefore, inspiration extends to concepts of special revelation.

The Partial Inspiration Theory

This is the view of some Liberals that God inspired the portions of Scripture that deal with faith and practice, but that He did not inspire areas such as science and history in the Bible. Therefore, inspiration extends to parts of the Bible but not to all of it.

The KJV Inspiration Theory

This is the view of some Fundamentalists that God inspired the King James Version to the same extent that He inspired the *autographa*. It is conducive to the mindset which says "If the KJV was good enough for Paul, it is good enough for me."[41] Therefore, inspiration extends to a translation of the Bible rather than to the *autographa*.

The Biblical View of Inspiration

The Bible gives several characteristics for the inspiration of Scripture. These characteristics set the

---

[41] The Bible believer should be cautious about theological over-statements which allow for continuing revelation beyond the *autographa*, such as "The truth is God slammed the door of revelation shut in 389 B.C. and slammed it shut again in 1611," Peter Ruckman, *The Monarch of the Books* (Pensacola, FL: Pensacola Bible Institute, 1973), p. 9. Although continuing revelation, albeit through visions, tongues, or translations, appeals to the 'walk by sight' rather than the 'walk by faith,' it undermines the authority, the inspiration, the inerrancy, and the preservation of the *autographa*.

parameters for the doctrine of inspiration.

Divine Origin

According to II Pet. 1:21, God, and not man, is the source of the inspiration of the Scripture. The process of inspiration originated with the will of God and not with the will of man. Moreover, this process involving the Holy Spirit's moving on man is inexplicable. The result of inspiration is the *autographa*; the working of the Holy Spirit in inspiration is mysterious.

Canonical Writings

Inspiration is limited to the canonical books of the writers, and it does not extend to all of the writings of the Scripture writers. For instance, David wrote numerous portions of the OT, as indicated in II Sam. 23:1-2; *"Now these be the last words of David...The Spirit of the Lord spake by me, and his word was in my tongue."* Yet not all of his writings were the manifestation of the Lord speaking through his tongue, as evidenced in his letter to Joab about the murder of Uriah (II Sam. 11:14-15). The Holy Spirit did not inspire this evil letter by David, but He did inspire the recording of this evil letter. Again, it seems that the Apostle Paul wrote more correspondence to Corinth than which is preserved in the NT canon. Paul states, *"I wrote unto you in an epistle not to company with fornicators"* (I Cor. 5:9). This seems to be an earlier epistle ('proto-First Corinthians') to the Corinthians than the canonical First Corinthians. To this 'proto-First Corinthians,' the Corinthians responded with questions about the married state (I Cor. 7:1). Paul then answered their questions with his 'first' Corinthians Epistle. Consequently, the writer Paul probably wrote many letters to his converts and churches, yet God has preserved only Paul's canonical letters, the Pauline Epistles. The *autographa* are inspired, not the writers of the *autographa*.

Divine Guidance

The Holy Spirit guided the writers of Scripture by helping them remember the eyewitness accounts that He wanted inscripturated. This truth is stated in Jn. 16:13, *"Howbeit when He, the Spirit of truth, is come, He will guide you into all truth: for He shall not speak of Himself; but whatsoever He shall hear, that shall He speak: and He will shew you things to come."*

Plenary, Verbal

Inspiration extends to all of the words. Inspiration of Scripture is 'plenary' (all, full) and 'verbal' (words). All of the words of Scripture, including nouns, verbs, adjectives, adverbs, pronouns, prepositions, conjunctions, etc., in all portions of Scripture, including the historic, the poetic, the scientific, the narrative, and the doctrinal sections, are equally inspired. Paul emphatically states that *"all Scripture is given by inspiration of God"* (II Tim. 3:16). The psalmist states that *"the words of the Lord are pure words,"* emphasizing the words spoken by the Lord (Psm. 12:6). Paul asserts that the Holy Spirit spoke in words to the writers, including himself (I Cor. 2:13). Christ promises that His words will be the standard against which man will be judged (Jn. 12:49-50). The Bible is replete with statements declaring that the Lord used words to give His special revelation.

Originals Only

As Paul affirms in II Tim. 3:16, the *autographa* are the product of inspiration, not the *apographa*. Although the Temple copies of Scripture are sufficient for salvation, as any reliable translation is, they are not in the process of inspiration and consequently they are not the product of inspiration.

Inspiration originated with God as the Holy Spirit directed the human writers to inscripturate truth in the canonical books of the OT and NT—the *autographa*. Every word in the original writings is the exact word which the Lord wanted used by the writers.

The Biblical Model of Inspiration

The passage of Jer. 36:1-32 gives a clear picture of the divine process of inspiration. Verses two and four are significant:

> *Take thee a roll of a book, and write therein all the words that I have spoken unto thee against Israel, and against Judah, and against all the nations, from the day I spake unto thee, from the days of Josiah, even unto this day...Then Jeremiah called Baruch the son of Neriah: and Baruch wrote from the mouth of Jeremiah all the words of the Lord, which he had spoken unto him, upon a roll of a book.*

God's Word Revealed

The Lord revealed His special revelation unto Jeremiah; the revelation originated with the Lord, not with Jeremiah and not with Baruch. God's revelation was the sermons that He gave Jeremiah to preach from the beginning of his ministry until that day. Jehovah guided Jeremiah in his sermons and then He brought to his remembrance what God wanted inscripturated.

God's Word Recorded

Three persons were involved in the recording of God's Word. The Lord gave words to Jeremiah who in turn gave them to Baruch who in turn inscripturated the words. Baruch did not write any error; he used the correct syntax and correct words, correctly spelled, to reveal the correct historical, scientific and theological facts. Baruch did not write any erroneous statements[42] because Jeremiah did not preach any erroneous statements because Jeremiah's inscripturated messages came from the Lord. The Lord God inspired His inerrant Word and then He preserved it.

---

[42] Verse 4 does not allow any latitude for Baruch or other Biblical scribes to take liberty in changing words given to them by the prophets or apostles. Stibbs' supposition on Silvanus editing Peter's First Epistle is fallacious. He states "It would originate from and be guaranteed by Peter, but the expression, the elegant diction, the easy use of the Septuagint—and who can tell how much else?—may be that of Silvanus." A. Stibbs, *The First Epistle General of Peter* (Grand Rapids: Wm. B. Eerdmans Publ. Co., 1978), p. 27.

God's Word Retained

Not only did the Lord reveal His Word and record His Word, but He also retained His Word. After King Jehoiakim destroyed the scroll of Jeremiah's message, the Lord re-commissioned Jeremiah to write it again. Jehovah brought the words to Jeremiah who gave them to Baruch who wrote them a second time. In fact, the Lord had Jeremiah include the additional events of Jer. 36 in the second edition of Jeremiah's message (Jer. 36:28-32).

Summary

God has inspired His Word. The Bible claims this inspiration which is based on the character of the Lord. The false views of inspiration reveal a faulty concept of the character of the Judeo-Christian God. The Bible is a manifestation of the truth that *"the Lord GOD hath spoken."*

CHAPTER FOUR

Inerrancy of Scripture

Introduction

Are there errors in the Bible? Many either ask this question or assert the affirmative of this question. However, what does the Lord say about inerrancy and His Word? This will be an effort to ascertain what the Bible says about its own inerrancy.

The Definition of Inerrancy

The Inerrancy of Scripture may be defined as "the Scripture is entirely inerrant, including statements regarding history, science, morals, and doctrine, being free from all errors or deceit."[43] Although many use infallibility and inerrancy interchangeably, they have different meanings. Infallibility has to do with the inability to fall or to err. Inerrancy has to do with the actuality of being without error. God is infallible and His Word is a product of infallibility; it is indeed inerrant since God does not have the ability to make errors.

---

[43] Thiessen simply defines inerrancy as the concept that Scripture "is without error in the original manuscripts." Henry Thiessen, *Lectures in Systematic Theology* (Grand Rapids: Wm. B. Eerdmans Publ. Co., 1983), p. 63.

The Importance of Inerrancy

Negatively

Some suggest that there is negative value in holding the doctrine of the inerrancy of Scripture. Evans and Berent warn about inerrancy:

> *We maintain that, in general, the greater the degree to which fundamentalists unquestioningly accept the doctrine of Biblical inerrancy, the greater the risk to their fullest understanding and appreciation of the Bible. By treating the Bible as inerrant, fundamentalists may become increasingly unable to conceive how human limitations in wisdom and knowledge could have influenced the Bible...Yet this rigid belief in inerrancy requires them somehow to dissolve any such 'errors' to retain their faith. In contrast, many non-fundamentalists can easily adapt their faith to a scientific appreciation of virtually any implausibility, inconsistency, or cultural bias that may appear in the Bible.*[44]

Obviously, this statement either confuses the authorship of the Scriptures, or it questions the character of God, or both.

Positively

Inerrancy is a corollary of the doctrine of plenary, verbal inspiration. If the Scriptures were errant, one wonders

---

[44] R. Evans and I. Berent, *Fundamentalism: Hazards and Heartbreaks*, p. xix.

why God would inspire them.   If God cannot write a Book free from all error, in spite of human authorship, then His character and His power are in question.   Is the God of the Judeo-Christian Scriptures trustworthy and omnipotent?   The Bible affirms that His character is without taint and that His power is without limitation.

Historically, theologians have defended inerrancy. Luther said, "The Scriptures have never erred...The Scriptures cannot err...It is certain that Scripture would not contradict itself; it only appears so to the senseless and obdurate hypocrites."[45]   The Baptist pastor C. H. Spurgeon affirmed,

> *It is also a book pure in the sense of truth, being without admixture of error. I do not hesitate to say that I believe that there is no mistake whatever in the original Holy Scriptures from beginning to end. There may be, and there are, mistakes of translation; for translators are not inspired; but even the historical facts are correct...there is not an error of any sort in the whole compass of them.*[46]

Various Views of Inerrancy

Full Errancy

This is the view that is held by religious Liberals and unbelievers who teach that the Bible is a product of human thinking.   Since errant man has produced the Bible, it is

---

[45]M. Luther, *Werke*, Weimar edition (WA), vol. 34.1, p. 356.

[46]C. H. Spurgeon, *The Metropolitan Tabernacle Pulpit*, Vol. 35 (Pasadena, TX: Pilgrim Publications, 1972), p. 257.

permeated with errors.

Limited Inerrancy

This is the view that is held by Liberals[47] and left-wing Neo-evangelicals who teach that the Bible is without error in the areas of salvation but that it is not necessarily without error in scientific and historical areas.

Full Inerrancy

This is the view that is held by Neo-evangelicals who teach that the Bible is fully without error in all areas, but that the scientific and historic passages are phenomenal (as appearing to the eye) but not necessarily exact. Scientific data and historical events are as correct as they are popularly reported with approximations.[48]

---

[47]Nels Ferre ridicules the fundamentalist's view of inerrancy even in the scientific passages, stating, "The fundamentalists, for our first example, are rejoicing in the breakdown of scientism. That gives the primitive biblical faith a chance once again. And to be sure, there is strong resurgence of traditionalistic Christianity. I see no chance for fundamentalism, however, unless we suffer a radical throwback in civilization. It is both too immoral and too unintelligent. Scientism may be collapsing, but thank God, as yet science remains." N. F. S. Ferre, *The Extreme Center* (Waco, TX: Word Books, Publ., 1973), p. 14.

[48]R. Nicole, "The Nature of Inerrancy," *Inerrancy and Common Sense*, ed. R. Nicole and J. Michaels (Grand Rapids: Baker Book House, 1980), pp. 71-95.

Absolute Inerrancy

This is the view that is held by most Fundamentalists who teach that the Bible is without error in all areas, including science and history. The data of the Bible are exact and can be harmonized. The Bible is not a science book or a history book, but where it speaks on science or history it is absolutely correct and true.

The Defense of the Inerrancy of Scripture

The Philosophical Defense

The Author of the Bible is the Truth—the Lord Jesus Christ (Jn. 14:6). Since it is authored by the One claiming to be the Truth, detractors must prove that it has errors. Philosophically, and theologically, the argument for the case of the inerrancy of Scripture goes back to the authorship of Scripture. If the One Who is Perfect Truth wrote the Bible, then it follows that the Bible must be Perfect Truth. Furthermore, this demands the presupposition that all alleged discrepancies may be harmonized. Sometimes alleged discrepancies are not discrepancies at all and parallel accounts are not really parallel. Because so much time and so much diverse culture or custom separates the modern reader from the original audience of Scripture, alleged imperfections may be due to man's ignorance rather than to God's 'mistakes.' In all cases, man should give the Lord God of the universe the benefit of doubt rather than to cast a shadow on His character (He is not deceitful) or His nature (He is not imperfect) or His power (He is not limited).

The Practical Defense

The Bible student recognizes certain alleged discrepancies are directed at the doctrine of inerrancy. These alleged discrepancies are in the areas of the Historic, Moral, Scientific, OT Quotations, Prophetic, Messianic Statements passages. In these areas, the author will Define the Problem and Defend a Possibility for the solution to the alleged discrepancy.

Alleged Historic Discrepancies

Genesis 14:14

The Problem Defined: The passage refers to the location of Dan to which Abram pursued the kings who had abducted Lot. The mention of Dan is an anachronism because it must refer to the Dan founded by the Danites at a much later date (Jud. 18:29).

The Possible Defense: It is possible that it refers to a different Dan, as in the case of Danjaan (II Sam. 24:6).

Genesis 36:31

The Problem Defined: The passage implies that there were kings in Israel before King Saul.

The Possible Defense: It is merely prophesying that there would be kings in Israel, as other passages prophesied, such as Dt. 17:17. All it is stating is that there were kings in Edom before there were kings in Israel.

I Kings 4:26 and II Chronicles 9:25

The Problem Defined: The reference in I Kings 4:26

states that Solomon had 40,000 stalls and the reference in II Chr. 9:25 says that he had 4,000 stalls. Did the historian make a mistake by the factor of ten?

The Possible Defense: A careful reading of both passages indicates that the Bible is referring to two different groups. The former declares that Solomon had 40,000 stalls of horses for his chariots, whereas the latter states that he had 4,000 stalls for horses and chariots. He had 40,000 stalls of horses for his chariots and 4,000 stalls for horses and chariots. In other words, he had more stalls for horses than he had for horses and chariots harnessed together.

II Kings 8:26 and II Chronicles 22:2

The Problem Defined: The first verse states that *"Two and twenty years was Ahaziah when he began to reign; and he reigned one year in Jerusalem."* The verse in II Chr. says that *"Forty and two years old was Ahaziah when he began to reign, and he reigned one year in Jerusalem."* Was Ahaziah 22 or 42 when he began to reign?

The Possible Defense: It is often stated that the copyist made a mistake and ascribed to Ahaziah the incorrect age of 42, since he must have been 22, according to II Kings 8:17. However, the problem goes beyond the copies, since the Hebrew manuscripts read 22 and 42, respectively, and extends to the originals. In II Chr. 22:2, the Hebrew literally reads "a son of 42 years." It is possible that the 42 refers to Athaliah's age,[49] since the Hebrew expression includes this possibility (cf. Psm. 127:4), and since Athaliah is stressed in this passage.

---

[49]Matthew Henry, *Commentary on the Whole Bible*, Vol. II (NY: Fleming Revell Co., n.d.), loc. cit.

In other words, Ahaziah was 22 when he began to reign and to replace his father who died at 40 (II Chr. 21:20), and his mother, Athaliah, was 42.

Alleged Moral Discrepancies

Exodus 4:21

The Problem Defined: The Lord says *"I will harden his heart, that he shall not let the people go."*[50] Jehovah's sovereignty over-ruled Pharaoh by hardening his heart and by not allowing him to let Israel go.

The Possible Defense: One of the three verbs translated "harden" is חָזַק (*chazaq*),[51] meaning "firm, strong." This same word is used in Dt. 31:6, which states *"be strong and of a good courage."* The Lord "firmed up" faith in Joshua's heart and He "firmed up" unbelief in Pharaoh's heart. God's sovereign will requires man to be responsible. In God's sovereign plan for Pharaoh, He raised him up (Rom. 9:17) and He gave Pharaoh very great spiritual light. The Lord's sovereignty is not immoral.

Numbers 31:15-18

The Problem Defined: The Lord said to Moses and the Israelites, *"Now therefore kill every male among the little ones, and kill every woman."* It is immoral to kill innocent children and women.

---

[50] Ten times the Scripture says God hardened Pharaoh's heart, and ten times it says Pharaoh hardened his own heart.

[51] The verb חָזַק occurs 290x in the OT. Other Hebrew words translated 'harden' include כָּבֵד (*cavad*) and אָמַץ (*'amatz*).

The Possible Defense: The Midianites were responsible for causing Israel to be involved in idolatry and immorality. Jehovah was so concerned about the purity of truth in Israel that He wanted the complete extermination of everyone associated with moral or doctrinal impurity. The religion of the people of Canaan was polytheistic and grossly immoral with orgiastic nature worship and ritual nudity worship of serpent symbols. This paganism was very appealing and contaminating.[52]

Judges 11:29 ff.

The Problem Defined: Jephthah vowed to offer his daughter as a burnt offering. Why did God endorse the murder of a child by a Judge?

The Possible Defense: The passage does not indicate that Jephthah murdered his daughter. In fact, on close examination, the passage supports the position that Jephthah dedicated his daughter to service in the place of worship. Several reasons for this are apparent from the passage. Jephthah was a godly Judge upon whom the Spirit of the Lord came (v. 29). He was committed to making a vow to the Lord and keeping the vow (vv. 30, 35). Both animals and humans could be offered to the Lord. Animals were sacrificed but humans were dedicated to the Tabernacle (Lev. 27). Several passages indicate that women were involved with public service such as I Sam. 2:22 and Ex. 38:8. The fact that she

---

[52]According to Unger, "It was a question of destroying or being destroyed, of keeping separated or of being contaminated and consumed." Merrill Unger, *Archeology and the Old Testament* (Grand Rapids: Zondervan Publ. House, 1973), p. 176.

bewailed her virginity and this became a custom indicates she recognized her perpetual celibacy; for her to be concerned about her virginity would be very unusual for someone facing death. The apparent problem of murder is alleviated by a careful examination of the passage.[53]

Proverbs 31:6-7

The Problem Defined: The passage commands strong drink and wine to be given to individuals, therefore denying total abstinence.

The Possible Defense: The immediate context indicates that this is an example of irony. Kings, and all who are to use rational judgment, are to avoid strong drink and wine;[54] *"it is not for kings...it is not for kings to drink wine; nor for princes strong drink"* (v. 4). Alcohol affects the mind in such a destructive manner that only those who do not need to

---

[53] For an excellent defense of the dedication to "tabernacle/temple" service position, see L. Wood, *Distressing Days of the Judges* (Grand Rapids: Zondervan Publ. House, 1976), pp. 287-295.

[54]The word behind *"wine"* is יַיִן (*yayin*) and the word behind *"strong drink"* is שֵׁכָר (*shekar*). The word יַיִן refers to grape juice at any stage, from fresh to fermented. Likewise, the word שֵׁכָר refers to date juice at any stage, from fresh to fermented. Only the context will tell if the particular juice is fresh or intoxicating. For instance, in Isa. 28:7, both juices are in an intoxicating stage. However, in Deut. 14:26, both juices are fresh rather than intoxicating. The KJV translators differentiated שֵׁכָר from יַיִן by the translation *"strong drink,"* in which stage שֵׁכָר was sometimes found in the Bible.

use their mental facilities may drink alcoholic beverages (vv. 6-7). The Bible demands total abstinence.[55]

Alleged Scientific Discrepancies

Genesis 7:20

The Problem Defined: The verse says *"fifteen cubits upward did the waters prevail; and the mountains were covered."* How could mountains be covered with 15 cubits (20-30 ft.) of water?

The Possible Defense: In the context, the cubit was used to measure the ark. The last mention of cubits referred to the ark's length of 300 cubits, width of 50 cubits and height of 30 cubits (6:15-16). The cubit was used to measure the ark and not the mountain. The 30 cubit high ark displaced 15 cubits of the water of the flood, which covered the mountains.

Joshua 10:12-14

The Problem Defined: How could the sun stop without causing chaos in all of heaven and earth?[56] Does not

---

[55]For a thorough treatment of and an exegetical defense for total abstinence, see R. P. Teachout, *Wine, The Biblical Imperative: Total Abstinence* (Allen Park, MI: Robt. Teachout, 1986), pp. 1-97.

[56]Barclay voices the common arguments of those who deny the supernaturalism of the Bible and who misunderstand the character of God. He states, "If it be insisted that this story be taken literally we are beset with difficulties. There is the simple fact that the sun does not move in any event...there is a moral difficulty. If the story be literal, it means that God suspended the normal working of the machinery of the universe in order that a mass slaughter of his

the expression *"sun...go down"* indicate the whole passage reflects a pre-scientific mentality?

The Possible Defense: Joshua needed more sunlight hours to destroy the kings' armies. Joshua prayed at about noon time for more day light. Since he had about six to eight hours left in the normal day, God apparently gave him the equivalent in sunlight (*"about a whole day"*). Consequently, the LORD stopped the revolution of the heavens, including the embedded sun and moon,[57] so that Joshua had the extra sunlight he needed to route the enemy. Reference to *"sun up"* and *"sun down"* are not merely phenomenological, but are literal since the earth is immobile (Psm. 93:1) and the Lord causes the sun to rise (Mt. 5:45). The miracle occurred when the Lord stopped the sun and the moon, apparently along with the heavens, as Habakkuk states, saying, *"The sun and moon*

---

enemies could be carried out. When we have discovered the character of God in Jesus Christ, that becomes something at which the mind shudders with horror." W. Barclay, *And He Had Compassion* (Valley Forge: Judson Press, 1975), p. 213.

[57]The Scriptures teach that the earth is stationary (Psm. 93:1; I Chr. 16:30), the sun has a circuit (Psm. 19:6), the heavens have a circuit (Job 22:14), the stars have their courses (Jdg. 5:20), and the earth, as a sphere (Gen. 1:2; Prov. 8:27; Isa. 40:22), hangs on nothing (Job 26:7). Evolutionary scientists teach that the earth rotates around its axis and revolves around the sun, tempting Christians to move from biblical Geocentricity to evolutionary heliocentricity, ultimately hurtling toward atheistic a-centricity. Cf. Thomas M. Strouse, "Geocentricity: A Case Study in Bibliology," *Emmanuel Baptist Theological Journal*, Fall/Winter, 2006:9-26. Also, *vide* Thomas M. Strouse, "Biblical Geocentricity," *The Biblical Astronomer* 109 (Summer 2004): 69-89.

stood still in their habitation..." (Hab. 3:11).

II Chronicles 4:2

The Problem Defined: The dimensions for the molten sea, which was circular, were ten cubits for the diameter and thirty cubits for the circumference. Robert H. Mounce countenances limited inerrancy by stating,

> *It would be impossible for a round vessel to have a diameter of ten and a circumference of thirty...In the culture of that day the measurement was not only adequate, but also 'inerrant.' In our determination of what constitutes an error we must judge the accuracy of Scripture according to the prevailing standards of the time.*[58]

The Possible Defense: Every school boy knows that the circumference of a circle equals the diameter times the constant *pi* 3.1416 ($d \times \pi = c$). Since the diameter of the molten sea was ten cubits, the circumference must really be 31.42 cubits, rather than 30 cubits. However, another factor must be considered, and that is the thickness of the brim, which was *"an handbreadth"* (v. 5). The apparent error is eliminated when one realizes that the writer gives the measurement for the outer diameter (10), and the measurement for the inner circumference (30), instead of the outer circumference (31.42). This is not an uncommon practice,

---

[58] As quoted in H. Lindsell, *The Battle for the Bible* (Grand Rapids: Zondervan Publ. House, 1979), p. 165.

since the varying dimensions give the total picture of the object, assuming that the artificer knows basic math. Architects and engineers of every age have needed precise scientific and mathematical calculations for their constructions in order for their projects to fit together and to remain.

Alleged OT Quotation Discrepancies

Matthew 2:23

The Problem Defined: Matthew states *"that it might be fulfilled which was spoken by the prophets, He shall be called a Nazarene."* The problem is where is this prophecy found written in the OT?

The Possible Defense: Numerous efforts have been expended to resolve this dilemma. Stanley Toussaint lists several explanations for this difficult verse. He eliminates the view that associates Nazarene with Nazareth (Jdg. 13:5) since Christ was not a Nazarite. He also eliminates the view that the Messianic prophecy of Isa. 11:1 uses the Hebrew word נֵצֶר (*netzer*) for *"Branch,"* thus being the basis for Matthew's citation, since there is no obvious connection between the Messiah's title and this town. Toussaint's view connects passages of reproach such as Psm. 22:6-9 and Isa. 53 with the "despicable" title of Nazarene to form the basis of Matthew's quotation.[59] Although all of these views are plausible, their advocates seem to make difficult the solution by overlooking what the text actually states. The verb that Matthew employs

---

[59] Stanley Toussaint, *Behold the King* (Portland, OR: Multnomah Press, 1981), pp. 56-57.

is ῥηθὲν (*rhethen*) *"was spoken,"* and not "was written." He did use the verb *"it is written"* for the written prophecy of Micah 5:2 (v.5), but in verse 23 Matthew is giving the *spoken* words, never inscripturated in the OT, but preached by several OT prophets. Not everything that the OT prophets preached was written down, but in this case the Holy Spirit brought this OT preachment to Matthew's attention so that he could say that the OT prophets preached the very words *"He shall be called a Nazarene."*

Hebrews 10:5-7

The Problem Defined: In the obvious citation of Psm. 40:6-8, the author substitutes *"a body hast thou prepared me"* in place of the OT statement *"mine ears hast thou opened."* Did the writer of Hebrews misquote Psm. 40:6-8?

The Possible Defense: Some argue that the author of Hebrews quoted from the *Septuagint* (LXX), giving an interpretation of Psm. 40:6-8.[60] It is apparent that the author of Hebrews is giving a spiritually heightened interpretation of the Psalm, indicating that God not only created the Messiah's obedient ears, but His whole incarnate body. It would be unwise, however, to suggest that the Apostle Paul, or any other NT writer, employed the LXX as an authoritative source for divine revelation instead of the Hebrew OT. The NT writers were bilingual, knowing Hebrew and Greek, and there is no reason to think that the Holy Spirit could not have led them to interpret the OT Hebrew and to express the new revelation in

---

[60]Leon Morris, "Hebrews," *The Expositor's Bible Commentary*, ed. F. E. Gaebelein (Grand Rapids: Zondervan Publ. House, 1981), p. 98.

their own statements. The Holy Spirit did not need the uninspired LXX to convey truth when He moved Greek-speaking Apostles to reveal new truth.

Hebrews 11:21

The Problem Defined: This passage states that Jacob blessed Joseph's sons, *"leaning upon the top of his staff."* The OT counterpart to this narrative is Gen. 47:31, which states that Jacob *"bowed himself upon the bed's head."* Did the author of Hebrews make a mistake?

The Possible Defense: Archer argues that the LXX gives the correct rendering of "staff," which reading the NT writer employed, rather than the erroneous reading of "bed" found in the Hebrew OT.[61] However, this view promotes the superiority of the LXX over the Hebrew text, creating more problems rather than eliminating this problem. It is far better to realize that Jacob could have done both activities, leaning upon the top of his staff *and* bowing himself upon the bed's

---

[61] G. L. Archer, *Encyclopedia of Bible Difficulties* (Grand Rapids: Zondervan Publ. House, 1982), p. 421. Although Archer's book offers many excellent explanations of Bible difficulties, its theological orthodoxy is suspect in places. For instance, Archer's capitulation to the influence of evolution is obvious. He suggests that there was *death* before Adam, negating the crux of Paul's soteriological parallelism between Adam and Christ (Rom. 5:12 ff.), by stating, "we are compelled to regard all these early anthropoids as pre-Adamic...but who completely died off before Adam and Eve were created...There may have been advanced and intelligent hominids who lived and died before Adam, but they were not created in the image of God," p. 64.

head, since he later sat on the bed (Gen. 48:2).

Alleged Prophetic Discrepancies

Isaiah 7:14

The Problem Defined: Although orthodox Christianity has accepted this as a prophecy of the virgin birth of Christ, liberals have denied this interpretation. Some argue that the proper translation of the passage merely refers to a young women (RSV) or that the virgin birth claim for Christ is discredited because this was a common way for glorifying ancient mythological heroes and famous people such as Mithra, Hercules, Buddha, Plato, etc.[62]

The Possible Defense: First of all, Jehovah did not give this sign to Ahaz, since he rejected the Lord's invitation, but to the house of David. Consequently, the time of fulfillment does not need to be immediate. Second, the Hebrew word עַלְמָה (*almah*) is used for good reason; in every use of עַלְמָה the word *"virgin"* could be translated without violating the context.[63] Third, a young woman with child,

---

[62]Evans and Berent, p. 141.

[63]Although בְּתוּלָה (*bethulah*) is the usual word for virgin (50x), as in Gen. 24:16, its reference in Joel 1:8 creates problems. The nine references to עַלְמָה in the OT (Gen. 24:43; Ex. 2:8; I Chr. 15:20; Psm. 46:1 and 68:25; Pro. 30:19; Song of Solomon 1:3 and 6:8; and Isa. 7:14). suggest no taint of impurity to the concept of virginity. For an excellent defense of עַלְמָה, see G. L. Lawlor, *Almah...Virgin or Young Woman?* (Des Plaines, IL: Regular Baptist Press, 1973), pp. 13-59.

married or unmarried, would never be a sign, and would never produce the situation of Immanuel, "God with us." A sign is always something unusual, such as the virgin birth. Fourth, the NT Apostle, Matthew, gives the authoritative interpretation of this passage, declaring that the virgin-born Jesus of Nazareth was the fulfillment of this prophecy (Mt. 1:22-23).

Luke 2:1-4

The Problem Defined: Liberals question the credibility of Luke's account that Christ was born in Bethlehem[64].

The Possible Defense: Although alleged historical questions arise concerning both the enrollment in the land of Israel and Augustus ordering it, the historian Luke corroborates the other writers of Scripture who declare that Christ was born in Bethlehem (Lk. 2:4, 7). The prophet Micah prophesied that the Messiah would come out of Bethlehem, stating *"But thou, Bethlehem Ephratah, though thou be little among the thousands of Judah, yet out of thee shall he come forth unto me that is to be ruler in Israel: whose goings forth have been from of old, from everlasting"* (Mic. 5:2). Again, the Apostle John declares *"Hath not the Scripture said, That Christ cometh of the seed of David, and out of the town of Bethlehem, where David was?"* (Jn. 7:42).

---

[64]Liberals such as D. F. Strauss and E. Renan reject the passage *in toto.* However, Ramsay gives a classic defense of this passage. W. M. Ramsay, *Was Christ Born at Bethlehem?* (Grand Rapids: Baker Book House, 1979 reprint), p. vii.

Alleged Discrepancies in Christ's Statements

Matthew 10:9-10; Mark 6:8

The Problem Defined: In Matthew's Gospel, Christ tells the disciples *"provide not...nor yet staves,"* and in Mark's Gospel, He tells them *"that they should take nothing for their journey save a staff only."* Were the disciples to take a staff or not?

The Possible Defense: The negated verb Matthew uses is κτήσησθε (*ktesesthe*) (*"provide"* or "acquire"), [65] indicating that the disciples were not to make an effort to acquire a staff especially for their journey. Just as they were not to make special provision with gold or silver for the trip, they were to go with the least encumbrance in their personal garb. Christ indicates that each may take his walking staff, but he was not to seek a new staff or make having a staff conditional to his going.

Matthew 12:40

The Problem Defined: In Jonah 1:17, the Scripture states that Jonah was swallowed by a great fish דָּג גָּדוֹל (*dag gadol*), whereas, in Matthew's Gospel Christ declares that Jonah *"was three days and three nights in the whale's belly."* Did Christ really mean that Jonah was swallowed by a whale?

The Possible Defense: Some believe that the creature was something other than a whale. For instance, Lange

---

[65]Robertson translates the verb as "procure." A. T. Robertson, *Word Pictures in the New Testament*, Vol. I (Grand Rapids: Baker Book House, 1930), p. 79.

affirms "we suppose it was a shark rather than a whale."[66] However, the word Christ uses for whale is κῆτος (*ketos*) which is the Greek word for whale. In fact, the modern science of the study of whales is called *cetology*. The Lord gives specific revelation concerning the fish that swallowed Jonah; the great fish was a great whale. To translate κῆτος otherwise is to reject revelation and to question the authority of Scripture.

Matthew 13:31-32

The Problem Defined: Christ declares in His parable that *"the Kingdom of Heaven is like to a grain of mustard seed...which indeed is the least of all seeds."* Is the mustard seed the smallest of all seeds?

The Possible Defense: The question revolves around whether Christ's statement was relative or absolute. Being the creator of the cosmos, Christ certainly would have known which seed is absolutely the smallest. However, He probably had in mind the relative size of the mustard seed for His Jewish audience.[67] For the Judean farmers, the mustard seed was the smallest of which they were aware.

---

[66]J. P. Lange, *Commentary on the Holy Scriptures, Matthew* (Grand Rapids: Zondervan Publ. House, n.d.), pp. 225-226. Modern translations render for κῆτος several variations such as "sea monster" (NASV), "great fish" (The Living Bible), "huge fish" (NIV), and "big fish" (TEV).

[67]E. W. G. Masterman, "Mustard," *The International Standard Bible Encyclopaedia*, Vol. III (Grand Rapids: Wm. B. Eerdmans Publ. Co., 1939), pp. 2101-2102.

John 12:38-41

The Problem Defined: Why did Christ attribute both Isa. 53:1 and Isa. 6:10 to the prophet Isaiah?

The Possible Defense: Christ believed that the prophet Isaiah was the author of the whole book of Isaiah (Jn. 12:38-41). Unlike modern scholars, [68] Christ was not enamored with a 'plural' authorship of Isaiah. The theology, the vocabulary, and the style of Isa. 1-39 and of Isa. 40-66 all argue for the same author. Christ's position of a single author of Isaiah, namely Isaiah, refutes the deutero-Isaiah and trito-Isaiah positions.

In defending the Scripture against alleged discrepancies, whether they are historical, moral, scientific, OT quotations, prophetic, or with regard to Christ's statements, there are possible solutions. It may be in some cases the believer can not determine with complete assurance the solution, but the uncertainty should be blamed on man's ignorance rather than on God's supposed inability.

Inerrancy and Translations

Are Bible translations, in any language, without error? The doctrine of inerrancy applies directly to the *autographa* and derivatively to the *apographa*. The *autographa* were the product of the process of inspiration and consequently they were without error, or inerrant. The *apographa* were copied from the *autographa*; they were not part of the process of inspiration. The biblical doctrine of preservation reveals that

---

[68]W. H. Schmidt, *Old Testament Introduction* (NY: Crossroad Publ. Co., 1984, pp. 257-270.

the inspired words of the *autographa* have been preserved without error in the *apographa*. Although copies have textual variants, the Spirit of God has led NT assembly members to recognize, receive, and perpetuate the very words of God through the centuries. With regard to translations, one must realize that they are only as good as their underlying Hebrew and Greek texts. The original words are inerrant and translations may have a precise accuracy. Since the author believes that God has preserved His inspired Words in the MT and TR texts, and therefore are essentially the words of the *autographa*, their resultant translation, the KJV, reflects their accuracy and truth.

Summary

There are no errors in the *autographa*. The Lord God has the character and the ability to produce an inerrant *autographa*. Of the numerous alleged discrepancies in the Bible, most are eliminated by a careful reading of the text. The remainder can be resolved through further study. The alleged errors in the Bible are apparent rather than real.

CHAPTER FIVE

Canonicity of Scripture

The Definition of Canonicity

The definition of Canon[69] of Scripture may be "The 66 books of the Bible, 39 OT Books and 27 NT Books, that have been measured by the Lord's assemblies, and consequently recognized and approved as the product of the process of inspiration, and accepted as the inspired books of the Judeo-Christian Scriptures."

The Views of Canonicity

The Neo-Orthodox View teaches that whatever part of the Bible that speaks to the reader is Scripture and therefore canonical. This extremely subjective approach should be avoided. The Roman Catholic View teaches that whatever the church councils, the traditions, and the popes say is Scripture is canonical. The Roman Catholic Church includes in its canon not only the 66 books of the Bible but also The Wisdom of Solomon, Ecclesiasticus, Tobit, Judith, I & II Maccabees, Baruch, Letter of Jeremiah, Additions to Esther, Prayer of

---

[69]The word 'canon' comes from the Hebrew word קָנֶה (*qanah*) for a *'measuring reed'* (Ezk. 40:3), and the corresponding Greek word κανών (*kanon*) for *'rule'* (II Cor. 10:13, 15-16; Gal. 6:16; and Col. 3:16). The Judeo-Christian Scripture of 66 books becomes the standard measurement for truth, rejecting spurious books such as the Ecclesiasticus and Gospel of Thomas.

Azariah, Susanna, and Bel and the Dragon.

The New Testament View teaches that the Holy Spirit worked in the hearts of NT church members so that they universally recognized the canonical Scriptures that God determined. Man *recognized* what God had *determined*. The Holy Spirit impressed upon believers' hearts several tests to determine canonicity. One test was Apostolicity, or what the connection was between the writer and the Apostles. Mark and Luke were not Apostles but they were associated with Peter and Paul, respectively. Another test was the Universal Reception of NT churches. Most of the NT books were accepted as canonical throughout the Mediterranean basin collectively but also independently by NT churches. Churches in Israel, Greece, Asia Minor, Italy, etc. independently recognized the same books as Scripture. A third test was the Consentient and Harmonious Message of Scripture. The canonical books did not disagree with either the OT canon message or with the message of other NT books. A fourth test was the Ring of Inspiration. The Holy Spirit impressed upon believers that the book in question was true and inspired. These last two tests were the objective and subjective parameters for recognizing the canon.[70]

---

[70] For a thorough discussion of canonicity, see Norman Geisler and W. Nix, *A General Introduction to the Bible* (Chicago: Moody Press, 1986), pp. 203-317.

The Phenomena of Canonicity

The Periods of Canonization

Composing (A.D. 50-100). During this period, the NT writers were writing the NT Scriptures. James was probably the first book written sometime around A.D. 45. Paul probably wrote Galatians about 49 and Matthew probably wrote the first Gospel about 50. Most NT scholars concur with the Lord's churches that John wrote his five books between AD 90-98.

Collecting (A.D. 100-200). After the Scriptures were written, believers and churches began collecting the various NT books available. Many of the NT books were written to churches which in turn would make copies and circulate them. According to Tertullian (160-220), the *autographa* were left in their original place of reception. He states this as he challenges heretics to compare their writings with the *autographa*, stating,

> *Come now, you who would indulge a better curiosity, if you would apply it to the business of your salvation, run over the apostolic churches, in which the very thrones of the apostles are still pre-eminent in their places, in which their own authentic writings are read, uttering the voice and representing the face of each of them severally. Achaia is very near you, (in which) you find Corinth. Since you are not far from Macedonia, you have Philippi; (and there too) you have the Thessalonians. Since you are able to cross to Asia, you get Ephesus. Since, moreover, you are close*

upon Italy, you have Rome, from which there comes even into our own hands the very authority (of apostles themselves).[71]

Comparing (AD 200-300). During this time professed believers were examining and comparing and sifting the various books alleging canonicity. Eusebius (263-339) categorized the various books into four groups. The *Homologomena* or Acknowledged Books were the four Gospels, Acts, the 14 Pauline Epistles, I Peter, I John, and Revelation. The *Antilegomena* or Disputed Books were James, II Peter, II and III John, and Jude. The *Apocrypha* or Spurious Books were some such as the Acts of Paul, the Epistle of Barnabas, the Shepherd of Hermas, the Revelation of Peter, etc. The *Pseudepigrapha* or Heretical Books were the Gospel of Peter, the Gospel of Thomas and a multitude of other Gnostic writings.

Completing (AD 300-400). By this time Catholics were recognizing canonical books and attempting to list them. The Council of Laodecia in 336 recognized and listed all of the NT canon except the Book of Revelation. Athanasius acknowledged all 27 of the NT Books in his canon in 367. The Council of Carthage recognized the complete NT canon in 397.

Copying (AD 400-1500). Before this period and during it scribes and later monks made numerous copies of NT manuscripts. With the marriage of Catholic Christianity to the

---

[71]A. Roberts and J. Donaldson, eds., *The Ante-Nicene Fathers*, Vol. III (Grand Rapids: Wm. B. Eerdmans Publ. Co., 1980 reprint), p. 260.

Roman Empire, scribes had liberty to copy Greek manuscripts, and monks considered the copying of Scripture in the scriptorium as sacred work. Most extant NT manuscripts come out of this period, reflecting the Byzantine Text (i.e., *Textus Receptus*).

The Development of the Canon

The recognition of the NT Canon developed slowly but accurately. Some of the NT Books were written to and read by certain assemblies. For instance, Romans, I and II Corinthians, Galatians, Ephesians, Philippians, Colossians, I and II Thessalonians, I and II Timothy, I and II Peter and Revelation were written to local churches. Some NT Books were written to individuals, such as Philemon and III John, while some locales did not receive any NT Books such as Egypt and Babylon. Since some Books would be read by more Christians than other Books, such as Ephesians over Philemon and Romans over III John, the recognition of the canonicity of these lesser read Books would be slow in coming. Other factors conducive to the slow but steady acceptance of the NT canon were the reception of the Epistle of Barnabas and the Shepherd of Hermas in the canon until the fourth century, as indicated by their appearance in Codex *Sinaiticus* (‭א‬). Athanasius' NT canon indicated that Catholics were developing their own canon before any official church canon was presented. Also, NT assembly members were *not* waiting for some church council to tell them what their Bible was.

Two factors lead to the speeding of the formation of the NT canon. Heretics such as Marcion were presenting their own canons which were very much shorter than the NT canon, and consequently they were forcing Christians to determine what was canonical and what was not. The other factor was Diocletian's decree (303) to destroy all Christian buildings and books, including the Scriptures. Christians were forced to decide what books should be protected and in many cases hidden. In the end, the Holy Spirit helped church members recognize all of and only the NT canonical Scriptures which God had determined. The Lord has inspired the *autographa* and He has preserved both the text and the canon of the Bible.

Summary

God has inspired His inerrant Words, and He has preserved these Words in the Masoretic Hebrew and the Received Greek texts, and thereby giving His canon of Scripture. The Holy Spirit impressed upon NT Christians the ability to recognize what He has determined to be the canon of Scripture. Although this recognition of the NT canon was slow it was sure. From the first century on, Christians have had all of the words of all of the books of the Bible.

CHAPTER SIX

Illumination of Scripture

The Definition of Illumination

The definition of Illumination may be "the work of the Holy Spirit to enlighten the mind of fallen man to understand the Scriptures." Although depraved man can read the words of the Bible, he cannot understand the spiritual message without Divine help. Regeneration is the starting place for illumination, but even after man is regenerated he still needs to be illuminated.[72]

The Necessity of Illumination

Illumination is necessary because all men are spiritually blind. The Bible declares that both the Jews and the Gentiles are spiritually blind.

The Spiritual Blindness of Israel

Numerous passages in the Bible teach that Israel has been and still is spiritually blind. For instance, Isaiah condemns Israel saying, *"Go and tell this people, Hear ye*

---

[72]Calvin declares, "Whatever is not illuminated by his Spirit is wholly darkness. The Apostles had been duly and amply instructed by the best of teachers. Still, as they wanted the spirit of truth to complete their education in the very doctrine which they had previously heard, they were ordered to wait for him." J. Calvin, *Institutes of the Christian Religion*, Vol. I, p. 241.

indeed, but understand not; and see ye indeed, but perceive not" (Isa. 6:9). Christ, citing this OT passage in Isaiah, underscores the truth of spiritual blindness in His day, saying *"Therefore speak I to them in parables: because they seeing see not; and hearing they hear not, neither do they understand"* (Mt. 13:13). The Apostle Paul adds to this truth about Israel's blindness, acknowledging that their blindness is temporary; *"For I would not, brethren that ye should be ignorant of this mystery, lest ye should be wise in your own conceits; that blindness in part is happened to Israel, until the fulness of the Gentiles be come in"* (Rom. 11:25). This blindness will be present until the Lord comes back to save Israel at the Second Advent.

The Spiritual Blindness of the Gentiles

The Lord teaches that spiritual darkness is a condition of the fallen state, saying *"For every one that doeth evil hateth the light, neither cometh to the light, lest his deeds should be reproved"* (Jn. 3:20). Paul corroborates this truth by stating that the Christian Gentiles were in a previous state of darkness; *"Who hath delivered us from the power of darkness, and hath translated us into the kingdom of his dear Son"* (Col. 1:13). Blindness is not only caused by the Fall, but it is also caused by Satan. Again, Paul asserts the blindness of the Gentiles *"in whom the god of this world hath blinded the minds of them which believe not, lest the light of the glorious gospel of Christ, who is the image of God, should shine unto them"* (II Cor. 4:4). Fallen man is spiritually blinded to the truth, but he is receptive to theological errors, such as *'another Jesus,' 'another Spirit,'* and *'another Gospel'* (II Cor. 11:4). Paul indicates that carnality promotes spiritual blindness as well, rebuking the Corinthians for their spiritual immaturity (I Cor. 2:14-3:2).

The Means of Illumination

The Holy Spirit Illuminates

The Holy Spirit illuminates unbelievers. Christ declares that the Holy Spirit *"will reprove the world of sin, and of righteousness, and of judgment"* (Jn. 16:8). The Spirit of God illuminates the unbeliever about sin and about salvation. John adds that *"Except a man be born again, he cannot see the kingdom of God"* (Jn. 3:3, 5). The Holy Spirit illuminates believers as well. Christ promised the Apostles that *"Howbeit when He, the Spirit of truth, is come, He will guide you into all truth: for He shall not speak of Himself; but whatsoever He shall hear, that shall He speak: and He will shew you things to come"* (Jn. 16:13). John promised his audience that as believers they did not need Gnostics to teach them, since they had the Holy Spirit who could illuminate them in all truth. He states *"But ye have an unction from the Holy One, and ye know all things...the same anointing teacheth you of all things, and is truth, and is no lie, and even as it hath taught you, ye shall abide in him"* (I Jn. 2:20, 27).

Bible Teachers Illuminate

God has given to local churches gifted men such as Bible teachers. Paul states this truth in Eph. 4:11, *"And He gave some ...teachers; for the perfecting of the saints, for the work of the ministry, for the edifying of the body of Christ"* (cf. I Cor. 12:28). These gifted teachers, prepared by prayer and study of the Scriptures, do not take the place of the Holy Spirit but are used by Him to illuminate believers in the truth. Although believers could be illuminated exclusively by the Holy Spirit, God gives Bible teachers to NT churches to illuminate believers as well.

Church Members Illuminate

The Lord used all of the NT writers to inscripturate truth in the form of the Scriptures and consequently these writers illuminate all those who read the NT. The Apostle John makes a statement to this effect, saying *"But these are written, that ye might believe that Jesus is the Christ, the Son of God; and that believing ye might have life through his name"* (Jn. 20:31). The example of Philip illustrates this truth. Luke records this incident, with Philip asking *"Understandest thou what thou readest? And he said, How can I, except some man should guide me? And he desired Philip that he would come up and sit with him"* (Acts 8:30, 31). Later, Luke adds that Philip *"preached unto him Jesus"* (v. 35) and instructed him in believer's baptism (vv. 35-38).

Subjective and Objective Understanding

God has so designed man that he benefits from the subjective and the objective aspects of understanding God's Word. The passage of Col. 3:15-16 illustrates these aspects. Verse 15 states, *"And let the peace of God rule in your hearts, to the which also ye are called in one body; and be ye thankful."* The subjective aspect of knowing God's will through the Word of God is based on the "rule" of the peace of

God. The word *"rule"* translates βραβευέτω (*brabeueto*) which is the action of a *brabeus* or "umpire."[73] Umpires control and direct athletic events. Likewise, God's peace, present in a believer because of the indwelling of the Holy Spirit, directs a believer concerning the truth. Verse 16 states, *"Let the word of Christ dwell in you richly in all wisdom; teaching and admonishing one another in psalms and hymns and spiritual songs, singing with grace in your hearts to the Lord."* The objective aspect of knowing God's will is based on the Word of God. Both aspects, the subjective and the objective, are necessary to understand truth. Those who emphasize the subjective to the neglect of the objective identify with the error mysticism. For one to claim God's peace about doing something forbidden by the parameters of the Bible is wrongheaded. On the other hand, those who emphasize the objective to the neglect of the subjective identify with rationalism. For one to claim to understand God and His Word and Will without the Holy Spirit is folly. The believer must be balanced in the subjective and objective aspects of understanding truth.

Summary

The Holy Spirit wants mankind to understand His Word. He illuminates unbelievers to the truth of the need for regeneration, and He illuminates believers so that they can understand the deep things of God. The Holy Spirit also uses

---

[73]J. H. Thayer, *Greek-English Lexicon of the New Testament* (Grand Rapids: Zondervan Publ. House, 1970), p. 105.

Bible teachers and other church leaders to illuminate believers. The Holy Spirit and His Word guide believers into all truth.

CHAPTER SEVEN

Interpretation of Scripture

The Definition of Interpretation

The definition of Interpretation may be "the science of exegeting the Bible to understand the message of its author." The study of the Interpretation of the Bible is called 'Hermeneutics.' Christ practiced the science of hermeneutics on the two on the road to Emmaus as Luke records that He *"beginning at Moses and all the prophets...expounded unto them in all the Scriptures the things concerning Himself"* (Lk. 24:27). The Lord expounded[74] or interpreted the OT Scriptures to the two disciples.

The Necessity of Interpretation

Amos declares that the Lord God has spoken. But what has He said? Man's responsibility is to understand what God has said. Since God used human language in its normal usage, man needs to understand the Bible, with the help of the Holy Spirit of course, interpreting it normally or literally. There are several considerations for the necessity of Interpretation.

One consideration is that the proper understanding of the Bible is necessary to properly practice it. Eccl. 7:16 states *"Be not righteous over much; neither make thyself over wise:*

---

[74] The compound verb διηρμήνευεν (*diermeneuen*) intensifies the concept of interpretation. It occurs 6x in the NT.

why shouldest thou destroy thyself?" Does this verse mean that a believer should not be too holy but should sin a little, and that he should not be too wise as well? Of course not. This passage indicates that righteousness or wisdom without God is destructive. The Pharisees were righteous without God and Christ condemned their self-righteousness. According to Ezk. 28:12, Satan was full of wisdom but his wisdom is corrupted (v. 17) because he rejected the Lord.

Another consideration for the necessity of interpretation is that many denominations and cults give false interpretations of passages. Doctrinal positions are often built upon false interpretations of Scriptures. Several Protestant denominations defend baptismal regeneration based on a faulty exegesis of Acts 2:38. The Mormons misinterpret I Cor. 15:29 to teach proxy baptism. Passages relating to important practical truths such *'church,' 'baptism,' 'Body of Christ,' 'baptism of the Holy Ghost,'*[75] etc., are often misinterpreted, causing aberrant practices by Christians.

Another consideration for proper hermeneutics is that the original message had and has one interpretation but many applications. The reader of Scripture must put himself in the

---

[75]Carson warns about making "by one spirit" (I Cor. 12:13) a technical term for "baptism in the Holy Ghost." He presents two faulty views without giving a satisfactory interpretation by stating, "Charismatics tend to want to make all occurrences of the expression refer to a post-conversion effusion of Spirit; some anti-charismatics contemplate I Corinthians 12:13...and conclude, with equal fallacy, that all New Testament references are to the effusion of Spirit all Christians receive at their conversion." D. A. Carson, *Exegetical Fallacies* (Grand Rapids: Baker Book House, 1984), p. 46.

'sandals' of the original recipient to attempt to understand the original message. All of the books of the Bible had a certain audience in a particular historical milieu. For instance, the Song of Solomon was written by Solomon about a particular woman in his life. What the original message was is essential before one can make an application from the book.

The Means of Interpretation

There are several means or helps of interpretation to understand the Bible. One help is by interpreting the Bible Historically. The Bible did not fall out of heaven in the twenty-first century, but it has a historical backdrop. If one does not interpret the Bible according to its historical background, he may be forced into dangerous practices. For instance, in Mark 16:18[76] the text promises *"They shall take up serpents; and if they drink any deadly thing, it shall not hurt them; they shall lay hands on the sick, and they shall recover."* Some fail to observe the historical background of this verse and practice 'snake handling' and die. This verse clearly states that the practice and the promise is not for this generation, but for the first generation. The signs were for the first century believers who were preaching and inscripturating the Word of God, as *"they went forth, and preached every where, the Lord working with them, and confirming the word with signs following. Amen"* (v. 20).

---

[76]For an able defense of the textual integrity and theological orthodoxy of Mark 16:9-20, see J. W. Burgon, *The Last Twelve Verses of the Gospel according to S. Mark* (Grand Rapids: Associated Publishers and Authors, Inc., n.d.), pp. 73-379.

Another means is by interpreting the Bible Literally. By literal, Bible believers do not mean a 'wooden' literalness which does not allow for figurative language. The Bible is replete with figures of speech[77], but the only way to determine figurative language is by interpreting the Bible literally. For the student of Scripture to allegorize the Bible obscures the figures of speech in the Bible. Ezra and the Levites read the Law of Moses and interpreted it *"distinctly, and gave the sense, and caused them to understand the reading"* (Neh. 8:8). They gave neither an allegorical interpretation nor a numerological interpretation, but they gave the *'sense'*[78] so the people could understand.

Another means for proper interpretation is by interpreting Grammatically. The Bible was written in human language as propositional truth. The reader of Scripture must consider the syntax and vocabulary of the Bible to understand it. Nouns, verbs, adjectives, adverbs, prepositions, articles, pronouns, participles, etc. make up language, and God used them to communicate His divine truth.

Another help is the Dispensational Interpretation of Scripture. One must interpret the Bible according to the distinctions of God's progressive revelation in order to rightly understand it. For instance, Judaism was the religion of the nation of Israel in the OT. Israel had a state religion, but Christianity is distinct from Judaism because it is not a state religion. The Lord's program for NT believers is the local

---

[77]For instance, the first chapter of Isaiah has at least 35 different figures of speech and totals over 50 elements of figurative language.

[78]*sekel* means "intelligent, prudent sense," and it conveys the concept of a normal or a literal interpretation.

church apart from the state. Contrary to Roman Catholicism and Protestantism, Christianity is not a state religion.[79]

The Method of Interpretation

Paul states in II Tim. 2:15 that the believer is to *"study to shew thyself approved unto God, a workman that needeth not to be ashamed, rightly dividing the word of truth."* The expression *"rightly dividing"* translates ὀρθοτομοῦντα (*orthotomounta*) which literally means 'straight cutting.' As Paul was a tentmaker, he would cut the pieces of material into rectangles to piece them together, making one large, integrated piece for a tent. Likewise, the Bible exegete must properly place the various portions of Scripture together and interpret them for one harmonious message. One simple way to do this is the *C.I.A.* method. First, the Bible student must study and understand the *Context* of the passage in question. This study would include both the greater context and the immediate context of the passage. The student must determine who the audience is, what the purpose of the message is, who wrote the passage, the time element involved in the message, and where the event happened. These determinations resolve the who, what, when, and where of the context. Second, the student must understand the *Interpretation* of the passage. This is

---

[79]Baptists differ from Catholicism and Protestantism in this regard. Baptists teach the separation of church and state based on the dispensational interpretation of the Bible. Fallaciously, state religions usually have a sole leader, persecute religious dissidents (heretics), and require all citizens to enter the state religion shortly after birth.

done by interpreting the passage Historically, Literally, Grammatically, and Dispensationally.   Once the interpretation is made, then the exegete may advance to the third step, which is making an *Application*.   By interpreting a passage according to its context, the Bible student will not tend to make mis-applications.   The value of the *C.I.A.* method is apparent by utilizing it on a passage such as Psm. 34.   Verse 19 states *"Many are the afflictions of the righteous: but the Lord delivereth him out of them all."*   The Context of Psm. 34 is I Sam. 21 which details David's flight from Saul.   The Interpretation of Psm. 34 gives David's refuge in the Lord as his life is at stake with Saul pursuing him.   Many times the Lord protected David when Saul wanted to kill him.   The Application is that the same Lord Who protected David at major crisis points in his life will be a refuge for any and all believers as well.   By applying the simple *C.I.A.* method to Scripture, the believer may develop valuable understanding of the Bible.

Summary

Believers must interpret the Bible correctly to understand what God has spoken.   Various means help the believer to determine a consistent interpretation of the Bible. Utilization of the C.I.A. method ensures that the believer will have a proper understanding of what the Lord has said.

CHAPTER EIGHT

Perfections of Scripture

Introduction

There are several perfections or qualities of the Bible which the author has not discussed previously. These perfections are the Perspicuity, the Sufficiency, the Animation and the Preservation of Scripture.

The Perspicuity of Scripture

The word *'perspicuity'* refers to the quality of clearness the Bible possesses with regard to all the major doctrines. Although the meaning of every verse of the Bible is not necessarily apparent, the main teachings of the Bible are clear, and the support passages for the main teachings are clear. God did not write a book which has as its major message a hidden or esoteric meaning. The doctrines of bibliology, theology, soteriology, ecclesiology and eschatology are clear to the believer who seeks illumination from the Holy Spirit.

The Sufficiency of Scripture

The message of the Bible is sufficient for faith and practice. Paul states that all Scripture is profitable for doctrine and duty (II Tim. 3:16). The Christian does not need further revelation from God. There are no missing books of the Bible, and there are no more Scriptures to be written.[80]   The Bible is sufficient for giving man the message of reconciliation with God and the plan for living as a reconciled creature before God.

The Animation of Scripture

The Bible has the vitality of life in its message which makes it alive.   The Scriptures have a life-giving and a life-changing message.   The author of Hebrews affirms this animation, stating *"For the Word of God is quick, and powerful, and sharper than any twoedged sword, piercing even to the dividing asunder of soul and spirit, and of the joints and marrow, and is a discerner of the thoughts and intents of the heart"* (Heb. 4:12). The word translated *'quick'* is ζῶν *(zon)* means 'living' throughout the NT.   Lenski comments, "It is an outflow of his [God's] life and therefore instinct with the same divine, imperishable, powerful life, either to kindle similar life in us or to react against all opposition."[81]   The Bible is alive because God is alive and His Words produce life (I Pet. 1:23).

---

[80]*The Book of Mormon* notwithstanding, Christians have all of God's message. Mormons undermine the sufficiency of Scriptures with heresy such as the demonic quote from the non-canonical book II Nephi 29:10, "Wherefore, because that ye have a Bible ye need not suppose that it contains all my words; neither need ye suppose that I have not caused more to be written."

[81]R. C. H. Lenski, *The Interpretation of The Epistle to the Hebrews and The Epistle of James* (Minneapolis: Augsburg Publ. House, 1966), p. 141.

The Preservation of Scripture

The Bible will endure forever as it is the inscripturation of the Mind of God. Psm 119:89 states *"For ever, O Lord, thy word is settled in heaven."* It is Eternal. I Pet. 1:23 states *"Being born again, not of corruptible seed, but of incorruptible, by the word of God, which liveth and abideth for ever."* It is Incorruptible. Mt. 24:35 states, *"Heaven and earth shall pass away, but my words shall not pass away."* It will not Pass Away. Jesus said in Jn. 12:48, *"He that rejecteth me, and receiveth not my words, hath one that judgeth him: the word that I have spoken, the same shall judge him in the last day."* It is the Final Judge.

Summary

"The Lord GOD hath spoken." God has given man divine revelation in the form of Holy Scriptures, the Bible. His inscripturated truth is the product of the process of inspiration and consequently it is the inerrant, canonical *autographa*. The Holy Spirit helps the believer to understand it by divine illumination and by proper principles of interpretation so that the believer may live a Christ-honoring life. The perfections of Scripture such as perspicuity, sufficiency, animation and preservation are necessary for the believer's full Christian life. *"THE LORD GOD HATH SPOKEN, WHO CAN BUT PROPHESY?"*

APPENDIX A

Gnosticism and the New Testament Text

Introduction

Satan has attacked God's Word since the beginning. He has utilized Gnosticism in this attack upon the Scriptures, especially upon the New Testament (NT). Many of the variant readings of the NT manifest Gnostic theology. These variant readings are in the manuscripts used by the Critical Text (CT), such as the United Bible Societies' Greek New Testament, and modern translations, in contrast with the readings of the fuller manuscripts of the *Textus Receptus* (TR) and the Authorized Version (AV). This essay will define Gnosticism, will demonstrate its influence on the NT text, and will denounce its impact on modern translations.

Gnosticism Defined

The Devil delineated the tenets of Gnosticism when he said *"Ye shall not surely die"* and *"Ye shall be as gods"* (Gen. 3:4-5). These tenets were manifested in all major religions in the form of reincarnation and deification of man. Even today, Hinduism, Buddhism, Shintoism and other religions have as a basis of belief the tenets of reincarnation and deification of man (humanism). Furthermore, the New Age Movement (NAM) is an apparent effort to unite all major and minor systems of religion under these two heads. The world view of Gnosticism is pantheism with a dualistic ontology (good vs.

evil, spirit vs. flesh). F. B. Huey defines Gnosticism as it affected NT Christianity, saying:

> *It comes from the Greek gnosis, knowledge, and it was a widespread and highly diverse religious movement with roots in Greek philosophy and folk religion. Its chief emphases are the utter transcendence of God, created matter as fallen and evil, and salvation by esoteric knowledge. It is associated with names of Marcion, Basilides, and Valentinus.*[82]

Gnosticism attacked the Person of the Lord Jesus Christ in one of two ways, namely, Docetism or Adoptionism.

Docetism

Docetism comes from the Greek verb δοκέω (*dokeo* ["to seem"]) teaching that Jesus Christ only "seemed" to be a man, but was in fact a phantom. Since to Gnostics flesh was evil, they could not accept the truth that God was manifest in the flesh. Irenaeus gives detail about the Docetism of his day, saying "The Savior he declared to be unborn, incorporeal and without form, asserting that he was seen as a man in appearance only."[83]

Adoptionism

Adoptionism is also known as Spirit Christology. An

---

[82]F. B. Huey and Bruce Corley, *A Student's Dictionary for Biblical and Theological Studies* (Grand Rapids: Zondervan Publishing House, 1983, pp. 88-89.

[83]Irenaeus, *Adversus Haereses*, I, xxiv. 1-2.

ancient writer states,

> *The Holy Spirit...is regarded as the pre-existent Son...The redeemer is the virtuous man chosen by God, with whom that Spirit of God was united. As he did not defile the Spirit, but kept him constantly as his companion, and carried out the work to which the Deity had called him...he was in virtue of a Divine decree, adopted as a son...*[84]

Irenaeus adds, "And that after his baptism Christ descended upon him in the form of a dove..."[85] Adoptionism permeated Christendom by the end of the second century. J. N. D. Kelly observes,

> *There was a great variety of Gnostic systems, but a common pattern ran through them all. From the pleroma, or spiritual world of aeons the divine Christ descended and united Himself for a time (according to Ptolemy, between the baptism and the passion) to the historical personage...These were tendencies of the fringe, yet Gnosticism at any rate came within an ace of swamping the central tradition.*[86]

Gnosticism attacked Christology in two different directions. In the one direction, Docetism taught that Jesus

---

[84] *The Shepherd of Hermas*, Mand. 12, Sim. 6.

[85] Irenaeus, *Adversus Haereses*, I, xxvi, 1-2.

[86] J. N. D. Kelly, *Early Christian Doctrines* (London: Adam and Charles Black), pp. 141,142.

Christ was not manifest in the flesh, but that He only seemed to be in the flesh.   In the other direction, Adoptionism taught that Jesus of Nazareth was not the Christ; the heresy disassociated Jesus from the Christ.

Gnosticism Demonstrated

Ancient and modern textual scholars admit that the NT text has been tampered with by heretics.   Tertullian complains, "Now this heresy of yours does not receive certain Scriptures; and whichever of them it does receive, it perverts by means of additions and diminutions, for the accomplishment of its own purposes."[87]   Again, Origen informs, saying,

> *Nowadays, as is evident, there is a great diversity between the various manuscripts, either through the negligence of certain copyists, or the perverse audacity shown by some in correcting the text, or through the fault of those, who, playing the part of correctors, lengthen or shorten it as they please.*[88]

The modern textual authority, E. C. Colwell frankly states,

> *The majority of the variant readings in the NT were created for theological or dogmatic reasons. Most of the manuals and handbooks now in print (including mine!) will tell you that these variations were the fruit of careless treatment which was possible*

---

[87]Tertullian, *On Prescriptions Against Heresies*, I:17:1.
[88]*In Matth. tom.* XV, 14; *P.G.* XIII, 1293.

because the books of the NT had not yet attained a strong position as 'Bible.' The reverse is the case. It was because they were the religious treasure of the church that they were changed.[89]

More importantly, the NT writers warned that this heresy would be Gnosticism, and the two forms of Gnosticism would be Docetism and Adoptionism.

Scripture

The Apostle Paul warned Timothy of the heresy threatening the church of Ephesus, stating, *"O Timothy, keep that which is committed to thy trust, avoiding profane and vain babblings, and oppositions of science* (γνώσεως [*gnoseos*)]) *falsely so called"* (I Tim. 6:20). Paul refers to *"the lie"* of Gnosticism as promoted in the Garden in two NT passages. Romans 1:25 states *"Who changed the truth of God into a lie, and worshipped and served the creature more than the Creator..."* In II Thessalonians 2:11, Paul states, *"And for this cause God shall send them strong delusion that they should believe a lie."* The deification of man is suggested in Paul's caution to Timothy in II Tim. 3:2, *"lovers of their own selves..."* Again, the Gnostic doctrine of reincarnation is the backdrop of the Gnostic teaching of Hymenaeus and Philetus, who attacked the doctrine of resurrection and about whom Paul warned, saying *"Who concerning the truth have erred, saying*

---

[89]E. C. Colwell, *What is the Best New Testament?* (Chicago: University of Chicago Press, 1952), p. 53.

that the resurrection is past already; and overthrow the faith of some" (II Tim. 2:16-17).

In Paul's Epistle to the Colossians, he defends Christianity by giving the true meaning to words utilized by Gnostics. Some of the words in the Gnostic vocabulary which Paul enlightened with Christian truth are 'philosophy,' 'fulness,' 'Godhead,' 'humility,' and 'will worship' (Col. 2:1 ff.). Since Gnosticism teaches that man becomes God after many reincarnations, it follows that flesh is evil and man must be delivered from evil flesh. Paul warned the church at Ephesus about the Gnostic teaching that flesh (both the marital union and animal flesh) was evil, delineating this demonic doctrine, *"Forbidding to marry, and commanding to abstain from meats..."* (I Tim. 4:1-5, especially v. 3).

Paul was not the only NT writer to warn against Gnosticism. The Apostle John singled out the two forms of Gnosticism in his Epistles. In I John 4:3, the Apostle explicitly warns against Docetism saying, *"And every spirit that confesseth not that Jesus Christ is come in the flesh is not of God: and this is that spirit of antichrist, whereof ye have heard that it should come; and even now already is it in the world"* (*vide* II Jn. 1:7). Concerning the other form of Gnosticism, Adoptionism, John issued this caveat to his readers saying, *"Who is a liar but he that denieth that Jesus is the Christ? He is antichrist, that denieth the Father and the Son"* (I Jn. 2:22).

The Apostle John concludes his First Epistle by declaring that Jesus Christ is the true God and then he commands *"Little Children, keep yourselves from idols. Amen"* (I Jn. 5:20-21). He is warning his hearers to stay away from the Gnosticism which produces false or Gnostic Christology, because a Gnostic Christ is an idol!

Gnosticism Denounced

Gnosticism has had an impact on modern translations because most English translations are based on Greek texts which favor Gnostic readings in the variants. Believers should obey John's warning concerning idolatry by shunning any translation which prefers and promotes Gnostic readings and the resultant Gnostic Christology. It is this writer's concern to denounce modern translations so that believers will not inadvertently promote Gnostic Christology and consequently come under the Lord's condemnation as expressed by John, *"Look to yourselves, that we lose not those things which we have wrought, but that we receive a full reward"* (II Jn. 1:8).

Several examples of Gnostic influence in modern translations are in order. In the first century, the Gnostics disassociated the person of Jesus of Nazareth from the person of Christ. This was manifested in their tampered texts when they attacked the full title of the Lord Jesus Christ. In over 200 places in the NT text the names *'Jesus'* and *'Christ'* were omitted by Gnostics to disassociate Jesus from the Christ and from the Lord. For instance, the following passages omit some part of the full title for the Son of God: Jn. 4:42 (the Christ), Acts 20:21 (Christ), Rom. 1:16 (of Christ), Rom. 16:18 (Jesus), I Cor. 16:22 (Jesus Christ), I Thess. 3:11,13 (Christ), Heb. 3:1 (Christ), Heb. 10:9 (O God), I Jn. 1:7 (Christ), Rev. 1:8 (Beginning and End), Rev. 1:9 (Christ...Christ), Rev. 1:11

(Alpha...Omega...First...Last), Rev. 16:5 (O Lord), Rev. 21:4 (God), and Rev. 22:21 (Christ). All one has to do is peruse the modern versions in these passages to see that these translations are following Gnostic readings.

The modern translations not only follow Gnostic readings which disassociate Jesus from the Christ, but they also follow Gnostic readings which attack the Deity and Humanity of Christ. The following are classic passages which demonstrate the modern versions consistent effort to eviscerate the Person of Christ. In Luke 22:43-44, the Critical Text (Westcott and Hort Text, Nestle's Text, *et al*) puts these two verses in double brackets denoting their questioning of the authenticity of these verses. The passage deals with the 'bloody sweat' of Jesus Christ, which would be offensive to Docetic Gnostics who taught that Jesus only seemed to have a body. In Jn. 1:18, the modern versions (RSV, NAS, NIV, etc.) follow the reading of Valentinus who substituted 'only begotten God' for 'only begotten Son.' Presumably, this Gnostic perverted the Scripture because he was opposed to the teaching of John that the *'Word'* (1:1) was identified with the *'only begotten'* (1:14) who was identified with the *'Son'* (1:18). John was stating that the *'Word'* was the *'Son;'* Valentinus could not accept that the *'Son'* was the *'Word'* (God).

The Lord teaches His omnipresence in Jn. 3:13. While He was speaking to Nicodemus on earth, He was omnipresent in Heaven (*'which is in heaven'*). The RSV, NIV and NAS omit this clause, which elimination would nullify Jesus' deity in this passage. The strongest teaching against the Gnostic tenet that flesh is evil is *'God was manifest in the flesh'* (I Tim. 3:16). The Gnostics attempted to remove that truth by cleverly substituting the relative pronoun 'who' for *'God.'* However, '(he) who was manifest in the flesh' is no mystery of godliness; there is no mystery for man ('he') to be manifested in the flesh, but there is for 'God to be manifest in the flesh,' the ASV, NAS, NIV, RSV, and NEB notwithstanding.

John's First Epistle is anti-Gnostic and consequently it was attacked by the Gnostics. The very passage which refutes Docetism (*'Christ is come in the flesh'*) is omitted in the ASV, NAS, NIV, RSV, and NEB. Again the Johannine Comma (I Jn. 5:7-8) is omitted by all modern versions, although this omission causes great grammatical problems. In spite of all the scholarly attacks by Gnostics and Christians on this passage, the Lord has preserved this Scripture (*'in heaven, the Father, the Word, and the Holy Ghost: and these three are one, and there are three that bear witness in earth'*). The teaching about the incarnation of God in Christ and the Trinity was, and still is, hated by Gnostics.

Although the writer could give a textual defense for the TR readings in the aforementioned passages, all that he intends to demonstrate is how conducive the modern versions are to the promotion of Gnostic Christology.

Conclusion

Gnosticism is the religious system built upon the tenets of *the lie* of Satan in the Garden of Eden. Gnosticism is manifested in the ancient and modern religions of the world, including first century Gnosticism and the current NAM. Gnostics attacked the NT manuscripts shortly after they were written and substituted Biblical Christology with Gnostic

Christology. NT manuscripts conducive to Gnostic Christology are the basis for modern versions. These versions in turn promote Gnostic Christology. If the Apostle John were asked about the Critical Text and it subsequent translations such as the ASV, NAS, NIV, RSV and NEB, he undoubtedly would say, *"Little children, keep yourselves from idols. Amen."*

APPENDIX B

The Lord Jesus Christ and the Received Bible
John 17:8[90]

Introduction

Around AD 96, Clement of Rome wrote *1 Clement*, an epistle to the Corinthians, encouraging them to be united as Paul advised them in I Corinthians. Although some may consider Clement's effort to write extra-biblical writings commendable, this early tendency among the patristics to produce penultimate authorities for Christianity is the quintessence of the extra-biblical authoritarianism of Roman Catholicism. The apostle Paul had already written, under the process of inspiration, the inspired and canonical book of 1 Corinthians.[91] The Corinthian

---

[90] Thomas M. Strouse, "The Lord Jesus Christ and the Received Bible, John. 17:8," *Thou Shalt Keep Them: A Biblical Theology of the Perfect Preservation of Scripture*. Kent Brandenburg, ed. (El Sobrante, CA: Pillar & Ground Publ., 2003), pp. 51-57.

[91] Paul knew his oral teachings which were inscripturated were inspired, stating *"Which things also we speak, not in the words which man's wisdom teacheth, but which the Holy Ghost teacheth; comparing spiritual things with spiritual"* (1 Cor. 2:13). Also, Peter knew Paul's writings were inspired, saying *"As also in all his epistles, speaking in them of these things; in which are some things hard to be understood, which they that are unlearned and unstable wrest, as they do also the other scriptures, unto their own destruction"* (2 Pet. 3:16). The fact that John attached a colophon to the Apocalypse (Rev. 22:18-19) indicates that he recognized that

Church, and all churches struggling for unity, needs to heed the *autographa,* and not some non-authoritative, non-canonical epistle of a proto-Roman Catholic bishop. This tendency to look for penultimate authorities to settle matters of truth is prevalent today within Christianity. Theologians want to bolster their arguments with quotes from John Calvin, C. H. Spurgeon, or D. A. Carson, etc. Even in the arena of bibliology, fundamentalists are looking for the ultimate, final quote or statement that will resolve all issues. Some look to B. F. Westcott and F. H. A. Hort, or Bruce Metzger, or to Daniel Wallace for the final, authoritative answer to the supposed complex issue about which text/translation is the best.[92] Those who look lightly at the great bibliological truths of Scripture concerning inspiration and preservation in theology, look strongly at extra-biblical authorities in practice.

The Bible, however, attests to its own inspiration, preservation, and authority. Furthermore, the author of Scripture, the Lord Jesus Christ, spoke clearly about the doctrines of perfect inspiration, perfect preservation and their resultant text and translations. The bibliologist does not need to listen to secondary authorities since the Ultimate Authority on Scripture has spoken. This essay will demonstrate, by

---

any change in the words of the Book of Revelation (whole Bible?) would result in a change of the message of Scripture.

[92] Some even maintain that a textual 'savior' will come along and save the day for text criticism as J. Whitcomb and H. Morris (*The Genesis Flood: The Biblical Record and Its Scientific Implications*, [Philadelphia: The Presbyterian and Reformed Publ. Co., 1961]) supposedly did for Biblical creationism.

exegeting John 17:8 in the context of Christ's great intercessory prayer for unity, that the Lord Jesus Christ is the author of the received Bible mindset and expects His followers to be united around the received Bible movement throughout history.

Exegesis of John 17:8

Background

John recorded the Lord's "high-priestly" prayer following His farewell discourse (Jn. 13-16). The prayer naturally divides into three parts; He prayed for Himself (vv. 1-5), for His immediate audience of apostles and disciples (vv. 6-19), and for future generations of believers (vv. 20-26). [93] Christ recognized the culmination of His redemptive purpose in the incarnation (cf. Jn. 2:4; 7:6, 8, 30; 8:20; 12:23, 27-28, 31-32; 13:1, 31) and prayed. The Lord's prayer for Himself included His desire for mutual glorification of the Son and the Father, His acknowledgment of the scope of the Son's redemptive purpose to give eternal life to those given Him (cf. Jn. 3:15-16; 6:37, 44; 10:28-30), His assertion that He had finished God's redemptive plan (cf. Jn. 19:30), and His request to return to His previous glory shared with the Father (cf. Jn. 10:30).[94]

---

[93]There may be a parallel with the high priest who offered sacrifices for himself, his family, and the nation on the Day of Atonement (cf. Lev. 16:1-34).

[94]Certainly the Lord Jesus Christ's request to return to mutual glory with the Father bespeaks of His pre-existence and deity (cf. Phil. 2:5-11).

The Son's prayer for His apostles and disciples is longer than His prayer for Himself.[95] The Lord interceded for them that they would be kept (vv. 11, 15) and would fulfill their ministry of the Word (vv. 8, 17). Christ was confident that the Father would hear His intercession because the disciples had been given to Him by the Father (vv. 6-7, 9-12), they had been obedient (v. 8), and that the Lord Jesus had kept them. (v. 12). The Son interceded for His apostles because He had given them the Father's Words to minister in the world (vv. 8, 20), which would hate them (vv. 14-19).[96]

The Lord Jesus' prayer extended to future believers as well, who would unite with Christ through the apostles' ministry of the Word (v. 20). He prayed that His disciples would be one in relationship with God (as the Son was in the Father) and that relationship would be manifested with love based the apostles' ministry of the Word (vv. 20, 23, 24, 26). As the Son of God had a spiritual relationship with God the

---

[95] These disciples, although they had limitations, were obedient to Christ (cf. Jn. 2:22; Mt. 16:22-23).

[96] Apostates manifest the world's hatred for the Words of God through higher and lower criticism. Their efforts to analyze and evaluate the Bible from the anti-supernatural, rationalist approach eviscerate the Words of the Bible and the character of its Author. The liberals and modernists approach is to *"minister questions, rather than godly edifying which is in faith"* (1 Tim. 1:4). Questions such as who wrote the Pentateuch or what was the ultimate source for Mark's Gospel or does the *pericope de adultera* (Jn. 7:53-8:11) belong in Scripture ring of *"Yea, hath God said"* (Gen. 3:1). This man-centered *"wisdom descendeth not from above, but is earthly, sensual, devilish"* (Jam. 3:15).

Father (vv. 21-23), so Christ prayed for spiritual unity among His disciples (vv. 11, 21-22) who were in the heritage of the Apostles who received the Lord Jesus Christ's words which He in turn received from the Father (vv. 8, 17, 20).

Context

The Received Bible

> *For I have given unto them the words which thou gavest me: and they have received them, and have known surely that I came out from thee, and they have believed that thou didst send me* (John 17:8).

God the Father gave Words (ῥήματά) to God the Son (cf. also Jn. 12:49; 14:10). Presumably these Words would be the *"all Scripture"* (πᾶσα γραφὴ) of the Bible canon (2 Tim. 3:16). These Words are the ones Christ promised would not pass away (Mt. 24:35). The Lord's canonical Words would be available for every generation, He declared, because His canonical Words, and not His *agrapha* (not written), will be the judge of every man. The views that not all of the Lord's spoken words have been written down and consequently His promise in Mt. 24:35 is for prophecy only[97] or is hyperbole,[98]

---

[97]Daniel Wallace argues that Christ must be referring to "His prophecies" because in John 21, "Everything that Jesus did and said, the whole libraries of the world could not contain. Obviously not all the words of Jesus are written down. So what happened to the preservation of those words? It doesn't mean that. It means…prophecy." John Ankerberg, "Which English Translation of the Bible is Best for Christian to Use Today," *The*

are certainly wrongheaded and refuted by Christ's claim that *"He that rejecteth me, and receiveth not my words, hath one that judgeth him: the word that I have spoken, the same shall judge him in the last day"* (Jn. 12:48). Mankind will not be judged by all of Christ's spoken words since many were not canonical. God is just in His judgment (Jn. 5:30; cf. Rom. 2:2) and will judge man on the basis of His ever available, perfectly preserved, inscripturated Words.

The process, to which the Lord alluded (in Jn. 17:8), was the process of inspiration, wherein the Father breathed out His Words[99] to the Lord Jesus Christ (Jn. 8:28), who in turn breathed out these inerrant and authoritative Words to His Biblical writers. The Lord's Biblical writers in His immediate audience, such as Matthew, John, Peter and others, received the Words and ultimately inscripturated them in their canonical writings which were passed on to future generations

---

John Ankerberg Show Transcript (Chattanooga, TN: The Ankerberg Theological Research Institute, 1995), pp. 44, 46.

[98]"Matthew 24:35 uses the same hyperbolic language as Matthew 5:18." William Combs, "The Preservation of Scripture," *Detroit Baptist Seminary Journal* 5 (2000): 24.

[99]These canonical words were no doubt the archetypal words to which the Psalmist referred when stating *"For ever, O Lord, thy word is settled in heaven"* (Psm. 119:89). Combs, like many others, rejects "the idea of an archetypal Bible in heaven," ("The Preservation of Scripture," p. 17), but is rebutted by Scripture. Daniel was informed of the same heavenly Bible that contained the prophesied history of the nations and leaders relative to Israel's future. The informing angel stated, *"But I will shew thee that which is noted in the scripture of truth...and now will I shew thee the truth..."* (Dan. 10:21-11:45; cf. Isa. 65:6).

through those who would believe on the Lord Jesus Christ through Apostles' respective Scriptures (cf. v. 20).[100]

The Lord's disciples *"have received* (ἔλαβον *elabon)*[101] *them,"* unlike the unbelieving Jews who *"receive not"* (οὐ λαμβάνετε *ou lambanete*) the Lord's spoken words (Jn. 3:11).[102] Those that had received (ἔλαβον) the Lord Jesus Christ in salvation (Jn. 1:12) readily received His words for sanctification (Jn. 17:20), John averred. Upon receiving the Lord's Words (Jn. 17:8), these ministers of God's Words acknowledged (ἔγνωκαν *egnosan*; Jn. 17:7; cf. Jn. 16:30) and believed (ἐπίστευσαν *episteusan*) cf. 3:16-17) that the Father sent the Son (cf. Jn. 5:36-37). The Lord Jesus Christ required His original audience to receive His Words and guard them (cf. Mt. 28:20; *"to observe"*

------

[100]Doubtless the Holy Spirit has used Paul's *Epistle to the Romans*, for example, as the means to justify multitudes of repentant sinners through the ages for the Lord's glory.

[101] This word is a 3rd person, plural, 2nd *aorist*, active, indicative verb from λαμβάνω (*lambano*) and means "to take" or "to receive."

[102]The Person of the Lord Jesus Christ and His Words are inextricably united so that rejection of one leads to the rejection of the other. Did not Christ warn the Jews, *"For had ye believed Moses, ye would have believed me: for he wrote of me. But if ye believe not his writings, how shall ye believe my words?"* The field of Biblical Criticism, of which Text Criticism is one facet, is a system of unbelief originated and promoted by apostates. Why are professing fundamentalists attracted to and entertained by any facet of this anti-supernatural movement?

[τηρεῖν *terein*]).[103] This "received text" or "received Bible" mindset originated with the Lord Jesus Christ, **not** with Erasmus, Beza, or the KJV translators.[104] Believers of every generation have expected to receive God's preserved Words. The requirement for and the expectation of the Lord's received Bible has had a theological and historical continuity which shall not be broken, according to Scripture (cf. 1 Tim. 3:15). The fact that believers in the first century, in the seventeenth century, and in the twenty-first century, have had a "received Bible" mindset is built upon Scriptural teaching, not historical necessity.

That the first century Christians had a "received Bible" mindset is corroborated by the practice of the first century churches.   These NT churches and the members thereof received the oral apostolic teaching which ultimately became the inscripturated Words of God. These inscripturated Words in the form of Gospels and Epistles became the NT Canonical Words which the churches were charged to guard (Mt. 28:19-20; 1 Tim. 3:15; Rev. 22:18-19).   Several examples of this "received Bible" mindset in the practice of the NT churches follow.

Peter preached his great Pentecost sermon from within

---

[103] Christ commended the members of the church of Philadelphia because they had guarded or "kept" (ἐτήρησάς *eteresas*) His word for perhaps some forty years (Rev. 3:8, 10).

[104]That believers coined the term "received text" (*textus receptus*) in 1633 and have remained comfortable with the term to this very day demonstrate historically this heritage of the "received Bible" mindset which originated with Christ.

the Jerusalem assembly to hostile Jews. When many of these Christ-rejecting Jews heard the preaching of Peter about repentance and remission of sins, they received (ἀποδεξάμενοι *apodexamenoi*)[105] his authoritative words, as Luke recorded; *"Then they that gladly received his word were baptized: and the same day there were added unto them about three thousand souls"* (Acts 2:41). They realized their responsibility before God and received the oral tradition that ultimately became the inscripturated Words of truth.

Not only were Jews saved when they fulfilled their responsibility before God and received His preached revelation, but so were the Samaritans. Luke stated, *"Now when the apostles which were at Jerusalem heard that Samaria had received the word of God, they sent unto them Peter and John"* (Acts 8:14). The church in Samaria was established because Samaritans, or half-Jews, had received (δέδεκται *dedektai*) the Words of God preached by a Jew named Philip.

Luke recorded that Jews and Samaritans entered into the Christian life with the "received Bible" mindset. Next, he stated concerning the Gentiles, *"And the apostles and brethren that were in Judaea heard that the Gentiles had also received the word of God"* (Acts 11:1). These Gentiles *"received"* (ἐδέξαντο *edexanto*), along with Jews and Samaritans, the Lord's revealed truth in preached form. Thus mankind has the responsibility to receive God's

---

[105] The root behind this *Aorist* participle is ἀποδέχομαι (*apodechomai*) which means "to take" or "to embrace."

revelation by faith and some have exercised this "received Bible" mindset.

The Jewish Bereans *"received* (ἐδέξαντο *edexanto*) *the word with all readiness of mind"* (Acts 17:11) and compared Paul's apostolic preaching with the OT Scriptures. They had already received the OT Scriptures as authoritative revelation, and now practiced this "received Bible" mindset with the oral tradition.

The Apostle Paul identified his preached word and the Words of God in his ministry at Thessalonica. He stated,

> *And ye became followers of us, and of the Lord, having received the word in much affliction, with joy of the Holy Ghost... For this cause also thank we God without ceasing, because, when ye received the word of God which ye heard of us, ye received it not as the word of men, but as it is in truth, the word of God, which effectually worketh also in you that believe* (1 Thess. 1:6; 2:13).

The apostle commended the Thessalonians since they received his preached Word as God's Words and not as man's words. Eventually Paul's canonical preached words became inscripturated in Acts and the Pauline Epistles. The Thessalonians are another testimony to the fact that first centuries churches maintained a "received Bible" mindset.[106]

---

[106]All saints enter into salvation in Christ with the "received Bible" mindset. It is only after some believers are indoctrinated contrary to this Biblical mindset and embrace the "restored Bible" mindset do denials of truth unfold.

In summary, the Lord Jesus Christ gave perfectly in inspiration and preservation the heavenly Words of the Father to His disciples. They in turn received these perfect Words and obediently kept them for future generations. That the early NT churches did this is incontestable. The Lord prophesied the means of His inspiration and preservation and fulfilled His bibliological work through His NT churches. The NT declares that the movement of the "received Bible" mindset originated with and is perpetuated by the Lord Jesus Christ through the instrumentality of His NT churches.

The Unity of Immersed Believers

The Savior prayed for the unity of those that the Father had given the Son. He stated, *"Holy Father, keep through thine own name those whom thou hast given me, that they may be one, as we are"* (Jn. 17:11). The foundation of this unity ("one" [ἐν *hen*]) is built on the indwelling (ἐν *en*) relationship of Christ with the believer and is likened to the Father and Son's indwelling relationship with each other (cf. v. 21).[107] As the believer receives the Lord through His Words (Jn. 1:12) in salvation and receives the Lord's Words as truth in sanctification (Jn. 17:20), he continues to believe and obey God's revelation.[108]

Those that receive the revelation of truth believe and obey the Lord. The Lord Jesus Christ required early on that

---

[107]Cf. Jn. 10:30; *"I and my father are one."*

[108]The Lord Jesus said, *"If a man love me, he will keep my words..."* (Jn. 14:23; cf. vv. 21 and 24; *vide* 1 Jn. 5:2-3).

those who received Him as Messiah needed to obey Him by publicly identifying with Him through John's baptism (Mt. 3:6-17; 21:25-27)[109] This baptism pictured the death, burial and resurrection of Jesus Christ (cf. Rom. 6:1-4).[110] John's baptism became the baptism of the Great Commission (Mt. 28:19-20) [111] and was consistently practiced by the NT churches throughout the *Book of Acts* (2:41-47; 8:12; 9:18; 10:47-48; 16:33; 18:8 *et al*).

Christ prayed for the unity of those the Father gave Him who in turn received the Lord and His Words, and believed and obeyed Christ by identifying with Him through believers' baptism.[112] Paul recognized the truth to the Lord's

---

[109] Almost all Protestant denominations as well as the Roman Catholic Church and the Eastern Orthodox Church recognize and practice baptism as the entrance requirement for church membership. These groups usually undermine the NT doctrine of believers' immersion.

[110] The meaning of βαπτίζειν (*baptizein*) is "to immerse" and the mode is immersion, according to the NT (cf. Mt. 3:16; Acts 8:37-39; Col. 2:12). Nowhere in the NT are the words for "sprinkle" or "pour" ever used for the ordinance of baptism.

[111] Baptized believers must recognize that they have the responsibility to guard the Lord's Words in their respective churches, according to Christ's Great Mandate.

[112] This does not mean that immersion is necessary for salvation, because it clearly is not. However, the Lord's whole prayer was concerned with those who receive, believe, and obey. Where do the un-immersed disobedient ones fit in relative to this prayer? Rather, why not ask why don't or won't the disobedient obey? The disobedient, and not theologians, create problems like this.

Prayer in Galatia, for example. The Apostle addressed the churches of Galatia (Gal. 1:2) and stated, *"For as many of you as have been baptized into Christ have put on Christ. There is neither Jew nor Greek, there is neither bond nor free, there is neither male nor female: for ye are all one in Christ Jesus"* (Gal. 3:27-28). The immersionist churches of Galatia manifested the "received Bible" mindset (Gal. 1:9) and were united in doctrine and practice. Based on contextual exegesis and grammar, the Lord Jesus Christ's prayer for unity was a prayer for those immersionists who have the "received Bible" mindset to be united around the Lord Jesus Christ. For one to reject Biblically this interpretation one would have to prove from Scripture that faithful followers of the Lord do not need to be baptized, that NT baptism is not believers' immersion, that the Lord Jesus would entrust His Words to disobedient believers, that believers' baptism is not the entrance into the local church, that Christ did not give His Great Commission to the local church, that believers did not have the responsibility or mindset to receive Christ's words and that they did not have the responsibility to keep His Words.[113]

Conclusion

The Lord prayed for the unity of *"the pillar and*

---

[113] It is apparent as one looks upon the landscape of fundamental Christianity that those on the forefront of the preservation/text/translation issue are the pastors and church members of received text/Bible, Baptist churches who are rightly battling the leaders and scholars of denominations, conventions, fellowships, para-church ministries, Bible colleges, and seminaries.

ground of the truth" movement cf. 1 Tim. 3:15). He gave His inspired and preserved Words to His initial churches of the first century for safekeeping. These apostolic churches had the expectation to receive His preserved Words and keep them for every generation. He wants His immersionist assemblies that have received His Words to be united in truth as is He and His Father. The received Savior with His received Words becomes foundational to the unity He wants for His institution of the immersionist assembly, as this divinely ordained and preserved institution preserves the Scriptures for every generation. The Lord Jesus Christ's preserved churches should be united in Him as they preserve His Words.

APPENDIX C

It is Written (Mt. 4:4)[114]

Introduction

Satan tempted the Lord Jesus Christ early in His ministry (Mt. 4:1-11). [115] The Lord answered the tempter with three references from Deuteronomy (8:3, 6:16, and 6:13, respectively). The first answer is significant. He stated, *"It is written, Man shall not live by bread alone, but by every word that proceedeth out of the mouth of God"* (v. 4, cited from Dt. 8:3).[116] This response summarizes the Lord's bibliology. 1) He affirmed the doctrine of the verbal, plenary inspiration of the autographa by stating the source of Scripture—*"proceedeth out of the mouth of God."* 2) He affirmed the authority of the written Scripture, and consequently its infallibility and inerrancy, by upholding it as a standard by which "Man shall live." 3) He affirmed the availability of Scripture since He declared His personal access and implied mankind's general access to God's Words—*"by*

------

[114]Originally entitled "Every Word, Matthew 4:4." Thomas M. Strouse, "Every Word, Matthew 4:4," *Thou Shalt Keep Them*, pp. 35-39.

[115]Cf. Mk. 1:12-13 and Lk 4:1-13.

[116]Although the Lord Jesus could have rebuked Satan with the power of His own personal authority (cf. Mt. 16:23), Christ submitted His personal authority to the written Scripture, and chose rather to rebuke His chief adversary with the highest authority—the written Words of God (Psm. 138:2).

every word." 4) He affirmed the doctrine of the verbal, plenary preservation of Scripture by the expression *"It is written."* The perfect tense, which He utilized, expresses a completed action with a resulting state of being. The result of the action continues from the past through the present and into the future. In effect, the Lord said "It was written and still is written." The living Word (Christ) validated His written Words since He believed He had the verbal, plenary Old Testament (OT) Words intact in His day. The purpose of this chapter is to examine in detail the Lord's claims about the full and complete text of the Hebrew OT available in His day.

Exegesis

Inspiration–*"Proceedeth Out of the Mouth of God"*

The participle behind proceedeth is ἐκπορευομένῳ (*ekporeuomeno*) and the infinitive means "to go out." The reference to the mouth στόματος (*stomatos*) indicates that God, who is Spirit, nevertheless gave man Words that could be inscripturated. God, who was the author of the original language (Gen. 1:3), and also of the various languages (Gen. 11:7), has revealed Himself through the medium of oral and written language (cf. Ex. 20:1 ff; Jer. 36:4).[117] The Lord God

---

[117]Since God spoke in words, the original Hebrew of the OT Scriptures must have had consonants and vowels (cf. Dt. 27:8). Consonants without vowels are not words and cannot be pronounced. Moses wrote the original words, including vowels (Dt. 31:24), apparently Ezra preserved the consonants and vowels (Neh. 8:8), and the Masoretes standardized the Hebrew OT text including the original consonants and vowel pointings.

is the source for the canonical *autographa* and decreed to put His self-revelation in the form of Words (II Pet. 1:20-21). He gave His divine Words through human language for the eternal benefit of mankind as Paul stated, *"All scripture is given by inspiration of God, and is profitable for doctrine, for reproof, for correction, for instruction in righteousness: That the man of God may be perfect, throughly furnished unto all good works"* (II Tim. 3:16-17).

Authority–*"Man Shall Live"*

Israel needed to learn the wilderness lesson of hunger and that through her obedience the Lord would supply the nation's physical and spiritual food (Dt. 8:1-3). The Lord cited this passage to show how He has provided every daily need including not only manna for Israel but also His Words for all mankind.[118] The Bible is the rulebook[119] by which man should live and for which man will give an account to God. It tells how man may be justified before God, stating *"Therefore being justified by faith, we have peace with God through our Lord Jesus Christ"* (Rom. 5:1).[120] Since the Scripture *"is profitable for doctrine, for reproof, for correction, for instruction in righteousness"* (2 Tim. 3:16), it follows that man should live in light of Scriptures'

---

[118]Jesus' food was obedience to God, as He stated, *"My meat is to do the will of Him that sent me and to finish His work"* (Jn. 4:34).

[119]*"Thy word is a lamp unto my feet, and a light unto my path"* (Psm 119:105; cf. Prov. 6:23).

[120]Cf. Rom. 3:23-25; 5:9-10.

injunctions. According to Psm. 119:98-100, God's Words make the believer wiser than his enemies, his teachers (even text critics) and the ancients. Scripture is necessary for salvation (1 Pet. 1:23-25) and sanctification (Jn. 17:17). The canonically inscripturated words of the Father and the Son constitute the standard by which man must live. The Lord stated *"He that rejecteth me, and receiveth not my words, hath one that judgeth him: the word that I have spoken, the same shall judge him in the last day"* (Jn. 12:48).

Availability–*"By Every Word"*

The Lord gave the *Torah* to the Jewish Nation through Moses so that she would be prepared to enter into Canaan (Dt. 1:1). Moses required the *Torah* to be placed in the Ark of the Covenant for future generations (Dt. 31:24-30). Centuries later Ezra read the *Torah* to the Jews in their new place of worship in Jerusalem (Neh. 8:1-9). There is no question that the Jewish scribes preserved the OT Scripture through God's ordained place of worship, either the Tabernacle or the Temple. God committed unto the Jews the oracles (τὰ λόγια) of God as their blessed privilege (Rom. 3:1-2). That the Jews were the custodians of the inscripturated divine utterances in their place of worship is non-controversial. Scripture adduces that they preserved and dispersed the Lord's Words for general availability as well: *"For Moses of old time hath in every city them that preach him, being read in the synagogues every sabbath day"* (Acts 15:21; cf. also Josh. 8:30-35).

The local New Testament (NT) church was and is the only custodian of the NT Canon and Text of the Canon. The

Lord promised to use His people in His institution to preserve His Words, stating:

> *Go ye therefore, and teach all nations, baptizing them in the name of the Father, and of the Son, and of the Holy Ghost: Teaching them to observe all things whatsoever I have commanded you: and, lo, I am with you alway, even unto the end of the world. Amen* (Mt. 28:19-20).

The Lord Jesus Christ gave His Great Commission to His churches to disciple all nations, by going worldwide, and immersing and instructing the believers. The Great Commission is the divine mandate to plant immersionist churches worldwide. Furthermore, the leadership of the churches must teach the members to observe (τηρεῖν literally "to guard") all things the Lord commanded (cf. Eph. 4:11-16). Ultimately, the *"all things"* would include the OT and NT Scriptures. Christ's Great Commission gives the sole responsibility of guarding the Bible Canon and Words of the Canon to the local NT church.[121] The NT Canon and Words therein were written to local churches and local church members.

Paul confirmed that the local church has the sole responsibility to preserve the truth. He stated, *"But if I tarry long, that thou mayest know how thou oughtest to behave thyself in the house of God, which is the church of the living*

---

[121]This responsibility was not given to the Roman Catholic Church, Protestantism, Bible societies, or para-church organizations.

God, the pillar and ground of the truth" (1 Tim. 3:15). The apostle identified the house of God as the church of the living God, the church that has bishops and deacons (vv. 1-13). Presumably, Paul alluded to the great Temple of Diana[122] (cf. Acts 19:24 ff.), which had massive architectural pillars and foundations, to make his analogy with the local church at Ephesus. Just as the Temple of Diana was a physical depository for the wealth of the Artemesian cult, the Ephesian church was the depository for the Lord's spiritual wealth—the truth. The local churches initially and continually recognized and preserved the NT Canon and the Words of the NT Canon, which God originally determined. History has corroborated the Scriptural truth that God preserved His Words through the Lord's assemblies. The Lord Jesus preserved His Words which were manifested in the manuscripts and translations used by His churches, starting of course with the NT churches. The Apostolic churches used the Received Text (cf. Jn. 17:8 *et al*), which text the Syrian (1st century), Italic (2nd century), Gallic (2nd century), Celtic (3rd century), Gothic (4th century), Waldensian (5th–16th centuries), Albigensian (13th century), Anabaptist (16th century) and Baptist (17th–21st centuries) churches preserved, either by translating or by promulgating the received translation over the past two thousand years.[123] The Lord God's institution of the local

---

[122]John Turtle Wood, (*Modern Discoveries on the Site of Ancient Ephesus* Charleston, SC: Nabu Press, 2010 reprint of 1923 edition), pp. 1-136.

[123] By faith one must believe that all legitimate extant manuscript readings and translations have been influenced by local NT churches. History cannot disprove this credo.

church has kept the Words of His Received Bible just as He promised and as history has corroborated.

Preservation–*"It Is Written"*

The passage at hand utilizes the expression *"it is written"* (Γέγραπται) four times (vv. 4, 6, 7, 10).[124] The Lord submitted Himself to the written OT Scripture in response to Satan's temptations and claimed the preservation of three passages (Dt. 8:3, 6:16, and 6:13) for His defense (cf. Eph. 6:17). Satan was forced to submit himself to the written Scripture and even declared the preservation of Psm. 91:11-12 (v. 6) with *"it is written."* The Greek word Γέγραπται is 3ms perfect indicative passive of γράφω meaning "it was, still is and will continue to remain written."[125] Christ declared that the Hebrew text of Dt. 8:3,

$$\text{כִּי לֹא עַל־הַלֶּחֶם לְבַדּוֹ יִחְיֶה הָאָדָם כִּי עַל־כָּל־מוֹצָא}$$
$$\text{פִי־יְהוָה יִחְיֶה הָאָדָם:}$$

("not by bread alone shall man live, but by all [words] proceeding out of the mouth of Jehovah") was still intact, including the consonants and vowels, up unto His day. There are at least three Biblical arguments that defend the position that the Lord always used the Hebrew text and not the Greek

---

[124] It is used 67 times in the NT. In one case the word Γέγραπται refers to the words of John's Gospel (Jn. 20:31).

[125] The perfect tense is resultative in aspect and past with ongoing results in time (cf. Rom. 9:33).

LXX. 1) The Lord referred to jots and tittles that make up the Hebrew language, not the Greek language (Mt. 5:17-18). 2) The Lord referred to the three-fold division of the *Tanak,* not the *LXX,* which included the *Torah* (law), the *Neviy'iym* (prophets), and the *Kethuviym* (writings), on several occasions (cf. Lk. 24:44). 3) The Lord referred to the first and last books of the *Tanak* (Lk. 11:50-51), indicating the brutal deaths of the prophets from Abel (Gen. 4: 8) to Zacharias (2 Chron. 24:20-22). Although the Lord cited precisely the Hebrew of Mt. 4:4, it is clear upon close examination of Dt. 8:3, Christ did not quote the *LXX* since at least two words are different.[126]

Not only did Matthew record Christ's temptation but Luke did also. Both writers record the Lord's inspired commentary on Dt. 8:3 with slightly different renderings. Several points must be considered. 1) The Lord had intact before Him the inspired and preserved Hebrew text of Dt. 8:3 (as well as the rest of Deuteronomy, and certainly verses 6:16 and 6:13). 2) Matthew cited Christ's inspired commentary on Dt. 8:3 *verbatim,* stressing the expression *"that proceedeth out of the mouth"* (ἐκπορευομένῳ διὰ στόματος). 3) Luke selectively cited Christ's inspired commentary, omitting the aforementioned words found in Matthew's quote, and included the article ὁ ("the") before *"man."* The inspired and preserved passage of Dt. 8:3 was intact in Christ's day, and the Biblical writers Matthew and Luke gave their inspired renderings of Christ's various inspired commentaries on Dt.

---

[126]The *LXX* adds ὁ and τῷ.

8:3.[127]

Conclusion

The Lord Jesus Christ's bibliology is clear and consistent. He clearly stated His belief in the verbal, plenary inspiration of the Hebrew OT since the Words proceeded from the mouth of God. He clearly stated His belief in the authority of Scripture, noting that Scripture gave God's standard for how man shall live. The Lord clearly stated His belief in the availability of Scripture by assuming the accessibility of every word. The Savior clearly stated His belief in the verbal, plenary preservation of God's Words since they had been and were still preserved intact in His day. The incarnate God in the person of Jesus Christ was consistent in His belief and practice since He submitted Himself to the perfectly preserved inscripturated Words He promised He would preserve. It behooves Christians, including pastors, believers and scholars, to emulate Christ's teaching in their bibliology, as the Father required, *"This is my beloved Son, in whom I am well pleased; hear ye Him"* (Mt. 17:5).

---

[127]The Gospel writers were not redactors (editors) in the sense of creating words supposedly stated by others as *redaktionsgeschichte* teaches. The Gospel writers gave the *ipsissimi verba* ("the very words") of Christ and not merely the *ipsissimi vox* ("the voice" or gist) of Christ's message.

APPENDIX D

One Tittle (Lk. 16:17)[128]

Introduction

The movement which *'ministers'* questions about the doctrine of Scripture (cf. I Tim. 1:4) began in the Garden by the subtle enemy of God, the serpent (Gen. 3:1-5), and continues to this very day. This satanic subtlety pervades Christianity to the extent that even some fundamental Baptists are beguiled by it. For instance, the clear and precise promise of the Lord Jesus Christ, *"till heaven and earth pass, one jot or one tittle shall in no wise pass from the law, till all be fulfilled"* (Mt. 5:18), has been obfuscated and blunted in such a way that leaders in fundamentalism are not sure what He meant. The editorial committee members of *God's Word in Our Hands*, after a promising exegetical study on this verse, make the ambiguous statement:

> *Returning now to the question, "Is our Lord here guaranteeing the preservation of all the written words of Scripture?" the answer is an emphatic "yes." Although, as has been shown, preservation is not His main point, it is nevertheless the point He chooses to contribute to the way in which He makes that main point (that all the Law would be fulfilled).*

---

[128] Thomas M. Strouse, "Luke 16:17—One Tittle." *Emmanuel Baptist Theological Journal* 2 (Spring 2006): 7-23.

> *What He does not do, however, is give even so much as a hint as to how or where preservation will take place. Answers to these questions are simply beyond the scope of what is revealed in this passage. The conclusion one must reach is that this passage does not teach that those words are preserved in one particular manuscript or lineage of manuscripts alone. Neither does this passage guarantee that all the words will be always available at all times.* [129]

These men make a least three denials about this verse and the biblical doctrine of preservation. 1) They deny the "how" of preservation. 2) They deny the "where" of preservation. 3) They deny the "availability" of preservation. Actually this passage teaches all three truths, which truths are corroborated elsewhere in Scripture. The Lord Jesus Christ referred to the jots and tittles of the law. In Scripture the law refers to both the Mosaic Law and the whole Old Testament (OT).[130] The answer to the second question, "where," is in the OT Hebrew text, which the Lord declared had been preserved up until His day (Mt. 4:4).[131] The answer to the first question, "how," is implied through the agency of God

---

[129]James B. Williams, editor, *God's Word in Our Hands, The Bible Preserved for Us* (Greenville: Ambassador Emerald International, 2003), p. 106.

[130] E.g., Dt. 31:24 ff. (for Pentateuch); Jn. 10:34 (for Psalms); I Cor. 14:21 (for Isaiah).

[131]The Greek verb the Lord utilized was the perfect passive *"it is written"* (Γέγραπται), meaning "it has been and still is written."

and necessitated through the agency of the Jews. The Lord, of course, is the One Who has promised verbal plenary preservation through the agency of His people, the Jews (*vide* Ps. 12:6-7; Rom. 3:2). The answer to their third denial is as follows. First, the "unavailable preservation" view is a *non sequitur*. If something is preserved it is available. If it is not preserved it is not available. Second, the Scriptures make it very clear about the agency God has raised up to preserve the Bible, both the OT and New Testament (NT) Scriptures—the local, NT immersionist church (Mt. 28:19-20; I Tim. 3:15). The Lord commanded His baptized disciples to disciple the nations and then baptize them, and instruct their converts in the Scriptures, and as they obeyed Him, His ecclesiological presence would be with them (Mt. 18:15-20; Rev. 1:13).[132] The Scriptures guarantee the presence of the Lord in His churches with His truth in every generation from the first until now, and history cannot disprove this divine promise.

In addition to these aforementioned truths, Mt. 5:18[133] and Lk. 16:17 claim that the very consonants and vowels of the inspired Hebrew text would be preserved. This additional truth causes another conundrum for those with a non-biblical view of the doctrine of preservation. Since jots and tittles, which are Hebrew consonants and vowels and consequently Hebrew words, will be preserved, at least two corollaries follow. 1) There is absolutely no warrant to look

---

[132] This presence is more intimate, and authoritatively powerful, than the Lord's general omnipresence.

[133] The Lord Jesus employed the strongest negative οὐ μὴ (*ou me*) possible as He denied absolutely the passing of one ἓν (*hen*) consonant or one μία (*mia*) vowel of the Hebrew OT.

to penultimate authorities, such as the *LXX* or Dead Sea Scrolls, to correct the Hebrew text.   2) The Hebrew text that has been preserved by the Jews and approved of by the Lord's churches has been the venerable Masoretic Hebrew text. These corollaries in turn eliminate the necessity to utilize the science of Textual Criticism "to restore" the OT and NT texts, and also repudiate the notion that God has promised merely to preserve His "word" or "concept," or "message."

This essay, focusing primarily on Lk. 16:17, will demonstrate that the Lord not only promised the preservation of every consonant of the Hebrew text, but also every vowel. Consonants and vowels make up words, and since the Lord promised to preserve His words, He has in fact preserved the constituent parts of words—jots and tittles.   The word "tittle" κεραία (*keraia*), both in English and Greek, refers to the Hebrew vowel חִירֶק (*chireq*), which is the dot (κεραία = חִירֶק).   This biblical interpretation is exegetically and linguistically sound, inherently harmonious with other Scripture, and it readily dispatches of the fallacious theory of "concept preservation."

Context

The Lord, in emphasizing that the purpose of His ministry was to fulfill the law, rebuked the Pharisees with the comparative statement, *"And it is easier for heaven and earth to pass, than one tittle of the law to fail"* (Lk. 16:17).[134]   He

---

[134]One may appreciate the fuller details of the background as Matthew cites Christ's similar promise in Mt. 5:18.

used two illustrations of extremes within His observable creation for emphasis. Heaven and earth comprise the largest realms of the Lord's created physical work (cf. Gen. 1:2-19).[135] The smallest thing in God's observable creation is the dot or חִירֶק in the Hebrew OT that constitutes a vowel. The Lord Jesus Christ's statement declared that before the smallest observable thing He created fails παρελθεῖν (*parelthein*), it would be easier for the largest thing He created to pass πεσεῖν (*pesein*) first! It would be difficult to miss His point: the minutia of the OT law will not fail but will be preserved until He completely fulfills it. The OT law was made up of statements, warnings and predictions that were made up of words that had consonants and vowels. The Lord promised that the Hebrew text would be preserved perfectly, as He had previously stated (Lk. 4:4), so that it could be fulfilled perfectly by Him, down to the very words of the law.

The tittle or κεραία is the smallest thing of the Hebrew text. It is not a consonant, such as a jot or *yodh* (יָד) the Hebrew equivalent (י) to the English "j" or "y" or "i," which He alluded to in Mt. 5:18.[136] It is not the overhang (i.e., serif)

---

[135]Since heaven הַשָּׁמַיִם (*hashshamayim*) is a dual noun, and not a plural, in the Hebrew text, it refers to the atmosphere and greater stellar space. The Lord also created the third heaven (II Cor. 12:2) during the creation week but it is not alluded to in Gen. 1. Before God created, all that existed was God (cf. I Kings 8:27).

[136]Matthew's reference to Christ's expression *"one jot or one tittle,"* utilizing the disjunctive particle ἤ (*"or"*), indicates that He differentiated between the consonant jot and the vowel tittle. Redundancy would have been meaningless.

on a consonant (ד versus ר) since He did not refer to a consonant in this passage, and serifs do not make up words. Since the Lord was talking about the smallest thing in the Hebrew text of the law, He was referring to the Hebrew vowel חִירֶק, and not to any other vowels such as the *kametz, pathach, segol, cholem, qibbutz, shureq, tzere, qametz chatuph, chataph qametz,* or *shewa.*[137] The חִירֶק is a mere dot (.), like a period in an English sentence, and is the basis for several other vowels.[138]

Commentators and lexicographers are very tentative about the precise identification of the Greek word κεραία. For instance, R. T. France suggests that "the dot (κεραία, 'horn') may be either the similar letter *waw* (which is equally optional), or the 'serif' which distinguishes some similar Hebrew letters."[139] Colin Brown, after rejecting Manson's interpretation that the κεραία refers to "scribal ornaments,"

---

[137] Nor was he alluding to accents since they are not necessary to constitute words.

[138] For example, the *cholem* vowel is a single dot over a consonant (א); the *tzere* vowel is two horizontal dots under a consonant (א); the *qibbutz* vowel is three diagonal dots under a consonant (א); the *segol* is a cluster of three dots under a consonant (א); and the *shewa* is two vertical dots under a consonant (א), acting as a half-vowel.

[139] R. T. France, *The Gospel According to Matthew: An Introduction and Commentary* (Grand Rapids: Wm. B. Eerdmans Publ. Co., 1985), p. 115. It is interesting to note that France's translation of κεραία renders it as "dot," and yet he interprets the dot to be the full-sized hook consonant *waw* (ו).

postulates the following speculation:

> *Another possibility for the keraia is that it denotes the "hook" (letter), i.e., Waw (w) which was also sometimes dispensed with...The Waw, when placed in front of a word means "and." Both letters could also be used as vowels (Yod = y; Waw = u, or = o), but unlike other vowels they would be written in the unpointed text (i.e., the normal text of the time which was written with consonants only). How such a text is read (i.e., whatever vowels are read into the text) obviously can make a considerable difference to the meaning. Whatever particular ideas may lie behind these terms, Manson would seem to be wrong in his interpretation...*[140]

Meaning of κεραία

The English Word *"Tittle"*

The Oxford English Dictionary traces the history of the occurrence of the word tittle to Wycliff's translation of the Bible in 1382. He rendered the Latin *apex*, for "point or tip,"

---

[140]Colin Brown, Editor, *The New International Dictionary of New Testament Theology*, Vol. III (Grand Rapids: Zondervan Publ. House, 1979), p. 182. His assumption that the consonants *waw* and *yodh* were employed for double duty as vowels in some cases, as the so-called *matres lectionis* ("the mothers of reading"), is unwarranted and easily refuted biblically.

in Mt. 5:18 and Lk. 16:17 as *titel*.[141] Other English translations followed this rendering, including Tyndale's translation (1526), the Great Bible (1539), the Geneva Bible (1560), the Rheims NT (1582), and the AV (1611). Why did these early translators employ the noun tittle, and not another word such as "serif," which means an overhang on a letter? The English word tittle comes from the old German word *titteldjen* meaning "tittle, dot."[142] Since Hebrew was the original language, all languages including German derive words from the original consonants. For instance, it is well known in linguistics to realize that dental consonants such as "d" and "t," are interchangeable. In fact, tittle or tit comes from dot since the d's and t's substitute for one another.[143] The English word tit, meaning small,[144] comes from dot that in turn comes from "dod" (tit = tot = dod = dot). The Hebrew *dad* (דַּד)[145] means breasts or teats and is so translated in Prov.

---

[141]"Tittle," *The Compact Edition of the Oxford English Dictionary* (Oxford: Oxford University Press, 1971), p. 3335.

[142]Felix Fluegel, *A Dictionary of the English and German Languages for Home and School,* eds. Im. Schmidt and G. Tanger, (Brunswick: George Westermann, n.d.), p. 819.

[143]Isaac Mozeson, *The Word: The Dictionary that Reveals the Hebrew Source of English* (NY: SPI Books, 2000), pp. 180, 183, 184.

[144]Cf. the name for the small rodent "titmouse" and the expression "tit for tat."

[145]The plural is *dadeyha* (דַּדֶּיהָ). Technically, *dad* refers to the teat or nipple whereas *shad* (שַׁד)refers to the whole breast.

5:19 and Ezk. 23:8, and Ezk. 23:3 and 23:21,[146] respectively. Tittle is the specifically accurate English word for a dot, coming through the German from the Hebrew for dot or teat. Interestingly, the *ESV* (2001) translates κεραία literally as "dot" in Mt. 5:18, stating "For truly, I say to you, until heaven and earth pass away, not an iota, not a **dot**, will pass from the Law until all is accomplished" (so also the *RSV*).

The Greek Word κεραία

When the Lord employed the Greek work κεραία He was giving the Greek equivalent to the Hebrew חִירֶק (*k-r-a* = *ch-r-q*). The Greek *kappa* (κ) is equivalent to the Hebrew *cheth* (ח). The Greek *rho* (ρ) is equivalent to the Hebrew *resh* (ר). The Greek *alpha* (α) replaces the Hebrew *qoth* (ק). This assertion will be established through several lines of argument.

Linguistic Argument

Linguistically, it is common for consonants in words to be dropped off or silenced as they pass from language to language or from generation to generation. In English, several examples of the consonant "h" being silenced are found in the words "hour" and "heir." Even hard guttural

---

[146]I. e., *"Thus thou calledst to remembrance the lewdness of thy youth, in bruising thy teats* (דַּדֵּ) *by the Egyptians for the paps* (שַׁד) *of thy youth."*

consonants are sometimes softened or even silenced with regard to some words.   For instance, Bryson states,

> *There were other changes as well—most notably the loss of the Old English sound x, the throat-clearing sound of the ch in the Scottish loch or the German ach.   The loss of this sound from English meant that others rushed to fill the vacuum, as in the Old English word burh (place) which became variously burgh as in Edinburgh, borough as in Gainsborough, brough as in Middlesbrough, and bury as in Canterbury.*[147]

As Bryson asseverates in his illustrations for English, similarly one should recognize that in other languages such as Hebrew the ק (*qoth*) in חִירֶק could be soften or omitted as it goes into the Greek. But it will be demonstrated that this change was not only a possibility but also an actuality.

Theological Argument

Theologically, the Bible predicts the preservation of words, or vocalized consonants, that is, consonants with vowels. Although it is popular to argue that since modern Israeli newspapers and the ancient Dead Sea Scrolls are

---

[147]Bill Bryson, *The Mother Tongue: English & How It God That Way* (NY: Avon Books, 1993), p. 93. All one needs to do to observe the "torture" many English words have received in pronunciation and spelling is to read Bryson's chapter on "Pronunciation."

un-pointed,[148] or lack vowels, and therefore the original Hebrew text had no points, this theory is fallacious for at least two reasons. 1) Neither ancient nor modern Jewish practices dictate the truth of Scripture (Rom. 3:3).[149] 2) The NT writers, under inspiration, read points in their Hebrew text and translated them as such.[150]

When the Lord God renewed His covenant with Israel, He used Moses to write the very same words that were on the initial tablets (Ex. 34:1 ff.). The Lord said to Moses, *"Write thou these words: for after the tenor of these words I have made a covenant with thee and with Israel"* (v. 27). The expression *"after the tenor of these word"* הַדְּבָרִים הָאֵלֶּה כִּי עַל־פִּי (*ciy `al piy hadevariym ha'elleh*) is translated literally "on [the basis of] the mouth of these words." The only way Moses could have written the Lord's spoken words was to hear the vowels in the consonants (i.e., vocalization) and then to write the words with the vowels intact.[151] The

---

[148]Most readers of their respective native language do not read every vowel or even every word in a sentence. Readers learn to read clusters of words, which words they have learned to spell and have memorized. The following statement proves this point: Cna yuo raed thsi snetecne?

[149]*"Let God be true, but every man a liar."*

[150]Cf. the Hebrew word behind Immanuel (Isa. 7:14) which is translated by Matthew as Emmanuel (Mt. 1:13), doubling the מ *mem* ("m") with the double Greek μ (*mu*) since he saw the *dagesh forte* (dot) in the Hebrew text (M).

[151]To postulate that the consonants were written but the vowels and therefore the pronunciation of such were passed on through oral tradition is biblically fallacious and constitutes a major

Mosaic Law, then, constituted the very written words of Jehovah, including the consonants and vowels. Furthermore, the Jews were to obey the Mosaic Law in minute detail, not adding to nor diminishing from it (cf. Dt. 4:2). They were to keep or preserve שָׁמַר (*shamar*) the Law and not forget the things they had seen and which were written down in it, and then to teach their children the Mosaic Law (vv. 6, 9, 10; 6:7; 32:46). Jehovah promised Isaiah that the words which He put in the prophet's mouth פֶּה (*peh*) would be accompanied by the Lord's Spirit, and these words would not depart out of Isaiah's mouth, or Isaiah's seed's mouth, or Isaiah's seeds' seed's mouth, from then forever on (Isa. 59:21). Obviously, these words of the book of Isaiah would be preserved intact through the Lord's remnant (Israel and the local churches) forever. The Lord told Jeremiah to write all the words which He had spoken to Jeremiah in a scroll (Jer. 36:2). God gave him vocalized consonants, namely words, which Jeremiah in turn gave to Baruch who wrote down the words (v. 4). These passages conclusively argue against any notion that the vowel sounds were merely given to Moses who passed on the oral tradition of the pronunciation until the Masoretes invented a

---

conundrum for its advocates. The position that vowels were passed by oral tradition is condemned by the Lord Jesus Christ, who denounced all traditions, stating *"Making the word of God of none effect through your tradition, which ye have delivered: and many such like things do ye"* (cf. Mk. 7:13). Furthermore, if the Masoretes invented the points and added them to the preserved consonantal text and consequently 'created' words, then they violated the commands of Scripture about adding to the preserved text (cf. Dt. 12:32; Rev. 22:18).

system to approximate the vowels. Elias Levitas' speculation that the Masoretes invented the points has nothing to commend it but has all scriptural authority to condemn it.[152]

The initial Psalm addresses the blessed man and his responsibility to delight in and meditate on the law of the Lord, stating: *"But his delight is in the law of the LORD; and in his law doth he meditate day and night"* (Ps. 1:2). The word *'meditate'* comes from הָגָה (*hagah*) that means, "to mutter" and suggests the deliberate pronunciation of the words of Scripture. It is impossible to recite meaningfully consonants without vowels and it is equally impossible to *"delight"* חֵפֶץ (*chephetz*) in consonants with non-authoritative vowels. Again, the fallacious view that man invented the Hebrew vowel points has nothing to commend it. Is there any reason that Bible believers must countenance the speculative view that the Lord God, the Creator of language, disdains vowels, at least to the extent that He would not preserve them in written form (Ps. 12:6-7; Mt. 24:35)? After all, has not the Lord Jesus Christ referred to Himself as the *Alpha* and *Omega* τὸ Α καὶ τὸ Ω (Rev. 1:8; 21:6), the first and last vowels of the Greek language?

---

[152]Owen questions the very existence of a 5th or 6th century school of Masoretes, stating "It is said to have been the common work of the school of Massoretes (*sic*) in Tiberias. At least Elias Levita says so…What then if someone should suggest that these Tiberian Massoretes perhaps never did exist at all, and that those who would persuade us that the Massoretes dreamed up the points first dreamed up the Massoretes themselves?" John Owen, *Biblical Theology* (Morgan, PA: Soli Deo Gloria Publications, 1996 reprint of the 1661 edition), pp. 508-509.

The speculation that the vowels were not inspired is ludicrous in light of the complexity of the Hebrew language. Biblical Hebrew demands the linguistic necessity for distinguishing Hebrew verbs and nouns. Hebrew verbs are made up of seven stems, of which are the *Qal* stem and six derived stems, including the *Niphal, Piel, Pual, Hithpael, Hiphil,* and *Hophal*. These stems apply equally to both the strong and weak verbs. The differentiation of some of these stems is based on complex vowel pointing, without which tremendous confusion abounds. The *Piel* and *Pual* differ from each and the *Qal* stem only by vowels and diacritical marks. The *Niphal* perfect 3ms (3rd person, masculine, singular), *Niphal* imperfect 1cp (1st person, common, plural), and *Niphal* participle ms differ by vowel points alone, and may be confused with the *Qal* imperfect 1cp except for the points. The imperfect forms for all of the stems except the *Hiphil* and *Hithpael* are identical without points and consequent confusion would abound with the divinely preserved vowel points. If the stems are significant, which they must be, then their respective vowel differences are significant, and must be carefully maintained to make sense of any given passage.[153]

For example, in Gen. 1:26, Scripture uses the first of several *Qal* imperfect 1cp verbs נַעֲשֶׂה (*na`aseh*) for Jehovah

---

[153] If, according to the prevailing theory, the Masoretes invented the pointing to prevent the loss of the traditional pronunciation about twenty-one centuries after the Lord gave it to Moses, what absolute guarantee is there that the Masoretes did not make mistakes in light of this extreme linguistic complexity?

to express *"let us make"* man. However, without authoritatively inspired vowels this verb could be "he was made" (*Niphal* [passive] perfect 3ms) or "we will be made" (*Niphal* imperfect 1cp). Furthermore, the *Niphal* participle masculine singular without the pointing would be the same consonants and mean "being made." Although some might say that the context would always show which conjugation and tense was divinely inspired, in this case the context would probably eliminate only the participle. Did Jehovah say "let us make" man, or man "he was made," or "we [i.e., the Godhead] will be made" man?

Another example should suffice for this point. In response to Isaac's query about the animal sacrifice, Abraham answered *"God will provide* יִרְאֶה *(yir'eh) himself a lamb"* (Gen. 22:8). Is the verb *Qal* imperfect 3ms and therefore active (God will provide **for** Himself the lamb) or *Niphal* imperfect 3ms and therefore reflexive (God will provide Himself **for** the lamb)? The Masoretic text has the former reading and therefore the answer is that God, and no one else, including Abraham, will provide the lamb. [154] Without authoritative pointing, the precise theology required here and elsewhere is forfeited.

With respect to nouns, the endings on masculine nouns are necessary to determine number, whether singular, dual, or plural. In Hebrew some nouns are singular, some are dual, such as those in pairs like hands, feet, eyes, ears, etc.

---

[154]The issue of whether the divine Lord Jesus Christ is the Lamb or not is not the question here since the NT clearly states that He is the Lamb of God (cf. Jn. 1:29, 36; I Pet. 1:19; Rev. 5:6; *et al*).

The distinctive ending of a masculine dual noun is *pathach, yodh, chireq,* and *mem* (מַיִם), in contrast to the distinctive ending of a masculine plural noun: *chireq, yodh, mem* (הִים). The first verse of the OT Scriptures is instructive. Scripture says, *"In the beginning God created the heaven and earth"* (Gen. 1:1). Without authoritative vowels, one would not know that the word *"God"* אֱלֹהִים *('elohim)* is a masculine plural noun and that the word *"heaven"* הַשָּׁמַיִם *(hashshamayim)* is a masculine dual noun. The pointed Masoretic text teaches that the plural Godhead created the two heavens (first and second). Or was it that the dual God (i.e., yin yang) created a plurality of heavens?

Regarding proper nouns, the consonantal text provides several interesting, but non-authoritative, alternatives to the Masoretic pointed text. In Proverbs 30:1, did Agur אָגוּר address Ithiel אִיתִיאֵל and Ucal אֻכָל? Kidner asserts,

> *The Hebrew consonants of this phrase can be revocalized to read: 'I have wearied myself, O God, I have wearied myself, O God, and come to an end', which introduces the opening theme well. The ancient versions likewise eliminate the proper names, but fail to agree in their translations. It remains an open question.*[155]

If vowel points may be rearranged in proper nouns, what

---

[155] Derek Kidner, *Proverbs, An Introduction and Commentary* (Downers Grove: InterVarsity Press, 1976), p. 178.

prevents the interpreter from the thorough rearrangement of major sections of the Hebrew text and thereby the creation of new and false doctrine?

Another example of the alleged need to revocalize the Masoretic text brings consternation to those who maintain the integrity and originality of the Hebrew vowel points. In the passage that deals with *"the great wall"* of Aphek, the Scripture states *"there a wall fell upon twenty and seven thousand of the men that were left"* (I Ki. 20:30). Chet Kulus, in citing Donald Wiseman's statement: "The 'thousand' (*'eleph*) might be revocalized without change of consonants to 'officer' (*'alluph*)…the number might represent twenty-seven officers killed," charges some who "will not hear this number because it is too large!"[156] In this context one would not know if 27,000 men were killed or twenty-seven officers.

Not only does the complexity of the Hebrew verb system demand that the vowels to have been written *ab origine*, but also so does the necessity to distinguish different words with the same consonants. In Psalm 119, the שׂ/שׁ *sin/shin* stanza (vv. 161-168), displays an illustration of the necessity for diacritical markings (i.e., tittles [Lk. 16:17]). The sibilant or 's' consonant designated *sin* looks like a three-pronged comb with a dot over the left tooth (שׂ). The *shin* has the same consonantal form but has the diacritical dot over the right tooth (שׁ) and produces the 'sh' sound and spelling. The psalmist declared in v. 164 *"Seven times a day*

---

[156]Chester Kulus, *Those So-Called Errors* (Newington, CT: Emmanuel Baptist Theological Press, 2003, p. 304.

do I praise thee because of thy righteous judgments." Without the diacritical dot over the right tooth of the first consonant in the noun *sheva`* שֶׁבַע (*'seven'*), the word could be the perfect verb *sava`* שָׂבַע (*'he is satisfied'*). Therefore the Hebrew text could read "He is satisfied in the day I do praise thee because of thy righteous judgments." The context cannot render an authoritative solution and hence the text becomes as wax ready to be twisted by every interpreter.

Moses punned on the nakedness of Adam and Eve and the subtlety of the serpent, using two words with the same consonants, *`arom* עָרוֹם and *`arum* עָרוּם [157] respectively (Gen. 2:25-3:1). The only difference between these two adjectives, other than the first is plural[158] and the second is singular, is the vowel pointing. What did Moses intend to say: the couple was naked and the serpent was subtle, the couple was subtle and the serpent was subtle, the couple was subtle and the serpent was naked, or the couple was naked and the serpent was naked? At this stage in the development of Moses' narrative, it would be impossible to know absolutely without the pointing.

Finally, a cursory glance at any elementary Hebrew grammar glossary would show basic words differentiated only by pointing. For example, one should consider the

---

[157] Without pointing these words are identical (*`rm* and *`rm*).

[158] Moses used the plural *`arummiym* עֲרוּמִּים (*'naked'*) in Gen. 2:25 and Solomon used the plural *`arumiym* עֲרוּמִים (*'prudent'*) in Prov. 14:18. In this case, the only difference is the *dagesh forte* (dot) in the *mem* (*'m'*) of the former word *'naked.'*

following: אֵל/אֶל/אַל ('God' or 'to' or 'no'), אֵם/אִם ('mother' or 'if'), אַף/אַף ('nose' or 'also'), אֵת/אַתְּ ('with' or 'you'), בִּין/בֵּין ('to perceive' or 'between'), בְּקָר/בֹּקֶר ('herd' or 'morning'), גָּלַל/גִּלֵּל ('to roll' or 'on account of'), הֵנָּה/הִנֵּה ('they' or 'behold'), זָכָר/זָכַר ('male' or 'to remember'), חַוָּה/חָוָה ('to bow' or 'Eve'), לְחֶם/לָחַם ('to fight' or 'bread'), מָן/מִן ('from' or 'manna'), נָגַשׁ/נָגַשׁ ('to beat' or 'to draw near'), עַד/עֵד ('witness' or 'unto'), עוּר/עוֹר ('to awake' or 'skin'), עַם/עִם ('people' or 'with'), פָּרָשׁ/פָּרַשׁ ('to spread out' or 'horseman'), רֵעַ/רַע ('friend' or 'evil'), and שֵׁם/שָׁם ('name' or 'there'). With these words, some verbs, some nouns, some adjectives, some adverbs, and some pronouns, making up thousands of contextual possibilities, it would be ludicrous to suggest vowels were not originally inscripturated.

Biblical Argument

Biblically, there are examples of the *qoph* dropping off of words as it is translated or replacing one of the Hebrew gutturals, such as the ח *cheth* ('ch'), the כ *caph* ('c' or 'k'), or the ה *hey* ('h').[159] For instance, the Hebrew word נָהַק (*nahaq*) for the verb *'bray'* is translated in English as 'neigh.' In this case the 'n' (*nun*) and the 'h' (*hey*) transfer over but the

---

[159] A guttural is a letter sound that is emitted from the back of the throat. In Hebrew other gutturals include the א *'aleph* and ע *'ayin* letters.

'q' (*qoph*) drops out in the translation. The Hebrew *qoph* is pronounced as a 'k' or 'q' without the 'u' sound. Over one hundred years ago biblical theologians pronounced the *qoph* with the 'k' sound. Govett stated, "I retain the English letter Q to represent the Hebrew *Koph* or *Quoph*, though I suppose it was generally pronounced K."[160]

The NT writers, under inspiration, confirmed that the Hebrew *qoph* was pronounced as the 'k' in the Greek letter *kappa* (ק = κ). Several Hebrew proper names beginning with *qoph* have been translated in the Greek NT with the *kappa* used as the equivalent. The name Cain has had the initial *qoph* translated with the *kappa* and the 'C' in English (*Qain* = *Kain* = Cain [קַיִן = Κάϊν = Cain]). Other examples include the names Cainan (Lk. 3:34), Cis (Acts 13:21), and Core (Jude 1:11). The point of all this is to demonstrate that the *qoph*, under inspiration, was sounded and spelled like the Hebrew gutturals *cheth, caph* and *hey*.

Furthermore, there are examples where the Hebrew guttural consonants, with which the *qoph* is interchanged, are omitted and replaced with vowels in Greek. The proper noun Abel in Hebrew is *Hebel* (הֶבֶל), and the NT writers omitted the *hey* leaving the *alpha* (A) or 'A' as the initial letter (e.g., Mt. 23:35), rendering his name 'Abel.' Another example is the name Hosea. The Hebrew is *hoshea`* (הוֹשֵׁעַ) and Paul translated the prophet's name as Osee ('Ωσηὲ) in Rom. 9:25,

---

[160] Robert Govett, *English Derived from Hebrew; with Glances at Greek and Latin* (London: S. W. Partridge and Co., 1869), p. 4. The English 'kitten' comes from the Hebrew word *qatton* for small.

omitting the *hey* and putting forth the vowel *omega*. Again, the Apostle John rendered the expression *'praise the Lord'* or *halelujah* (הַלְלוּ־יָהּ) from the Hebrew (e.g., Ps. 115:18) as *Alleluia* (Ἀλληλουϊά) in Rev. 19:1. In this case he omitted the guttural *hey* and retained the *alpha* as the initial letter. Similarly, Paul rendered Hagar (הָגָר) as Agar (Ἀγάρ), giving the *alpha* the rough breathing mark in Gal. 4:25. These examples illustrate that the biblical writers omitted the Hebrew guttural consonant *hey* and started the word with the Greek vowels such as *alpha* or *omega*.

More specifically however, are the occasions the biblical writers omitted the Hebrew guttural consonant *cheth* and allowed the subsequent vowel to head up the word. The *qoph* ('q') is interchangeable with the *cheth* ('ch') and both sound and are spelled like the English 'k.' Some examples are put forth to demonstrate that the hard 'k' sound in Hebrew words is often softened or eliminated so that the vowel sounds of the Greek *alpha* or *epsilon* head up the word. The Hebrew names *Henoch* (חֲנוֹךְ) and *Chawwah* (חַוָּה) for Enoch and Eve are translated respectively as Ἐνώχ and Εὖα, removing the hard guttural *cheth* and retaining the corresponding vowel which is the Greek *epsilon*. The names Hannah (חַנָּה), Annas (חָנָן), and Ananias (חֲנַנְיָה) all begin with the *cheth* in the Hebrew OT, being derived from *chen* (חֵן) for 'grace' (cf. Lk. 2:36; Jn. 18:13; Acts 5:1). The NT writers omitted the *cheth* in their translation and let the underlying vowel rendered as an *alpha* carry the word, producing Anna (Ἄννα), Annas (Ἄννας), and Ananias (Ἀνανίας), respectively. Another example is that of the Aramaic place name Aceldama (Acts 1:19). The Aramaic spelling is *chaqaldema'* (חֲקַל־דְּמָא), starting the noun off with the *cheth*, and reflected as such in the 1899 Douay-Rheims Version's spelling 'Haceldama.' The biblical writer Luke, under inspiration, spelled the word Ἀκελδαμα, dropping off the hard *cheth* letter and sound, and allowed the soft *alpha* vowel to surface as the head letter.

These examples illustrate the NT biblical writers' proclivity in translating Hebrew words was to drop the hard 'k' letters of Hebrew (*cheth, hey, caph,* or *qoph*) and allow the subsequent corresponding vowel to surface, whether the Greek *epsilon, omega,* or *alpha.* The two references to tittle or *keraia* that the Lord Jesus Christ made (Mt. 5:18 and Lk. 16:17) manifest this omission of the corresponding Greek letter for the Hebrew *qoph* in חִירֶק. The Greek word κεραία is the equivalent to the Hebrew vowel חִירֶק, translating *kappa* for the *cheth, rho* for the *resh,* and omitting the *qoph* and allowing the *alpha* to surface (ch = k, r =r, q = 0, and 'a' appears). When the Lord said 'tittle,' He was referring to the dot (.) that is the Hebrew vowel חִירֶק. Accordingly, He asserted, *"Till heaven and earth pass, one* **consonant** (jot = יָד) *or one* **vowel** (dot = חִירֶק) *shall in no wise pass from the law, till all be fulfilled"* (Mt. 5:18). Likewise, He also asserted *"And it is easier for heaven and earth to pass, than one* **dot** (חִירֶק) *of the law to fail"* (Lk. 16:17).

Conclusion

Surely it is a self-evident fact that words are vocalized

consonants, or consonants with vowels. This is true in most languages and the Scriptures indicate that this indeed is true for the words of the biblical languages. The OT Scriptures predicted that the Lord God would preserve all of His inscripturated words, including the vowels with the consonants. The Lord Jesus Christ confirmed these OT promises by referring to the jots and tittles of the OT Hebrew words. He mentioned specifically the word κεραία for tittle, arguing for the preservation of the smallest vowel of the Hebrew language, the *chireq* or dot, in Mt. 5:18 and Lk. 16:17. That the Greek word κεραία is the equivalent to the Hebrew vowel חִירֶק is demanded along several lines of argument. First, the translators of English Bibles, from Wycliffe to the 2001 ESV, understood the Greek word as referring to the dot and utilized the English equivalent 'tittle' or 'dot.' Second, the Greek κεραία corresponds to the Hebrew vowel for the point, the חִירֶק, as the 'k' and 'r' letters are transliterated and the 'q' is dropped and replaced by its underlying vowel. This linguistic phenomenon of softening or dropping the hard 'q' sound is common not only in English, but also in the biblical languages, as numerous examples demonstrate.

Since the Lord confirmed His OT promises by referring to the preservation of every consonant and every vowel, the Hebrew text He had was perfectly preserved and is still perfectly preserved down to this very moment. This truth eliminates the necessity then to emend the OT Hebrew text with Textual Criticism and with the aid of the *LXX*, the Vulgate and the Dead Sea Scrolls. If there is no necessity for OT Textual Criticism, since God has indeed preserved all of His words, then there is no necessity for NT Textual Criticism as well. Therefore the Hebrew and Greek texts (Critical and Majority texts) produced by Textual Criticism and the subsequent English versions from such texts are corrupt impostors based on a fallacious and dangerous theory which denies the Bible. Believers need to receive by faith the Jehovah God's promise of the preservation of every OT Hebrew consonant and vowel since for the Lord Jesus Christ *"it is easier for heaven and earth to pass, than one tittle of the law to fail"* (Lk. 16:17).

APPENDIX E

Christ's Use of Targums (Lk. 4:18)[161]

Introduction

In the time of the building of the Second Temple, the enemies to this construction project wrote a letter of complaint to Ahasuerus. Apparently this Persian document was written with Aramaic script and *"interpreted"* מְתֻרְגָּם (*methurgam*) in the Syrian tongue (Ez. 4:7). The interpretation was a *Targum* from the verb *tirgam* (תִּרְגַּם).[162] This biblical foundation gives the precedent for the interpretive translation of a document to be called a *Targum*. Historically, the Jews referred to the Aramaic portions of Genesis, Jeremiah, Daniel, and Ezra as *Targums*, and later rabbis developed the Babylonian Targum, interpreting the *Tanak* or Old Testament (OT) Scriptures. The writers of the New Testament (NT), along with the Lord Jesus Christ, employed the practice of interpreting/translating the *Tanak* in their citations of the OT. These biblical NT interpretations, or *Targums*,[163] were inspired (II Tim. 3:16). One may note

---

[161] Thomas M. Strouse, "Christ's Use of Targums," *Emmanuel Baptist Theological Journal* 3, no. 1 (Spring 2007): 9-28.

[162] The actual *Pual* participle is *methurgam* (מְתֻרְגָּם).

[163] Several commentators affirm Christ's employment of the Targum, including Geldenhuys who states "As far as we know, He read in Hebrew and translated into Aramaic, the common spoken language at that time...G. Dalman finds reflections of the

the instances of "targuming" in both the Gospels and the Book of Acts (cf. the many NT citations of the OT).[164] Knowledge of this biblical practice of employing the *Targum* helps the serious Bible student understand the bibliology of Christ and the NT writers. Although the prevailing view concerning the Lord's use of the OT is that He quoted from the *Septuagint* (*LXX*), this essay will demonstrate Scripturally the irrefutable position that the Hebrew OT text was preserved intact in Christ's day, that Christ and the Apostles cited from the preserved Hebrew text and consequently did not use the *LXX* as their OT source, and that Christ and Apostles did employ inspired targuming as their contribution to the NT text.

Synagogue Practice

James affirmed that the *Torah* was the text by which preaching was done on every Sabbath in every town of Judea, and elsewhere, in the synagogue (Acts 15:21). Therefore,

---

traditional Aramaic paraphrase (*Targum*) in the present passage in Luke [4:18 ff.]." Norval Geldenhuys, *The New International Commentary on the New Testament, The Gospel of Luke* (Grand Rapids: Wm. B. Eerdmans Publ. Co., 1979), p. 167. Cf. also Robert H. Stein, *The New American Commentary, Luke* (Nashville, Broadman Press, 1992), p. 155; Craig A. Evans, *New International Biblical Commentary, Luke* (Peabody, MA: Hendrickson Publ., 1990), p. 73; and William Manson, *The Moffatt New Testament Commentary, The Gospel of Luke* (London: Hodder and Stoughton, Ltd., 1955), p. 41.

[164] Gleason Archer and Gregory Chirichigno, *Old Testament Quotations in the New Testament* (Chicago: Moody Press, 1983), 167 pp.

synagogues, distributed over a widespread geographical area, functioned as the first century training center for Jewish understanding of the *Torah* on their religious day (cf. Acts 13:27). The early Christians regularly frequented the synagogues (Acts 6:9; 9:2, 20; 13:5, 14, 43; 17:2; 21:26) because the synagogue leaders afforded them the opportunity to give a *"word of exhortation"*[165] (Acts 13:15). Paul's word of exhortation was a summary interpretation of many passages from the Law (*Torah*) and Prophets (*Neviy'iym*) and the Writings (*Kethuviym*), pointing the Jews to Jesus of Nazareth as the fulfillment of these Messianic Scriptures (cf. vv. 17-37). The Gentile Luke gave elaborate detail of a typical Sabbath synagogue service involving the Lord Jesus Christ (Lk. 4:16-21).[166] 1) The reader stood, received the scroll, and opened it (vv. 16-17). 2) The reader read the OT Scripture and then gave his 'running' interpretation or *Targum* of the passage at hand (vv. 17b-19). 3) The reader rolled up the scroll, handed it back, and sat down (v. 20). 4) The reader preached his sermon or *"the word of exhortation"* (cf. 21 ff.). This synopsis of these aforementioned biblical

------

[165]This invitation to preach a sermon, called *"the word of exhortation"* τοῦ λόγου τῆς παρακλήσεως (*tou logou tes parakleseos*), allowed the Christian to expound upon the particular passage read from the law and prophets (Acts 13:15-16). The Book of Hebrews is the classic example of Paul's inscripturated *"the word of exhortation"* (cf. Heb. 13:22).

[166]Luke's Gentile status is affirmed by his testimony (Acts 1:19) and Paul's statement (cf. Col. 4:11 with 4:12-14), and is significant because both he and his recipient Theophilus needed the details of Jewish practices delineated.

texts reveals foundation knowledge about the NT Christians' practice of employing the OT Scriptures in the synagogue.

Case Study: Lk. 4:18

The Phenomenon

Luke's record of the practice of the Lord Jesus Christ in the synagogue is instructive for the serious Bible student. The Scripture Luke recorded generally cites Isa. 61:1-2a and one clause of Isa. 58:6d (g).   Several observations are in order concerning the Scriptural phenomenon.   1) Luke gave the reference of the OT text and stated that this Scripture (Isa. 61:1-2a) was written (cf. Lk. 4:4).   The perfect tense of his verb *"is written"* Γέγραπται (*gegraptai*) indicates that the Hebrew had been written (by Isaiah) and was still intact in Christ's day. 2) The actual words Luke inscribed obviously were not the exact equivalent words of the Hebrew text, or any text for that matter.   By comparing the *Masoretic* Hebrew text (MT), the Greek translation (*LXX*), the Critical Text (CT), and the *Textus Receptus* (TR), several truths come to light.   a) Concerning agreement, the MT, *LXX*, CT and TR basically agree[167] in clauses 61:1a, b, c, e, f, and 61:2a. b) Concerning differences the MT, TR and *LXX* agree against the CT for clause d,[168] and the TR and CT agree against the

---

[167]For the infinitive *"to preach good tidings"* (Isa. 61:1c) the TR translated with the present infinitive εὐαγγελίζεσθαι (*euangelizesthai*) instead of the *LXX*'s translation of the *aorist* infinitive εὐαγγελίσασθαι (*euangelisasthai*).

[168] Since the CT omits the Greek for *"to heal the*

MT and *LXX* in adding clause g (Isa. 58:6d). Furthermore, the TR, *LXX* and CT extend the concept of clause f, deviating from the original Hebrew text.   It should be obvious then, that no translation quoted *verbatim* the Hebrew text.

Since the Hebrew text had been preserved, word perfect, according to Luke's own testimony Γέγραπται, the *LXX*, TR, and CT are renderings which add and/or subtract words in their respective translation of the preserved words of Isa. 61:1-2a. For instance, the TR, *LXX*, and CT all add an unusual twist to the Hebrew clause f, changing the concept and word "bound" אֲסוּרִים (*'asuriym*) to "blind" τυφλοῖς (*tuphlois*). It becomes obvious that the post-Hebrew writers did not directly quote the Hebrew text but paraphrased or even targumed the OT Scriptures. How then, does one understand and explain the following summary of salient points of this phenomenon?

> 1. The Hebrew text was preserved intact in the scroll from which Christ read.
> 2. Luke recorded what Christ said, not read, since He added clause g (*"to set at liberty them that are bruised"*).
> 3. Christ did not quote *verbatim* either from the Hebrew text or the *LXX*.

---

brokenhearted," perhaps this is an indication that the post-first century *LXX* cited the TR.

The Explanations

VIEW ONE: *Christ and the Apostles Used the LXX*

The prevailing view, which has a degree of antiquity,[169] denies that the Hebrew text was intact in Christ's day, but rather affirms that He quoted from the *LXX*, since that was His and the early Christians' Scriptures. For instance, Stewart Custer asseverates that "Luke (and Stephen [Acts 7:42]) always quote from the Septuagint."[170] A more recent work continues the claim of this popular mantra, stating,

> *The Septuagint (LXX) was the Bible for the Greek-speaking world. The Septuagint, which was the Greek translation of the Hebrew OT for the Greek speaking Jews of the Diaspora or Dispersion, was certainly different from the Masoretic text we use today...Why did Christ use the Septuagint? Why did our Savior not launch a crusade against the false Septuagint?...Yet, Paul used the Septuagint.*

---

[169]For instance, the KJV translators held, wrongly, that the *LXX* was the early OT Bible for the first century Christians. "The Translators to the Reader," *The Holy Bible, 1611 Edition, King James Version* (Nashville: Thomas Nelson Publ., 1982), p. iv. They apparently accepted early Septuagint tradition which includes the historical testimonies of the Letter of Aristeas, Philo, and Josephus, *et al*. Those that defend the KJV as the supreme English translation do not necessarily defend the practices or theology of the translators.

[170]Stewart Custer, *Witness to Christ, A Commentary on Acts* (Greenville: BJU Press, 2000), p. 95.

Matthew used the Septuagint.[171]

The argument goes accordingly, that since the early Christians, including Christ, employed the *LXX* as their OT Scriptures, and although it is universally accepted that the veracity of the *LXX* is questionable in many places, it follows that this precedent allows for modern Christians to accept as and even call all modern translations, regardless of omissions and additions, "the word of God."

So sensitive to the obvious conclusion that the aforementioned view holds a weak bibliology, Archer and Chirichigno have responded in detail with an attempt to quell such a conclusion in a qualifying manner.[172] They have the unenviable task of articulating the apologetic against liberals who deny inerrancy and question the verbal, plenary inspiration of Scripture, while at the same time defending evangelicals (and a growing number of fundamentalists)[173] who hold to the inspiration, but not to the verbal, plenary preservation, of Scripture. Archer and Chirichigno want to say, yes, liberals are wrong, who want to use the argument that since the Hebrew OT and *LXX* do not agree, the doctrine of inerrancy and therefore inspiration is compromised. However, they also want to say that evangelicals are orthodox

---

[171]Michael D. Sproul, *God's Word Preserved: A Defense of Historic Separatist Definitions and Beliefs* (Tempe, AZ: Whetstone Precepts Press, 2007), pp. 96-97.

[172]Archer and Chirichigno, pp. ix-x.

[173]The biblical doctrine of preservation is *not* one of the so-called fundamentals, and therefore fundamentalists and Bible believers must look askance at this truth.

who argue, that since the Hebrew and *LXX* do not agree, there is no compromising of the doctrine of preservation, and that all translations are really the word of God.

Archer and Chirichigno employ three arguments, one historical, one "biblical," and one practical, to justify their bibliology with respect to the *LXX*: 1) "The missionary outreach of the evangelists and apostles of the early church," 2) "Matthew and Hebrews often quote from the OT in a non-*LXX* [but Greek] form," and 3) "That inexact quotations imply a low view of the Bible is really without foundation."[174] These arguments not only "beg the question" but prompt biblical refutation.

The Missionary Outreach Bible

Accordingly, the consensus of most scholarship assumes that the *LXX* was available to and had the veritable character for Christ and the apostles to use as their OT Scriptures. This consensus is faulty because of two important Bible truths. First of all, the Bible plainly demonstrates that the Lord Jesus Christ used the Hebrew OT for His Scripture and that He never used the *LXX*. Secondly, the Lord and the apostles did not need to utilize the *LXX* for the evangelism of the Jews and Gentiles and consequently did not.

Expanding on the second point as it relates to the current heading, the biblical evidence needed to argue for Christ and the apostles' evangelistic use of the *LXX* is wanting. Supposedly, the Alexandrian Hellenization was so

---

[174]Archer and Chirichigno, pp. ix-x.

great that the Jews ceased using the Hebrew Scriptures in the first century. Instead, according to this theory, they replaced their Hebrew *Tanak* with the *LXX*. This unbiblical presupposition is easily refuted with Scripture. 1) There is no question that Hebrew was a known and read language of the first century since Pilate required the title on the cross to be written in three known and read languages of the Greco-Roman world—*"Hebrew and Greek and Latin"* (Jn. 19:20). [175] 2) The Apostle Paul, in his great apologetic speech, spoke to the Jews in Jerusalem *"in the Hebrew tongue"* (Acts 21:40 ff.). 3) The Lord Jesus Christ spoke both Hebrew Ἠλί, Ἠλί, λαμὰ σαβαχθανί (*"Eli, Eli, lama sabachthani"*) and Aramaic Ἐλωΐ Ἐλωΐ, λαμμᾶ σαβαχθανί (*"Eloi, Eloi, lama sabachthani"*) from the Cross, as the Gospels of Matthew and Mark testify (Mt. 27:46 and Mk. 15:34, respectively). 4) The Lord also spoke to Paul *"in the Hebrew tongue"* at the time of his conversion (Acts 26:14). Several pertinent biblical facts emerge: Christ and the apostles were multilingual, the Jews could read Hebrew, and the Jews could understand spoken Hebrew. Therefore, as the Scriptures state *"for Moses of old time hath in every city them that preach him, being read in the synagogues every Sabbath day"* (Acts 15:21), there is no biblical reason to assume that any language other than Hebrew was the language of the Jews in Jerusalem in the first century. In a word, the Jews throughout Judea read the Hebrew *Tanak* every Sabbath in their respective synagogues.

---

[175] The Lord Jesus Christ did die for the sins of all mankind—Jew, Greek and Roman (cf. Rom. 5:6-8; Jn. 3:16).

Since the Jews of first century Palestine knew how to read and speak Hebrew, the Lord and the apostles did not need to use the *LXX* for evangelistic purposes toward the Jews. For instance, the initial ministry of Christ was to the Jews in Galilee and Judaea (Jn. 1:19-4:3). He sent His Jewish apostles to the Jews to declare to them that their Jewish King was on hand (Mt. 10:2-6). When He ministered to the Jews, there was no exegetical necessity that He had to use the *LXX*, and not use the Hebrew *Tanak.* On the day of Pentecost, Peter preached to the Jews citing the OT book of Joel, but not using the *LXX* (cf. Acts 2:14-36). When the Lord Jesus Christ ministered to the Syrophenician Greek woman, He did not use the Hebrew *Tanak* or the *LXX,* but His own inspired words in Greek (Mk. 7:26-30). For the Gentiles in Jerusalem on Pentecost, and who did not know Hebrew,[176] the Spirit of God guided the apostles "to speak with other tongues" (Acts 2:4), and eliminated the need to use the *LXX.* The apostles instructed the new converts, from both the Jews and the Gentiles, in the Greek words of *"the apostles' doctrine"* (Acts 2:42). This teaching was not from the *Tanak* or the *LXX,* but from Christ's earthly teaching ministry which He taught in Greek to His disciples (cf. Lk. 1:1-4; Acts 1:1). It should be apparent from Scripture that Christ and the early Christians did not have the necessity to evangelize Jews or Gentiles with the *LXX,* and in fact they did not.

---

[176]The Ethiopian treasurer apparently knew Hebrew since he came to Jerusalem "to worship" the Jews' God (Acts 8:26 ff.). As he read the Hebrew *Neviy'iym* and needed help with the interpretation of Isa. 53:7-8, the Lord sent Philip to "targum" the passage for him.

The Early Christians used Greek OT Sources for their 'Bible'

The essence of this argument is that Christ and the apostles used other OT Greek sources since their respective "quotes" from the *Tanak* deviated from both the Hebrew and *LXX*. This position is based on the fallible premise of the first argument and rejects the biblical teaching that the Hebrew text is preserved intact and that the Lord and early Christians employed targuming on the Scriptures. Therefore Archer and Chirichigno must posit the inane sentiment that there was a pre-Hebrew Bible which has evidence of existence in the deviant readings of the *LXX*. They state, "it should also be observed that, at least in some cases, those Greek renderings (whether *LXX* or not) point to a variant reading in the original form of the text that is better than the one that has come down to us in the standard Hebrew Bible."[177] The world of Christian scholarship has not only accepted the liberal position of the mythical "Q" document of Higher Criticism, but also the mythical original Hebrew "proto-Masoretic" text represented in the mythical original Greek "proto-*LXX*" text.

By all accounts the original *LXX* text is unknown. Thackeray states,

> *The main value of the LXX is its witness to an older Hebrew text than our own. But before we can reconstruct this Hebrew text we need to have a pure Greek text before us, and this we are at present far from possessing...the original text has yet to be*

---

[177]Archer and Chirichigno, p. ix.

recovered...Not a verse is without its array of variant readings.[178]

Ewert adds more to this agnosticism concerning the "original" text of the *LXX*, saying, "it is very difficult today always to know exactly which readings were present in the *LXX* originally."[179]   This position clearly denies that there is either a preserved Hebrew original or a OT Greek "original," and consequently requires reconstruction of both texts through the so-called science of Lower Criticism. The only assurance that the Christian world has, according to this position, is that someday textual scholars will restore the original OT text along with the original NT text, because the Lord has not promised to preserve either, nor in fact has preserved either.

Inexact Quotations of the LXX

This view maintains that the NT writers "quoted" the *LXX*, in some cases exactly, and in other cases inexactly, and thus promotes that inexactitude, with regard to words, is part and parcel of the bibliology of Christ and the apostles. Belief in the NT writers' use of the *LXX* is foundational for the promotion of 1) the science of textual criticism, 2) the various Greek editions (Critical and Eclectic text), 3) the multiple English versions, and 4) this belief culminates in the unbiblical 'Totality of Manuscripts' position. Therefore, the

---

[178] H. S. J. Thackeray, "Septuagint," *The International Standard Bible Encyclopaedia*, Volume IV (Grand Rapids: Wm. B. Eerdmans Publ., 1939), pp. 2724-2725.

[179] David Ewert, *From Ancient Tablets to Modern Translations* (Grand Rapids: Zondervan Publ. House), p. 110.

argument goes, that God has preserved His 'word' (thought, concept, doctrine), but not His 'Words' (although compare Ps. 12:6-7; Mt. 4:4; 5:18; 24:35; and Jn. 12:48). Shaylor defines this position stating, "This preservation exists in the totality of the ancient language manuscripts of that revelation."[180] He goes on to allude to Harding's input, saying "Michael Harding in chapter 9 illustrates how ancient translations can be helpful. He points out how the Septuagint can help in harmonizing a seeming discrepancy in Scripture. His conclusion recognizes a problem but expresses the faith of one who believes that God has preserved His Word in the totality ancient MSS..."[181] Even though the totality of manuscripts has many variant and opposed readings[182] in the original languages and resultant translations, this should not be a reason for the Christian to give pause. Shaylor confidently concludes that, in spite of the inexactitude of words, believers should have great assurance in God's preservation, stating "When we use a faithful conservative translation such as the King James Version, New King James Version, the New American Standard Version, or another version of demonstrated accuracy we can trust our Bible as the Word of God. We can

---

[180]James B. Williams and Randolph Shaylor, eds. *God's Word in our Hands, The Bible Preserved for Us* (Greenville: Ambassador Emerald International), p. xxi.

[181]Williams and Shaylor, p. 414.

[182]Schnaiter affirms that "all translations (even poor ones) are the Word of God and deserve respect." Sam Schnaiter and Ron Tagliapietra, *Bible Preservation and the Providence of God* (Philadelphia: Xlibris Corp., 2002), p. 319.

be confident that we have God's Word in our hands."[183]

VIEW TWO: *Christ and the Apostles Targumed the Preserved Hebrew Text*

In order for the Biblicist to combat almost two *millennia* of historical tradition, the believer must rely solely upon the Scriptures.[184] There is no question that View One has antiquity as its "proof" for veracity. Of course, all that antiquity really proves is that both truth and error go back to the beginning. Scripture, and Scripture alone, is the source for and measurement of all inscripturated truth (I Cor. 2:13) because it is truth (Jn. 17:17). The arguments for the veracity of View Two follow the Scriptural teaching that the Hebrew text was preserved, that Christ did not look to the *LXX* as his OT Bible since the original preserved Hebrew text was available, and that both Christ and the apostles targumed the OT Hebrew text.

The Preserved Hebrew Text

When Satan tempted the Lord Jesus Christ, He submitted Himself to the written words of God[185] by saying,

---

[183]Williams and Shaylor, p. 422.

[184]*Vide* Thomas M. Strouse, "Scholarly Myths Perpetuated on Rejecting the Masoretic Text of the Old Testament," *Emmanuel Baptist Theological Journal* 1, no. 1 (Spring 2005): 37-61.

[185]This action harmonizes with Ps. 138:2, which states, *"I will worship toward thy holy temple, and praise thy name for thy lovingkindness and for thy truth: for thou hast magnified thy word above all thy name."* Nevertheless, the NIV editor makes the following inane and inaccurate statement on this verse: "The

"It is written, Man shall not live by bread alone, but by every word that proceedeth out of the mouth of God" (Mt. 4:4). The expression *"It is written"* Γέγραπται is in the perfect tense indicating past action with continuing results.[186]   In

---

Hebrew at the end of the verse is unclear in its syntax and thus difficult to translate.   It can be translated the way the KJV has it, or it can be rendered as it is in the NIV.   Since either rendering is possible…we chose ours on theological grounds.   It is inconceivable that God would exalt His Word above His name which, in Hebrew usage, represents one's very person and character.   The KJV choice is actually saying that God has exalted His Word above His very own person, essence, and character ("name").   **This is theologically inconceivable**" (bold mine). Ken Barker, *Accuracy Defined and Illustrated* (Colorado Springs: International Bible Society, 1995), p. 48.   Contrary to Dr. Barker's sentiments, the Hebrew is quite elementary even for first year Hebrew students, the KJV gives the only possible formal equivalent translation, and the Lord Jesus Christ did indeed submit Himself to the written Hebrew text preserved in His lifetime (cf. Mt. 4:4 ff.).

[186] "This common introductory formula [it is written] to OT quotations seems to be used to emphasize that **the written word still exists** [bold mine].   It implies a present and binding authority."   Daniel B. Wallace, *The Basics of New Testament Syntax: An Intermediate Greek Grammar* (Grand Rapids: Zondervan Publ. House, 2000), p. 248.   *Vide* also F. Blass, and A. Debrunner, *A Greek Grammar of the New Testament and Other Early Christian Literature,* trans. and rev. R. W. Funk, (Chicago: University of Chicago Press, 1961), p. 175; and William D. Mounce, *Basics of Biblical Greek: Grammar,* (Grand Rapids: Zondervan Publ. House, 1993), p. 219. The majority of the 67 NT occurrences of Γέγραπται refer to OT passages still intact in the days of Christ and the apostles.

effect, the Lord said that this Hebrew verse to which He alluded (Dt. 8:3), and obviously the Hebrew Book of Deuteronomy and consequently the Hebrew Pentateuch, had been written (by Moses the Hebrew) and was still written to His very day. The Lord Jesus Christ had the preserved words of the Hebrew OT available to Him just as He had promised (cf. Dt. 4:2; 12:32; 17:18-20; 29:1,29; 30:11-14 [*vide* Rom. 10:6-8]; 31:9-13, 24-27; Josh. 1:7-8; Ps. 12:6-7; 119:111, 152, 160).

The Lord taught that the jots and tittles[187] of the Hebrew OT would be preserved, stating, *"For verily I say unto you, Till heaven and earth pass, one jot or one tittle shall in no wise pass from the law, till all be fulfilled"* (Mt. 5:18). He believed that the very consonants and the very vowels of the OT Hebrew words of prophecies (and of course all the other words of Scripture) were preserved perfectly intact in His day and would continue until final fulfillment (cf. Jn.

----

[187]"The word 'tittle' (κεραία), both in English and Greek, refers to the Hebrew vowel *chireq*, which is the dot." Thomas M. Strouse, "Luke 16:17—One Tittle," *Emmanuel Baptist Theological Journal* 2, no. 1 (Spring 2006): 9. Κεραία may encompass the inspired and preserved Hebrew accents (*te'amiym*) that permeate the prosody and psalmody sections of the whole *Tanak* and assist in the cantillation of the Hebrew text (cf. Ex. 15:1 ff.; Judg. 5:1 ff.). For instance, the Lord described the Book of Deuteronomy as a *"song"* שִׁיר (*shir*) to be sung perpetually (Dt. 31:19, 22, and 30). To sing words, one needs notes; presumably the accents were the equivalent to musical notes for the purpose of Israel singing the whole *Tanak* (cf. I Chron. 25:1-3).

12:48).[188]   Since the Greek OT (*LXX*) does not have jots and tittles, He was not referring to this inferior translation, which does have a questionable background and character.

Again, the Lord Jesus Christ alluded to the three-fold division of the Hebrew OT, which division the *LXX* does not follow, when He affirmed, *"These are the words which I spake unto you, while I was yet with you, that all things must be fulfilled, which were written in the law of Moses, and in the prophets, and in the psalms, concerning me"* (Lk. 24:44; cf. v. 27; also Acts 26:22).   The law (*Torah*), the prophets (*Neviy'iym*), and the writings (*Kethuviym* [of which Psalms was first]) made up the Hebrew OT and is called the Tanak. He elaborated on His use of the Hebrew OT when the Lord identified the Pharisees' persecution of the prophets with their murderous Jewish ancestors, saying, *"From the blood of Abel unto the blood of Zacharias, which perished between the altar and the temple: verily I say unto you, It shall be required of this generation"* (Lk. 11:51).   He surveyed the whole scope of the Hebrew OT, using the examples of the murder of the righteous Abel from the first book (Genesis 4:8) to the murder of the righteous Zacharias from the last book (II Chronicles 24:20-22).

The Lord claimed that the Hebrew text was intact in His day, that the jot and tittles were intact in His day, and alluded to the three-fold division of the *Tanak*.   This ample biblical evidence has not been and cannot be overturned by

---

[188]The prophesied events could not be perfectly fulfilled if the prophecies themselves were not perfectly preserved for one to match the minute details of the prophecy with the minute details of the fulfillment (cf. Isa. 34:16).

textual scholars, since they reject biblical revelation. Christ absolutely did allude to the Hebrew text, and did not allude to the *LXX,* throughout His whole ministry.

The Scriptures state clearly the means by which the Hebrew text was preserved: *"What advantage then hath the Jew? Or what profit is there of circumcision? Much every way: chiefly, because that unto them were committed the oracles of God"* (Rom. 3:1-2).[189] The Lord blessed His chosen people, the Jews, in many ways, including using them to preserve the inspired jots and tittles of the Hebrew words of the *Tanak* (cf. Rom. 9:3-5). With Christ's first advent (cf. Mk. 1:1), He gave the privilege and responsibility for the preservation of the inspired OT Hebrew words and the canonical NT Greek words to His assembly (Mt. 16:18). The mandate for preservation comes from the words of the Great Commission: *"Go ye therefore, and teach all nations, baptizing them in the name of the Father, and of the Son, and of the Holy Ghost: Teaching them to observe all things whatsoever I have commanded you: and, lo, I am with you always, even unto the end of the world. Amen"* (Mt. 28:19-20). The root verb behind "observe" is τηρέω (*tereo*), which has both lexical and contextual meanings of "to keep," "to reserve," "to watch," or "to preserve" (cf. Jude 1:1; Rev. 3:10 [2x]). The Lord commanded exclusively that His assemblies had the responsibility of evangelizing the nations (apparently with translations) as they preserved the Hebrew

---

[189] *Vide* also *"This is he, that was in the church in the wilderness with the angel which spake to him in the mount Sina, and with our fathers: who received the lively oracles to give unto us"* (Acts 7:38).

OT[190] and Greek NT words.   Paul declared that the Ephesian church was *"the pillar and ground of the truth"* (I Tim. 3:15), and this assembly had in its midst the Jew named Apollos who was *"mighty in the* (Hebrew OT) *scriptures"* (Acts 18:24). Therefore, the Ephesian church was representative of the Lord's assemblies which had the wherewithal to preserve both the Hebrew and Greek Scriptures for perpetuity (cf. Eph. 1:1 and Rev. 2:1 ff.).[191]

The Non-Use of the LXX

The greatest challenge for those promoting Christ's use of the *LXX* is overcoming the biblical passages which declare His exclusive use of the Hebrew text.   Since the Lord had the preserved Hebrew text, and since He could speak and

---

[190] The Lord's candlesticks recognized and received the preserved Hebrew text which came through the Masoretes, and thus honored the so-called "Masoretic Hebrew" text.   These Masoretic Jews did not invent anything, including a vowel system since they were familiar with the קְרִי (*Qere*, Aramaic for 'called' or 'spoken'—i.e., the marginal text) readings, but merely passed on the preserved text כְּתִיב (*kethiv*, Aramaic for 'written text').   These AD six century Masoretes are not venerated any more than the AD seventeenth century King of England named James, but the Lord's churches identify these texts accordingly as "Bible."

[191] Contrary to Sproul's assertion that there was no "secret Alpine trail" of believers who copied manuscripts in languages they did not know (Hebrew [?]), the Bible predicts, by virtue of Christ's mandate, that NT assemblies would have capable Hebrew and Greek scholars for this biblically required task. *Vide* Sproul, p. 264.

read Hebrew, He had no necessity to use the *LXX,* whether it was in existence or not in the first century.

Other challenges to those who must disprove Christ's non-use of the *LXX* include the history, character and known errors of the *LXX.* Concerning it history, several questions arise immediately from the letter of Aristeas. These questions include when was it originally translated, by how many Jewish elders, and how much of the OT? Thackeray critically admits that the date of the *LXX* ranges from the fourth century BC to the second century BC, that the number of Jewish translators were seventy (LXX) or seventy-two (LXXII), and that the translation may have only included the Pentateuch. He states, "Yet it has long been recognized that much of it is unhistorical, in particular the professed date and nationality of the writer...yet the story is not wholly to be rejected, though it is difficult to disentangle truth from fiction."[192]

The character of the *LXX* is suspect as well. The current *LXX*[193] contains the Apocrypha intermingled with the canonical books of the *Tanak.* Furthermore the *LXX* scrambles the Hebrew text at places especially in the Psalms (e.g., 9 and 10 are a single Psalm), and in Jeremiah (vv. 46-51 come after v. 25:13).

The *LXX* is rife with errors, omissions and transcriptional gaffes. For instance, the *LXX* adds 586 years

---

[192]Thackeray, p. 2724; also pp. 2722-2723 and 2725 ff.

[193]If there was an original *LXX,* it is not presently extant. The current *LXX* is a compilation of Origen's *Hexapla,* which includes his revision of the *LXX,* along with the Greek renderings of Aquila, Symmachus, and Theodotion. See Ewert, pp. 105-110.

to the time from Adam to the Flood in Gen. 5. There is hardly a page in the *LXX* where errors do not abound. This author records several alleged errors in the Masoretic text "corrected" by the *LXX* (Ps. 2:9; Ps. 145; Amos 5:26).[194] A recent discovery by this same author recognized that the translators of the Book of Daniel apparently misread the *resh* in Meltzar's name as a *daleth,* and translated it as "[A]melsad." Another discovery involves the effort of the *LXX* "to smooth out"[195] the change of person in Hosea 2:6. The Lord addressed Israel with the second person suffix (*"thy way"*) and then employed the third person *"she shall seek."* The *LXX* uses the third person throughout this verse. Unger frankly adds these comments about portions of the *LXX* concerning its questionable veracity: "The Psalms, on the other hand, and the Book of Isaiah show obvious signs of incompetence…In the latter part of Jeremiah, the Greek…is 'unintelligibly literal.' The Book of Daniel is mere

---

[194]Kent Brandenburg, Editor, *Thou Shalt Keep Them* (El Sobrante, CA: Pillar and Ground Publ., 2003), p. 155.

[195] According to the tenets of Textual Criticism, the so-called difficult reading is preferred. Therefore, any efforts to smooth out a difficult reading must be considered late and consequently inferior. But the popular theory of OT Text Criticism holds that the *LXX* predates the Masoretic Text. As one can see with this representative example, modern OT text scholarship is encumbered with inconsistencies and faulty rationale. Furthermore, the *LXX* is a translation; why should a translation correct the original language text? Is this not another example of Ruckmanism reversed?

Midrashic paraphrase."[196]

Granting for a moment the unproved assumption that there was a complete *LXX* prior to Christ's ministry, one must still prove that the Lord Jesus Christ, who indeed did have the preserved Hebrew text (Mt. 4:4), would have any inclination, in precept or practice, to use a questionable translation in a secondary language to minister NT revelation to Jew or Gentile.

Christ Targumed

The Scripture demands that the interpreter of it understands the truth that the Lord Jesus Christ did indeed *Targum* many of the OT texts to which He referred. In the Case Study of Luke 4:18, several lines of argumentation for this proposition are set forth.

First, Luke's use of the perfect verb *gegraptai* (*"it is written"*)[197] refers to the original inspired Scripture which has continuing results in written form; i.e., the preserved, inspired original of Isaiah 61:1-2a and 58:6d. When Luke stated *"it is written"* and then records Christ's *Targum,* he is not teaching that the Lord's *Targum* was written, but the original is intact from which Christ built His *Targum.* This would be analogous to someone saying, "you know that verse in John's

---

[196]Merrill F. Unger, *Unger's Bible Dictionary* (Chicago: Moody Press, 1972), p. 1147.

[197]This perfect verb form of *grapho* occurs 67 times in the NT. Its occurrences range from Mt. 2:5 to Rev. 17:8 and among six biblical authors, namely Matthew, Mark, Luke, John, Paul and Peter. In each case the verb denotes the preservation of something written, unless of course the verb is negated (see Rev. 13:8).

Gospel that says that God loved the world and sent His son and whoever believes in Him won't perish—oh, yes, that is John 3:16." The allusion to the intact written words of Jn. 3:16 does not diminish the reality of the intact words of the verse.

Second, the Lord Jesus Christ did not quote *verbatim* the Masoretic Hebrew text or any known text for that matter in Lk. 4:18-19. He did not quote Isa. 61:1f ("And the opening of the prison to them that are bound") because He rendered it *"and the recovering of sight to the blind"* (v. 18). Even though His citation was in agreement with the *LXX* at this point, it is certain that He was not quoting the *LXX*. The Lord added clause g ("to set at liberty them that are bruised" [*Targum* of Isa. 58:6]) which is not found in either the MT or *LXX* at this point. Furthermore, He used a different infinitive than that of the *LXX* in clause c (*LXX: euangelisasthai* vs. TR: *euangeliszesthai*). And it is certain that the CT did not quote the *LXX* since it omits clause d ("he hath sent me to heal the brokenhearted"), which clause occurs in the *LXX* and TR.

Third, Christ's expanded and inspired interpretation of Isa. 61:1-2a not only becomes part of the canonical Scripture, but is also an object lesson in bibliological interpretation, enhancing one's understanding of the Lord's eschatology. Dispensationally, He divided up Isaiah's prophecy of the coming of the Lord into the first coming and the second coming (cf. Lk. 4:21). The Lord Jesus Christ fulfilled the prophecy of Isa. 61:1-2a with His first advent, and will fulfill Isa. 61:2b with His second advent in connection with the conclusion of *"the day of vengeance"* (Isa. 61:2b; cf. 34:8; 35:4; 63:4). Christ's employment of targuming OT Hebrew texts gave further complementation to the interpretation of these texts and additional contribution to the whole of Christian theology.

Summary of the Two Views

As the student of Scripture juxtapositions View One with View Two, it is biblically clear that View One has no biblical merit, and that View Two has full scriptural support and full harmony with bibliological truth (see Chart # 2). View One must argue that the Lord did not promise to preserve His words intact for future generations, and that in fact He did not preserve them. Next, View One must argue that the Greek OT *LXX* had the history, character and purity to be the source from which the Son of God would draw his OT quotes. Then View One must demonstrate, unambiguously, that the Lord and the Apostles employed the *LXX* to evangelize Jews or Gentiles. Next, this view must completely ignore the expression *gegraptai* ("it is written"). Then View One must use the expression "quote" to mean "loose citation," since there is really very little direct, verbatim quoting practiced by Christ or the Apostles. Then this position must rationalize this extremely weak bibliology of our Lord by stating that since the Savior had such a low view of His Bible the Christian may have that same low view. This view then propagates the blasphemous notion that all texts, manuscripts and translations make up the on-going, evolving word of God, which culmination for completion is hampered only by newer archaeological finds and the latest theories in Text Criticism.[198]

View Two, which teaches that the Lord Jesus Christ and the Apostles targumed the OT, builds its biblical defense on the interpretation of many Scriptures. The Lord believed the OT words were preserved (Ps. 12:6-7; Mt. 4:4) including the Hebrew jots and tittles (Mt. 5:18), and referred to the three-fold division of the *Tanak* (Lk. 11:51 and 24:44). He and the Apostles never used the *LXX* to evangelize Jews or Gentiles, but instead employed the Hebrew text for Jews and the Greek NT words for Gentiles (Mk. 7:26-30; Acts 2:42). In targuming the Hebrew OT, they expanded God's NT revelation to include not only His NT doctrine but this divinely-complemented OT explanation within the text of the NT Scriptures.

Conclusion

The prevailing consensus of biblical scholarship maintains that Christ and the Apostles quoted from the *LXX* as their OT Scriptures. These scholars must insist upon this untenable assumption to justify their biblically weak position on the Hebrew and Greek texts and their subsequent translations. The Bible refutes this ancient and popular false notion. Instead, Christ and the Apostles had the preserved Hebrew words intact in their possession and preached from

---

[198] "God preserved His Word in the abundance of manuscripts…However, textual variation from geographic distribution and multiplicity of manuscripts, hence textual criticism, is THE observable method God has used to ensure the accuracy and permanency of His Word," Sproule, p. 298.

them. In addition, they expanded the text of Scripture by giving their inspired *Targums* of various OT Hebrew passages. These *Targums* were recorded by the writers of Scripture in the Gospels, Acts and the Epistles. This interpretation of the biblical phenomenon denies that the Lord used an inferior translation such as the *LXX* for His OT Bible, and instead posits that He utilized the preserved Hebrew text and expanded on it with inspired *Targums*. This high view of bibliology requires Christians of all centuries and languages to recognize that God preserved His Hebrew, Aramaic, and Greek words in the original languages and that these preserved words must be the foundation for all bibliological truth, including all translational efforts of Scripture. *"Yea, let God be true, but every man a liar; as it is written, That thou mightest be justified in thy sayings, and mightest overcome when thou art judged"* (Rom 3:4).

APPENDIX F

Scholarly Myths Perpetuated on Rejecting The Masoretic Text of the Old Testament[199]

Introduction

Paul warned Timothy about promoting fables (i.e., myths [μύθοις *muthois*]) in the Ephesian church. He stated *"Neither give heed to fables and endless genealogies, which minister questions rather than godly edifying which is in faith: so do"* (I Tim. 1:4). Biblical critics have rejected the Hebrew Masoretic text of the OT and perpetuated historical myths about the language and text of the OT. Several fallacious corollaries stem from these diabolical myths.

The popular expression of the mythical views of the language and text of the OT follows these fallacious assumptions: 1) The language God gave Adam in the garden is unknown. No one knows what the divinely given "mother tongue" was. 2) The Hebrew language, in consonantal form only, evolved from the Canaanite language around 1200 BC.[200] 3) Through Alexander the Great Greek culture and language permeated the Mediterranean Basin resulting in the

---

[199]Thomas M. Strouse, "Scholarly Myths Perpetuated on Rejecting the Masoretic Text of the Old Testament," *Emmanuel Baptist Theological Journal* 1, no. 1 (Spring 2005): 3-61.

[200]Christo H. J. van der Merwe, Jackie A. Naude and Jan H. Kroeze, *A Biblical Hebrew Reference Grammar* (Sheffield, England: Sheffield Academic Press, 2002), pp. 15-17.

wide spread usage of the Greek OT (*LXX*). Christ and the early Christians used the *LXX* for evangelistic purposes.[201] 4) The *LXX* flourished between 200 BC and AD100 in the Near East. After this period the Hebrew language came back in vogue among the Jews.[202] 5) Somewhere between AD 600-1000, the Masoretic scribes invented a vowel pointing system for the consonantal Hebrew text,[203] resulting in the inaccurately transliterated name "Jehovah" among other infelicities.[204] 6) The Reformers used the inferior Masoretic text for their translations of the OT. 7) Critical Biblical scholarship (19th century) realized the MT was inferior and began to correct it with the Greek OT translation (*LXX*), the Dead Sea Scrolls (DSS), and other ancient authorities. Critical scholars are still tweaking the Hebrew text in order to give some assurance to Christians of what God has said in the OT.[205] 8) Christians should thank God for textual critics who have restored the OT and NT texts to such an advanced degree

---

[201]Merrill F. Unger, *Archaeology and the New Testament* (Grand Rapids: Zondervan Publ. House, 1979), pp. 38-39.

[202] David Ewert, *From Ancient Tablets to Modern Translations* (Grand Rapids: Zondervan Publ. House, 1983), pp. 105-107.

[203]Kyle M. Yates, *The Essentials of Biblical Hebrew* (NY: Harper and Row, Publ. 1938), p. 1.

[204]Francis Brown, S. R. Driver and Charles A. Briggs, *The New Brown-Driver-Briggs-Gesenius Hebrew and English Lexicon* (Peabody, MA: Hendrickson Publishers, 1979), p. 218.

[205]Gary D. Pratico and Miles V. Van Pelt, *Basics of Biblical Hebrew Grammar* (Grand Rapids: Zondervan Publ. House, 2001), p. 409.

of certainty and authority. 9) Furthermore, since Christ and the Apostles used the loose and poor *LXX* as their translation, Christians then have the precedence to use a similar quality of translation today, especially as found in the modern translations.

These historical myths and supporting corollaries diametrically oppose the reception of the Masoretic text as the Hebrew text behind the Authorized Version. The perpetuation of these deceptive propositions seriously weakens confidence in the Authorized Version. Yet if these are truly myths then why do Bible scholars of all stripes, including fundamentalists, perpetuate them? The writer's purpose for this brief essay is to expose the non-biblical nature of these scholarly lies and repudiate them with Scripture. Several of the aforementioned fallacious and presumptuous corollaries will be scrutinized with Scripture and Biblically repudiated: 1) The original language of Adam in the Garden and the mother tongue until the Tower of Babel is unknown. 2) Biblical Hebrew evolved out of the Canaanite language as a consonantal text only. 3) Christ and the Apostles used the *LXX* to evangelize the Gentiles. 4) The Masoretic scribes invented vowel points for the inspired consonantal Hebrew text. 5) Christians should thank textual critics for restoring the original texts of Scripture that God chose not to preserve.

Myth Number 1: The Original Language the Lord gave to Adam is unknown.

The Lord God created Adam and gave him a working

vocabulary and capability for language. This divinely originated language was perfectly suited for Adam to think concepts and enunciate words for clear expression and communication. The first recorded human words were Adam's response to God's creation of Eve. Adam said, *"This is now bone of my bones, and flesh of my flesh: she shall be called Woman, because she was taken out of Man"* (Gen. 2:23). Adam's first recorded statement has a significant element in it called the *paronomasia* or word pun. He punned on the name "man" אִישׁ (*'ish*) with the word "woman" אִשָּׁה (*'ishshah*) which means "from the man." Gill argues that this pun is not found in other ancient versions:

> *This paronomasia does not appear in the Syriac version, or in the Chaldee paraphrases of Onkelos and Jonathan. The Syriac uses Gabra for a man, but never Gabretha for a woman, not even in places where men and women are spoken of together...The Syriac or Chaldee language will not admit such an allusion as is in the text. Just a Gabra is used for a man, and not Gabretha for a woman, so Itta, and Ittetha, and Intetha or Antetha, are used for a woman, but never Itt for a man...this seems to prove that the language Adam spoke to his wife must have been the Hebrew language, and consequently is the primitive one.*[206]

---

[206] John Gill, *A Dissertation Concerning the Antiquity of the Hebrew Language, Letters, Vowel Points, and Accents* (London: G. Keith, 1767), p. 11.

Hebrew students recognize that there are numerous other puns in the Hebrew language, many of which are not translatable in any language, even the English of the KJV, in Gen. 1-11.[207] Gen. 11:1 is pivotal because Moses states *"And the whole earth was of one language, and of one speech."* Prior to the tower of Babel there was one mother tongue created by God.[208] Jehovah divided this original language into many to disunite man's rebellion (Gen. 11:6-9). Zephaniah the prophet predicted for the Millennial reign of Christ there would be the restoration of the original tongue, stating *"For then will I turn to the people a pure language, that they may all call upon the name of the LORD, to serve him with one consent"* (Zeph. 3:9). What would this language be for the people to call upon Jehovah, the God of Shem (Gen. 9:26)? Would it be Akkadian, German, or English? It would be the language of the Shemites or the Jews, who trace their lineage back to Shem (cf. Gen. 10:21-31; 11:10-32). In fact, the Scripture calls Abram "the Hebrew" (`eber`) because he was a descendent of Eber, in whose generation the mother tongue (Hebrew) was last universally spoken before the tower of Babel (cf. Gen. 14:13;

---

[207] John H. Sailhamer, *Genesis, The Expositor's Bible Commentary*, Vol. 2 (Grand Rapids: Zondervan Publ. House, 1990), p. 106.

[208] If this God-given mother tongue were Hebrew, those who are anti-Semitic might oppose this interpretation and create other linguistic alternatives. This anti-Semitism is pronounced in the Hebrew lexicons edited by rationalistic German linguists, who promote the evolution of the Hebrew language in the Akkadian—Canaanite—Hebrew lineage.

10:21).[209]

Whatever the mother tongue of humanity was, it should have many descendants in the present languages and therefore traceable for modern linguists. Modern linguists, holding to the evolution of language, dismiss the possibility that Hebrew could have been Adam's language. They would rather hold that language evolved from a series of grunts into highly sophisticated languages, including the lately developed Hebrew. Not only is this approach unbiblical but it is refuted by languages which trace their roots back to Hebrew. In a significant and enlightening new work, Isaac Mozeson demonstrates beyond any "coincidence" that over 22,000 English words trace their roots back to Hebrew. He states,

> *Don't worry if you've never read anything on language, or if you've never heard a Hebrew word. You will soon know that you've never heard a word that wasn't Hebrew...Hebrew vocabulary has as much affinity with English as it has with Arabic. More English words can be clearly linked to Biblical Hebrew than to Latin, Greek or French. Most known English words or roots are treated in this book...The last group of Westerners to take up the lost paradise of Hebrew included 17th-century Englishmen like John Milton and his Puritan counterparts in colonial America...The curriculum of Harvard was full of Hebrew, and an early graduate theses at Harvard concerned Hebrew as the Mother tongue. Noah*

---

[209] Asshur was the father of the Assyrians who spoke Assyrian (Num. 24:23-24).

> *Webster's etymologies (discredited for 200 years now) were full of English words traced to "Shemitic" sources. Most significant of all, if a vote in the Continental Congress had gone the other way, America, and much of today's world, would now be speaking Hebrew.*[210]

Darwin's book *The Origin of Species: The Preservation of Favored Races in the Struggle for Life* (1859) dethroned from its rightful reign the position that the Hebrew language was the original language God gave Adam in the Garden of Eden. This very title bespeaks of the impact evolution would have on all academic disciplines, including not only sociology but also linguistics. Bible commentators prior to this publication embraced the views of a recent creation of the universe and of Hebrew as the original tongue. Davis affirms the history of this latter point in the following:

> *That all men were of one language and dialect should not be surprising since they were fundamentally united in the sons of Noah. Research in the area of comparative grammar has demonstrated that known languages are related and could have descended from one language. Of course it is unknown whether that language resembles any modern language, but until the nineteenth century the theory that the original language was Hebrew was*

---

[210] Isaac E. Mozeson, *The Word: The Dictionary that Reveals the Hebrew Source of English* (NY: SPI Books, 2000), pp. 1-2.

practically unquestioned.[211]

The Scripture demands that the original language of Adam was Hebrew. That this is the case is based on the puns Moses used in Gen. 1-11 that have not been duplicated in ancient versions. Furthermore, Zephaniah's prophecy concerning the restoration of the original language to praise Jehovah, and the designation of Abram the Hebrew requires the aforementioned premise that Hebrew was the mother tongue. Extra-biblical arguments such as linguistic studies tying English with Hebrew and the contrived schemes of evolutionists powerfully corroborate the truth that Adam spoke Hebrew.

Myth Number 2: Biblical Hebrew, as a consonantal text only, evolved from the Canaanite language.

This myth has two components, namely that the consonants only were originally inspired and this Hebrew consonantal text evolved from the Canaanite[212] language. Since the theory or implementation of evolution is not an option for the Bible believing Christian, the latter component cannot be affirmed. This view denies the perfect preservation of God's Words and therefore must assume the evolution of

---

[211]John J. Davis, *Paradise to Prison: Studies in Genesis* (Grand Rapids: Baker Book House, 1975), p. 144.

[212]The descendants of Canaan were cursed by the Lord (Gen. 9:25). Biblically it is impossible to reconcile how God could use the cursed Canaanites to produce a language from which the blessed Shemites and their language would come (Gen. 9:26).

the Hebrew language. Those who are so enamored with the scholarship that assumes evolutionary principles are legitimate within Biblical criticism[213] would accept, without Biblical authority, that all languages including Hebrew evolved. Old Testament scholars and Hebrew grammarians constantly claim that Hebrew is a derived language. For example Unger states:

> *Necessary to the formation of the canon was a suitable language to serve as a medium for the reception and recording of the inspired message. Such a vehicle was providentially provided for the Hebrew people in the development of a simple alphabetic script rather than an unwieldy and cumbersome language like Akkadian...From the testimony of the Pentateuch and the witness of archeology there is every reason to believe that Hebrew was already in spoken and written use by Moses and the Israelites who came out of Egypt about 1440 BC.[214]*

---

[213] The OT textual critic Wurthwein exemplifies unbelieving critical scholarship as he states: "The available witnesses to the text must first be examined in order to reconstruct a single form of the text which we can assert with confidence to be as close to the form of the autographs as scientific principles can lead us, if not (ideally) identical with them." Ernst Wurthwein, *The Text of the Old Testament* (Grand Rapids: Wm. B. Eerdmans Publ. Co., 1981), p. xviii.

[214] Merrill F. Unger, *Introductory Guide to the Old Testament* (Grand Rapids: Zondervan Publ. House, 1951), p. 51.

Payne advocates this derived approach to the theology and language of the Jews stating,

> *It is our historical knowledge of the religions of the pagans who surrounded Israel that serves to explain certain terms or forms that God chose to use in His own true religion. The very names of God in Biblical Hebrew, which is a Canaanitish language, illustrate this point.*[215]

Archer treats Hebrew as a branch of West Semitic in the development of language, stating,

> *The traditional classification of the various Semitic languages divides them, according to the geographical location of the nations speaking them, into north, south, east, and west…West Semitic (often classed with Aramaic in what is called Northwest Semitic by modern scholars) comprises Ugaritic, Phoenician, and Canaanite (of which Hebrew and Moabite are dialects).*[216]

Post-Darwinian Hebrew grammarians have continually maintained that Hebrew is merely a derived language in the long history of the evolution of the languages. For instance, H. F. W. Gesenius states:

---

[215]J. Barton Payne, *The Theology of the Older Testament* (Grand Rapids: Zondervan Publ. House, 1962), p. 20.

[216] Gleason L. Archer, *A Survey of Old Testament Introduction* (Chicago: Moody Press, 1994), p. 20.

> *The Hebrew language is one branch of a great family of languages in Western Asia...The better known Semitic languages may be subdivided as follows:—The Middle Semitic or Canaanitish branch. To this belongs the Hebrew of the Old Testament with its descendants, the New Hebrew, as found especially in the Mishna, and Rabbinic...* [217]

The former component that assumes that the inspired Hebrew text contained only the consonants and that the vowels (and consequently the pronunciations) were passed on through oral tradition is unbiblical and wrongheaded. [218] This view maintains an insufficient position on the perfect preservation of the Hebrew text. The Bible is replete with divine promises of the preservation of the Lord's Words (e.g., Pss. 12:6-7, 119:111, 152, 160; Mt. 4:4, 5:18, 24:35, etc.). Consonants are not words. Words include consonants and vowels. The Bible declares that *"every word of God is pure"* (Prov. 30:5-6) and these pure Words are complete Words with consonants and vowels. When the Lord God spoke the heavens and earth into existence He used Words (Gen. 1:3).

---

[217] E. Kautzsch and A. E. Cowley, editors, *Gesenius' Hebrew Grammar* (Oxford: At the Clarendon Press, 1970), pp. 1-2.

[218] Waltke represents some who seemly suggest that there was a "proto-Masoretic" text which is superior to the current Masoretic text and must eventually be recovered through textual criticism. Bruce Waltke, "The Textual Criticism of the Old Testament," *The Gaebelein Bible Commentary,* Vol. I, (Grand Rapids: Zondervan Publ. House, 1987), p. 223.

When the Lord gave His commandments to Moses He wrote Words on the tablets (Ex. 34:1; cf. 20:1 ff.; Dt. 10:2). When the prophets, such as Amos, saw God's revelation, they wrote Words (cf. Amos 1:1; Obad. 1:1; Hab. 1:1). None of these examples, as well as scores of others, allows that God's revelation was in the form of consonants only.

The denial of the perfect preservation of the Hebrew OT text carries with it several specific ramifications. One such ramification will be explored. Since God has not preserved His OT Hebrew text, the argument goes, the current MT is an inferior Hebrew text to the supposed "proto-Hebrew" text.[219] This earlier Hebrew text allegedly utilized a cipher system whereby Hebrew letters were used for Hebrew numbers. This supposed cipher system then allows for "scribal errors" in the numbers of various Biblical texts because the scribes mis-read the letters depicting the numbers. In attempting to explain how numerical errors entered into the Sacred Text of the OT, Kaiser states the following:

In the Old Testament documents now available

---

[219] Contradicting the clear promises of the Lord Jesus Christ, Bible critic Beacham fallaciously affirms that "God nowhere in Scripture assures us that the Jewish scholars of the first century AD produced a corpus of Scripture that perfectly mirrored the originals. Thus, the Masoretic text should not be considered a flawless reproduction of the autographs. Rather, the Masoretic text evolved from a late, standardized Rescension of variant, imperfect, and updated copies made by imperfect men." Roy Beacham and Kevin Bauder, *One Bible Only?* (Grand Rapids: Kregel Publ., 2001), p. 63.

to us, all the numbers are spelled out phonetically. This is not so say, however, that a more direct numeral system or cipher notation was not also in use originally for at least some of these numbers. While no Biblical texts with such a system have been found, mason's marks and examples of what may well be simple tallies have been attested in excavations in Israel.[220]

Although in the preserved Masoretic Text there are no examples whereby a Hebrew letter represents a number, and every number is a written word, Bible critics nevertheless assume, with no evidence, a cipher system existed in a "proto-Masoretic" text. Davis quotes Merrill Unger who asserts:

But, though, on the one hand it is certain that in all existing manuscripts of the Hebrew text of the Old Testament the numerical expressions are written at length, yet, on the other, the variations between themselves and from the Hebrew text, added to the evident inconsistencies in numerical statements, between certain passages of that text itself, seem to prove that some shorter mode of writing was originally in vogue, liable to be misunderstood by copyists and translators. These variations appear to

---

[220]Walter C. Kaiser, Jr., Peter H. Davids, F. F. Bruce, and Manfred T. Baruch, *Hard Sayings of the Bible* (Downers Grove, IL: InterVarsity Press, 1996), p. 51.

have proceeded from the alphabetic method of writing numbers.[221]

The Lord Jesus Christ put His full approval on the Hebrew text He had preserved unto Himself (Mt. 4:4). Since evolution is not true and there was no consequent proto-Masoretic Hebrew text from which the current one evolved, there is no cipher system for the numbers of the OT and no excuse to argue for misread letters to allow "scribal errors" for the apparent numerical conflicts in the OT. [222]

Myth Number 3: Christ and the Apostles used the LXX to evangelize the Gentiles.

In attempting to refute the charge that Christ and the Apostles' inexact use of the *LXX* argues for errancy in the originals, Archer and Chirichigno argue vociferously that the aforementioned preachers used the *LXX* to evangelize Gentiles. Their argument follows this line of thought:

---

[221]John J. Davis, *Biblical Numerology: A Basic Study of the Use of Numbers in the Bible* (Grand Rapids: Baker Book House), p. 35.

[222] For a complete refutation of the alleged cipher numbering position, see Chester Kulus, *I Heard the Number of Them: General Principles for Handling Apparent Biblical Contradictions with Specific Applications of the Principles to the Alleged Numeric Contradictions in I Samuel to II Chronicles* (Newington, CT: Emmanuel Baptist Theological Press, 2003), pp. 128-138.

> *The very reason for using the LXX was rooted in the missionary outreach of the evangelists and apostles of the early church...It was virtually the only form of the OT in the hands of Jewish believers outside Palestine, and it was certainly the only available form for Gentile converts to the Jewish or Christian faiths.*[223]

Others dogmatically maintain, albeit recognizing the questionable history and character of the *LXX*, that this version was readily available to the early first century evangelists and apostles. For instance, Waltke asserts the following:

> *Although many details of the story are fictitious, it is widely accepted that the translation of the Law was made in the time of Philadelphus. Contrary to the story, however, it is concluded that LXX arose out of the needs of the Alexandrian Jews and was done by various literary Greeks at Alexandria on a text type already present in Egypt...Scholars agree that a complete version of the Bible existed at least at the beginning of the first century A.D.*[224]

Accordingly, the consensus of most scholarship

---

[223] Gleason L. Archer and Gregory Chirichigno, *Old Testament Quotations in the New Testament* (Chicago: Moody Press, 1983), p. ix.

[224] Waltke, p. 220.

assumes that the *LXX* was available to and had the veritable character for the first century Christians to use as their OT Scriptures. This consensus is faulty because of two important Bible truths. First of all, the Bible plainly demonstrates that the Lord Jesus Christ used the Hebrew OT for His Scripture and that He never used the *LXX*. Secondly, the Lord and His apostles did not need to utilize the *LXX* for evangelism of the Jews and Gentiles and consequently did not do so.

First, the Bible clearly shows that the Lord Jesus Christ used the Hebrew text as His Scriptures. When Satan tempted Him, the Lord submitted Himself to the written Words of God[225] by stating, *"It is written, Man shall not live by bread alone, but by every word that proceedeth out of the mouth of God"* (Mt. 4:4). The expression *"It is written"* Γέγραπται is in the perfect tense indicating past action with continuing results. In effect the Lord said this Hebrew verse to which He alluded (Dt. 8:3), and obviously the Hebrew Book of Deuteronomy and consequently the Hebrew Pentateuch, had been written (by Moses the Hebrew) and was still written to His very day. The Lord Jesus Christ had the preserved Words of the Hebrew OT available to Him just as He had promised (cf. Dt. 4:2; 12:32; 17:18-20; 29:1, 29; 30:11-14 [*vide* Rom. 10:6-8]; 31:9-13, 24-27; Josh. 1:7-8; Ps. 12:6-7; 119:111, 152, 160).

---

[225]This action harmonizes with Ps. 138:2, which states, *"I will worship toward thy holy temple, and praise thy name for thy lovingkindness and for thy truth: for thou hast magnified thy word above all thy name."*

The Lord taught that the jots and tittles[226] of the Hebrew OT would be preserved, stating, *"For verily I say unto you, Till heaven and earth pass, one jot or one tittle shall in no wise pass from the law, till all be fulfilled"* (Mt. 5:18). He believed that the very consonants and the very vowels of the OT Hebrew words of prophecies (and of course all the other words of Scripture) were preserved perfectly intact in His day and would continue until final fulfillment (cf. Jn. 12:48).[227] Since the Greek OT (*LXX*) does not have jots and tittles He was not referring to this inferior translation which has a historical background and time table that are very suspect.

Again the Lord Jesus alluded to the three-fold division of the Hebrew OT, which division the *LXX* does not follow, when He affirmed, *"These are the words which I spake unto you, while I was yet with you, that all things must be fulfilled, which were written in the law of Moses, and in the prophets, and in the psalms, concerning me"* (Lk. 24:44; cf. v. 27; also Acts 26:22). The law (*Torah*), the prophets (*Neviy'iym*), and the writings (*Kethuviym* [of which Psalms was first]) made up

---

[226]"[L]it. 'horn'; projection, hook as part of a letter, a serif (of letters…of accents and breathings…" Walter Bauer, William Arndt and F. Wilbur Gingrich, *A Greek-English Lexicon of the New Testament and Other Early Christian Literature* (Chicago: The University of Chicago Press, 1957), p. 429.

[227]The prophecies could not be perfectly fulfilled if the prophecies themselves were not perfectly preserved for one to match the minute details of the prophecy with the minute details of the fulfillment (cf. Isa. 34:16).

the Hebrew OT and is called the *Tanak.*[228] He elaborated on His use of the Hebrew OT when the Lord identified the Pharisees' persecution of the prophets with their murderous Jewish ancestors, stating, *"From the blood of Abel unto the blood of Zacharias, which perished between the altar and the temple: verily I say unto you, It shall be required of this generation"* (Lk. 11:51). He surveyed the whole scope of the Hebrew OT, using the examples of the murder of the righteous Abel from the first book (Genesis 4:8) to the murder of the righteous Zacharias from the last book (II Chronicles 24:20-22).

The Biblical truths that the Lord Jesus always used the Hebrew text for His Scriptures includes His reference to the perfectly preserved Hebrew text, His reference to the perfect preservation of the smallest components of Hebrew words, and His reference to the three-fold division of the Hebrew OT are indisputable. The NT does not countenance the assumed position that Christ used the *LXX* because it clearly contradicts this false assumption. The Lord consistently alluded to the Hebrew OT. Since the nature and character of the *LXX* are extremely questionable, the alleged argument that the NT quotes the *LXX* must be rejected. The supposed NT quotes of the *LXX* must be understood in another way. The simple fact of the matter is that the *LXX* was in part or whole post-first century and never used by Christ or the Apostles.

Second, the Lord and the Apostles did not need to implement the use of the *LXX* in their evangelistic endeavors.

---

[228] This is an acrostic for the letters "T" (*Torah*), "N" (*Neviy'iym*) and "K" (*Kethuviym*) and Jews use this designation even today for their Scripture.

The initial ministry of Christ was to the Jews in Galilee and Judaea (Jn. 1:19-4:3). He sent His Jewish apostles to the Jews to declare to them that their Jewish King was on hand (Mt. 10:2-6). When He ministered to the Jews there is no exegetical necessity that He had to use the *LXX*. The Lord ministered to the Syrophenician Greek woman, no doubt speaking to her in Greek (Mk. 7:26-30). But He did not need to use the *LXX* since He gave her His inspired Greek Words.[229]   There is positively no indication in Scripture that the Lord Jesus Christ had the necessity to use or in fact did use the *LXX* to evangelize Jews and Gentiles.

Furthermore, there is no indication that the Apostles had the necessity to use the *LXX*. On the day of Pentecost, Peter preached to the Jews citing the OT book of Joel, but not using the *LXX* (Acts 2:14-36).[230] The Lord eliminated the necessity for Peter using the *LXX* for the Gentiles present that day by the supernatural occurrence of tongues. The Apostles taught the early church members, both Jews and Gentiles, *"the apostles doctrine,"* presumably in Greek (Acts 2:42). When the Apostles and Paul eventually evangelized the Gentiles (e.g., Acts 13-21) they taught them the apostles' doctrine, which eventually was inscripturated as the Greek

---

[229]There is no question that Christ and the Apostles, as well as many in the ancient Near East, were multilingual, as the message over the cross in various languages suggests (Jn. 19:19-20). Jesus of Nazareth read the preserved Hebrew OT in the synagogue (Lk. 4:16 ff.), spoke Aramaic on several occasions (i.e., Mt. 27:46; Mk. 7:34), and had a brother who wrote elegant Greek (cf. the Book of James).

[230]A careful examination of the Greek NT demonstrates that Peter did not quote Joel 2:28-32 from the *LXX*.

NT. Where is the alleged need for the *LXX*? No exegesis requires that the Lord and His Apostles had to have used the *LXX* to evangelize the Greek-speaking Jews or Gentiles. This fallacious assumption has not been and cannot be proved and must, therefore, be rejected. Biblically, there is neither need nor exegesis for this ill founded but popular assumption.

Myth Number 4: The Masoretic scribes invented vowel points for the inspired consonantal Hebrew text.

Rejecting the aforementioned Biblical promises for perfect Words preservation, critical scholarship argues that the original Hebrew text was only in consonant form, that the vowels were not inspired,[231] and the pronunciations were passed on by oral tradition until the Masoretic scribes invented a vowel pointing system. For instance, van der Merwe affirms,

> *Originally BH (Biblical Hebrew) text consisted of consonants only. In order to prevent the eventual complete loss of the correct pronunciations, a group of Jewish scholars began to devise a system of*

---

[231]"Yet another argument is advanced by bringing forward the testimony of Elias Levita, who lived in Germany about 1520, and who roundly states that the post-Talmudic Massoretes of Tiberias invented the points, and goes on to attempt to prove it. And why is this testimony considered important? Because Levita says so!" John Owen, *Biblical Theology: The Nature, Origin, Development, and Study of Theological Truth, in Six Books* (Morgan, PA: Soli Deo Gloria Publ., 1996 reprint), p. 522.

> *signs (from about 600 CE) to record and standardize the received pronunciation (inasmuch as it was known).*[232]

Ewert posits the same argument for the Masoretic invention of vowels stating "But they made one very important innovation. They developed a system by which the vowels of the Hebrew words could be indicated in writing."[233]

Consonants without vowels are not words. One cannot distinguish between some nouns and verbs, conjugations or stems without vowel pointing. The other ancient languages of the Samaritans, Syrians, Chaldeans, and Arabs had consonants and vowels. The Hebrew vowels must be *ab origine* for several reasons.

Linguistically, the very nature of words requires both consonants and vowels since God and man spoke and wrote words from the beginning. Words need to be precise to convey accuracy and this precision comes only with the vowels. Gill cites several arguments for the divine origin of the vowels. 1) The perfection of language requires vowels. 2) The nature and genius of the Hebrew language require points. 3) The vowel points are necessary and useful to easier learning, reading, and pronouncing of the Hebrew language. 4) The vowel points and accents are useful and necessary. 5) It will be difficult to assert and maintain the clarity of the Scriptures if the vowel points and accents are removed. 6) One would be unable to support the infallibility of the Scripture. 7) The inspiration of Scripture is affected

---

[232]van der Merwe, p. 17.
[233]Ewert, p. 90.

by the points and accents.[234]

Historically, the main fallacy with positing the invention of the Hebrew vowel points with the Masoretes is the lack of recorded testimony. [235] Furthermore, this historical assumption makes the Masoretes the final authority with regard to the Words of Scripture. Moncrief gives a list of five Hebrew words, as select examples, whose meanings vary depending on the vowel pointing.[236] The final meaning of a Word of Scripture cannot be dependent on man in light of the promises for the authoritative inspired and preserved Words of Scripture. The preacher of Scripture must declare *"thus saith the LORD,"* not "thus saith the Masoretes."

Scripturally, Christ recognized the preserved Words of the Hebrew OT (Mt. 4:4) and affirmed the inspiration and preservation of the consonants (*jot*) and vowel points (*keraia*) in Mt. 5:18. The Gospel writers consistently followed a pattern for the vowel pointings of the proper Hebrew nouns to which they alluded. For example, they recognized the inspired *dagesh forte* (a small dot to indicate doubling) in words like Immanuel (Mt. 1:23; cf. Isa. 7:14), Anna/Hannah (Lk. 2:36; cf. I Sam. 1:2), Abaddon (Rev. 9:11; Ps. 1:6), Armageddon (Rev. 16:16; cf. Zech. 12:11), and Sabbaton

---

[234]Gill, pp. 67-70.

[235]On the other hand, Gill gives an abundance of historical evidence that the points were known at least back to 454 BC, and consequently could not have been invented by the Masoretes. Gill, pp. 38-66.

[236]John Moncrieff, *An Essay on the Antiquity and Utility of the Hebrew Vowel-Points* (Glasgow: John Reid & Co., 1833), pp. 34-35.

(Mt. 12:5; Ex. 20:11). Paul knew the pointing of the inspired Hebrew word behind the inspired Greek ἀῤῥαβὼν (*arrabon*, "earnest") in Eph. 1:14 because he doubled the "r" (*rho*) in his inspired transliterated spelling of the Hebrew word עֵרָבוֹן (`*errabon*, "pledge") from Gen. 38:17. The authority of the inspired NT text demands that the vowel pointings were part of the inspired OT text.

Bible critics assume that man invented the pointing and that consequently the proper pronunciation for the divine name of the *tetragrammaton* JHWH (יְהֹוָה) is unknown. This view alleges that the Jews refused to pronounce the name of the Lord because of a faulty interpretation of Lev. 24:16, which states, *"And he that blasphemeth the name of the LORD, he shall surely be put to death..."*[237] After many centuries of not pronouncing the divine name the Jews claimed the proper pronunciation was lost. The Masoretes interjected the so-called *Qere perpetuum* reading into the text and produced the impossible name Jehovah.[238] Based on

---

[237] The *LXX* incorrectly renders this caveat as "he that names the Lord shall be put to death." Both the OT saints and sinners named the name of Jehovah without fear of punishment (Moses [Ex. 3:13-14, 4:1]; Pharaoh [Ex. 8:8]; Rahab and Canaanites [Josh. 2:10]).

[238] Some argue that the *holem* and *waw* must be treated as the *holem waw* vowel and thus the *waw* loses its consonant status giving an impossible *Jehoah* construction. There are numerous examples, however, of the *holem* vowel with the *waw* consonant construction (e.g., Isa. 47:11; Ezk. 7:26; Lam. 3:25; Pss. 37:9, 88:16; Neh. 6:6; Est. 3:8). Could it be possible that Satan has inspired and promoted through his Bible critics a different name for

extra-biblical authorities, critics assume the best rendering for the *tetragrammaton* should be Yahweh.[239]

The popular position that the Masoretes invented the vowel pointing of the OT Hebrew text denies the Bible claims of perfect Words preservation. Furthermore, this view posits the inspired source and final authority for the Words of Scripture upon man and not God. Since the Masoretes merely passed on the divine vowel points with the consonants, the falsely assumed Masoretic-invention position must be rejected along with the fallacious tradition that the divine name of the *tetragrammaton* must be pronounced Yahweh. According to the Masoretic Hebrew text behind the KJV the proper pronunciation for the OT name of the LORD is Jehovah.

Myth Number 5: Christians should thank textual critics for restoring the original texts of Scripture that God chose not to preserve.

Waltke confidently states "to restore the original text of ancient documents, such as the OT Scriptures, is the task of textual criticism." [240] Another Bible critic affirms the following role for seminaries such as his:

Our purpose at Central is "to reconstruct from all the witnesses available to us the text essentially

---

Jehovah?

[239] Gustave F. Oehler, *Theology of the Old Testament* (Grand Rapids: Zondervan Publ. House, n.d.), pp. 92-93.

[240] Waltke, p. 211.

*preserved in all, but perfectly preserved in none"
[footnote 3, Rene Pache, The Inspiration and
Authority of Scripture (Chicago: Moody Press,
1969), 197]. It is evident from the historical evidence
that God has providentially preserved His Word for
the present generation. However, we do not believe
that God has preserved His Word perfectly and
miraculously in any one manuscript or group of
manuscripts, or in all the manuscripts. Therefore, in
our study of the text we work with all the manuscripts
to compile a text closer to the original than any one
manuscript or group of manuscripts.*[241]

Again, Mark Norton states, "Christians are thus in debt to the
textual critics who have worked, and are working, to provide a
dependable biblical text."[242] These writers obviously think
that the role of Textual Criticism is to restore or reconstruct a
Bible text that God apparently chose not to preserve. This
view begs the question as to how the critic will know that the
text is restored or reconstructed since the Lord apparently left
no exemplar for comparison! The anti-supernatural German
rationalistic movement (17th-19th centuries) known as Biblical
Criticism spawned several literary-critical fields, one of

---

[241]Michael A. Grisanti, editor, *The Bible Version Debate:
The Perspective of Central Baptist Theological Seminary*
(Minneapolis, MN: Central Baptist Theological Seminary, 1997),
p. 131.

[242]Mark Norton, "Manuscripts of the Old Testament," *The
Origin of the Bible*, ed. Phillip Comfort (Cambridge: Tyndale
House Publ., 1992), p. 177.

which was Textual Criticism. The picking and choosing of Bible texts is not Textual Criticism. Textual Criticism is a sophisticated system based on elaborate and evolutionary schemes following human logic to determine the possible origin of variants. [243] The so-called science of Textual Criticism is only needed when one believes that God has not accomplished His promise to preserve the inspired original Hebrew, Aramaic, and Greek Words of the *autographa*.[244]

The Lord Jesus Christ has promised the full preservation of the divinely inspired Words of the OT and NT Scriptures (Ps. 12:6-7; Mt. 4:4, 5:18, 24:35). He has given the responsibility of preserving His Words to His only ecclesiological institution—the local, immersionist assembly (Mt. 28:19-20; I Tim. 3:15). God has given His chosen people (Jews) and His chosen institution (the local

---

[243] Archer lists seven canons for OT Textual Criticism. Gleason Archer, *A Survey of Old Testament Introduction*, pp. 63-66. The Alands give twelve basic rules for NT Textual Criticism. Kurt Aland and Barbara Aland, *The Text of the New Testament* (Grand Rapids: Wm. B. Eerdmans Publ. Co., 1987), pp. 275-277.

[244] One does well to consider the negative influence of the textual critics. For example, the Masoretic Hebrew text incorporates the titles of the Psalms in the text. However, textual critics reject the Masoretic text and consequently do not know the background of the titled Psalms. For instance, the "contribution" the textual critics Rogerson and McKay give the Bible-believing Christian is that the Psalm titles "are almost certainly not the work of the authors of the psalms." J. W. Rogerson and J. W. McKay, *The Cambridge Bible Commentary on the New English Bible, Psalms 1-50* (Cambridge: Cambridge University Press, 1977), p. 3.

immersionist assembly) the responsibility and empowerment to preserve His OT and NT Words, respectively. The Bible nowhere gives credence to the role of the professional "textual critic," especially outside of the immersionist assembly, to restore what He has determined not to preserve. In spite of Biblical evidence, some want to praise textual critics for their role in giving Christians the approximate Words of God. Mark Minnick states:

> *For many centuries now God has ensured that there have been qualified textual critics to analyze available manuscripts. In other words, textual criticism is not a new discipline—it is an old one—employed by anyone who has ever compared two or more manuscripts in an effort to reproduce an accurate copy of God's Word. If our present translations do indeed reproduce the original readings, it is because textual critics did their work well.*[245]

This claim is repudiated by the inspired history of NT immersionist churches recorded in the NT. For instance, the church at Ephesus not only received but also copied perfectly the Book of the Apocalypse from John. The church at Smyrna made a copy and passed it on to the church at Pergamos, and so on, until there were six perfect copies and one original, and all this accomplished by faithful church

---

[245]James B. Williams, editor, *From the Mind of God to the Mind of Man* (Greenville, SC: Ambassador-Emerald International, 1999), p. 72.

members (cf. Rev. 22:7,18-19). This inspired scenario was repeated thousands of times through history so that now we have immersionist churches which receive the preserved inspired OT and NT texts and accurate translations of God's Words through the instrumentality of fallible yet faithful church members. Since the text of Scripture was never lost, the Lord never used textual critics to restore His text. Faithful church members have never had to use the premise or tools (i.e., rules, canons, axioms, etc.) of Textual Criticism since neither are Biblically valid.[246] The Lord has always used, whether history can corroborate this or not, faithful church members as He promised (Mt. 28:19-20), not to restore, but to preserve His Received Words (Jn. 17:8).

Conclusion

As Paul warned Timothy (I Tim. 1:4), even so Bible-related *"fables"* or myths are a concern today for all Bible believers. Christians have the responsibility and the means whereby to dispel these myths. Those Bible critics

---

[246]As Paul taught his understudy Timothy, he never gave him any tools for Textual Criticism. He did warn Timothy, nevertheless, stating: *"If any man teach otherwise, and consent not to wholesome words, even the words of our Lord Jesus Christ, and to the doctrine which is according to godliness; He is proud, knowing nothing, but doting about questions, and strifes of words, whereof cometh envy, strife, railings, evil surmisings, perverse disputings of men of corrupt minds, and destitute of the truth, supposing that gain is godliness: from such withdraw thyself"* (I Tim. 6:3-5).

and their followers who have rejected the Masoretic Hebrew text behind the King James Version have postulated several myths and fallacious corollaries, and at the same time given no assurance of final Words or absolute authority. The Bible refutes these myths. The Bible teaches that the original language of the Garden of Eden was Hebrew. Therefore, Hebrew did not evolve from the Canaanite language. Christ used the Hebrew text and His NT Words to evangelize Jews and Greeks. The early Christians used the Hebrew and the Apostles' tradition to evangelize Jews and Gentiles. Since the vowel points were part of the original Words God preserved, the Masoretes did not need to invent a pointing system. Since the Masoretes passed on the preserved Words, the name Jehovah for the *tetragrammaton* stands. Bible critics have only questioned the Words and the authority of Scripture, and even the authorship of the Psalms, and have given no valuable contribution. When the preserved Hebrew text represented by the Masoretic text is received by faith, then the scholarly myths are dispelled. Is it not time for Bible-believing Baptist church members to stop giving *"heed to fables"* and honor Jehovah God, the Lord Jesus Christ, with faith in His inspired and preserved Words of promise?

APPENDIX G

The Permanent Preservation of God's Words (Psalm 12:6-7 Expanded)[247]

Introduction

Psalm 12 is a psalm of contrasts. It contrasts the Godly with the ungodly and the Words of the Lord with the words of men. The latter contrast provides the backdrop to one of the clearest promises in the OT of the preservation of God's Words (cf. Pss. 78:1-8; 105:8; 119: 89, 111, 152, 160, Isa. 40:8; Mt. 4:4, 5:18, 24:35; Lk. 4:4; I Pet. 1:23-25).[248] Although some dismiss or deny the declaration of the Lord that He will preserve His Words forever, the exegesis of the Hebrew text of this Psalm will demonstrate unambiguously this proper understanding of verses 6-7, that God has indeed promised to preserve His Words (vv. 7-8 in the Hebrew text). The KJV, in contradistinction to some

---

[247]Thomas M. Strouse, "The Permanent Preservation of God's Words, Psalm 12:6-7," *Thou Shalt Keep Them*, pp. 29-33. The expanded research appears first in the present volume.

[248]The Christian exegete should not be surprised that the enemy has attacked some of the clearest passages on key doctrinal subjects (cf. Eph. 6:12; I Tim. 4:1-2). For instance, the clear teachings on the ubiquity of Christ (Jn. 3:13), on the incarnation of God (I Tim. 3:16), on the requisite faith for baptism (Acts 8:37), and on the Trinity of the Godhead (I Jn. 5:7) have been under attack since their respective inscripturation.

modern versions,[249] gives this aforementioned rendering: *"The words of the Lord are pure words: as silver tried in a furnace of earth, purified seven times. Thou shalt keep them, O LORD, thou shalt preserve them from this generation for ever."*

Psalm 12

Title

The title[250] of this psalm reveals several important facts. The psalm was for the *"chief Musician"* (*lamanatstsach* לַמְנַצֵּחַ)[251] to be sung with the eight stringed harps or *"Sheminith"* (*hashsheminith* הַשְּׁמִינִית).[252] It was a *"Psalm"* (*mizmor* מִזְמוֹר) that David authored (*ledawid* לְדָוִד).[253] David obviously lamented the evil words of his enemies, but the psalm's specific occasion is not revealed.

---

[249]For instance, the NIV reads "And the words of the Lord are flawless, like silver refined in a furnace of clay, purified seven times. O Lord, you will keep us safe and protect us from such people forever" (Ps. 12:6-7).

[250]The title of this psalm as well as others is part of the *Masoretic* text and should be considered part of the *autographa*.

[251]This word is found in the titles of fifty-five psalms as well as in Hab. 3:19.

[252]It may refer to the octave (cf. Psm. 6:1 [Heb.]).

[253]David was the predominant writer of the Psalter, having written at least seventy-three psalms (cf. Lk. 20:42).

Structure

The structure of the psalm is asymmetric. This structure causes the focus to be on the middle or odd strophe, "C" The Promises of God (v. 5). David's lament carries the reader from the need for divine help, because of the words of the ungodly, to a focus on the promises of God for deliverance, which include the permanent preservation of His Words, the antidote to the word of the ever-present wicked.

Graphic Structure of English Text

    A.   The Recognition of the Need for Divine Help (v. 1)
        B. The Threat of the Words of the Ungodly (vv. 2-4)
            C. The Promises of God (v. 5)
        B.' The Antidote of the Words of God (vv. 6-7)
    A.' The Recognition of the Need for Divine Help (v. 8)

Summary of the Content of Psalm 12

A. The Recognition of the Need for Divine Help (v. 1)

David appealed to the Lord for *"help"* (*hoshiy`ah* הוֹשִׁיעָה),[254] fearing that the *"godly man"* (*chasiyd* חָסִיד)[255] would come to an *"end"* (*gamar* גָּמַר) and *"faithful men"*

---

[254]The verbal root *yasha`* (יָשַׁע) is behind the names Joshua, Jesus, and Hosanna.

[255]The consonants of this word relate to *kesed* (חֶסֶד) that refers to the Lord's covenant love.

(*'emuniym* אֱמוּנִים) would *"vanish"* (*phassu* פַּסּוּ)[256] from mankind. The reference to the individual Godly man no doubt refers to David, and the *"faithful men"* refers to the larger community of believers, all of whom were on the brink of annihilation, or so the psalmist thought.[257] This apparent obliteration of the righteous was in contradistinction to the Lord's covenant promise for the remnant (cf. Gen. 12:1-3; Isa. 10:20).

B. The Threat of the Words of the Ungodly (vv. 2-4)

The psalmist David acutely sensed this great threat of words from the ungodly around him. Using two different verbs (*"they speak"* [*yethabberu* יְדַבְּרוּ] {3x} and *"said"* [*'ameru* אָמְרוּ]) the wicked told *"vanity"* (literally "empty lies" *shawe'* שָׁוְא)[258] with flattering lips (2x), a double heart, and a flattering tongue (2x). The psalmist recorded the claim of the wicked, who stated, *"With our tongue will we prevail; our lips are our own: who is lord over us?"* (v. 4). These wicked men asserted that they would *"prevail"* (*nagebbiyr* נַגְבִּיר)[259] and that they were autonomous. *"Who is lord*

---

[256]This *hapax legomena* verb comes from *pasas* (פָּסַס) and means "to disappear."

[257]Elijah manifested this attitude of *'solipsism'* ("I only exist") and was rebuked by the Lord (I Kings 19:14-18).

[258]This masculine singular noun means "worthless, empty" speech.

[259]The stem of this first person common plural imperfect verb is *Hiphil,* suggesting the force of "we will cause to prevail."

(*'adon* אָדוֹן) *over us?"* suggests the rebellious attitude of those who said, *"There is no God"* (Ps. 14:1). The "atheists" in this latter instance were those who rejected God's lordship (cf. Ps. 14:2, 4). David asserted or prayed that the Lord would *"cut of"* (*yakereth* יַכְרֵת) the braggarts he was facing. This *Hiphil* (causative stem) imperfect verb could be understood as an assertion, "the Lord will cut off," or as a prayer, "may the Lord cut off."

C. God's Promises (v. 5)

The structure of the psalm focuses on the promises of God.[260] The Lord promised that, because *"of the oppression of the poor,"* and *"of the sighing of the needy,"* He would *"arise and set him in safety from him that puffeth at him."* Since the *"poor"* (*'aniyyiym* עֲנִיִּים) were despoiled and the *"needy"* (*'evyoniym* אֶבְיוֹנִים) were groaning, the Lord made significant promises. *"Now will I arise"* (*'aqum* אָקוּם), the Lord promised, and set the psalmist *"in safety"* (cf. v. 1). The LORD promised to arise (cf. Ps. 9:19) and intervene on the part of the faithful. The enemy made boastful threats, and if fulfilled, this verbal antagonism would lead to the injury and destruction of the saints. Jehovah's promise was to place David in safety, the very help for which the psalmist asked (v. 1). The safety was physical deliverance from those that *"puff*

The root consonants are related to גֶּבֶר ("strong man").

[260]Paul emphasized the importance of the promises of God to the believer, saying *"For all the promises of God in him are yea, and in Him Amen, unto the glory of God by us"* (II Cor. 1:20).

at" (*yaphiyach* יָפִיחַ)[261] the author with manipulative and boastful words.

B.' The Antidote of God's Words (vv. 6-7)

The content of God's help was the assurance of His ever-present Words (cf. Dt. 30:11-14), with the inherent promises of deliverance, as an antidote to the words of the wicked. After all, the wicked asserted that their words would prevail, or *be preserved indefinitely*. The Lord's response to this boastful claim was that *His* Words, and not man's, would be preserved, each and ever one of them, for ever. The psalmist reflected on the quality and endurance of the greatest tangible help that the Lord desires to give man—His perfect Words (cf. Prov. 30:5-6). The quality of the Lord's Words is likened to purified silver from a refining furnace. The results of the seven-fold refining process produced one hundred percent perfect silver in the ancient world, and apt illustration for the quality of the perfect Words of the Lord. Furthermore, David revealed the endurance of God's Words, indicating that they would be preserved from that generation forever.

A.' The Recognition of the Need for Divine Help (v. 8)

---

[261]The root of this *Hiphil* imperfect verb is *puach* (פוּחַ) meaning to blow or breathe. The antidote to these man-breathed words are the God-breathed Words of the inspired and preserved Scripture (II Tim. 3:16).

David concluded the psalm by recognizing his need for the Lord's help because the wicked were *"all around"* (*saviyv* סָבִיב) him. Their *"vilest"* (*zulluth* זֻלֻּת) nature was not only prevalent but *"exalted"* (*rum* רוּם)[262] among the sons of *"men."* David recognized that the proud words of the wicked flatterers were a constant problem, but the perfect Words of God will always counter man's lies. Jeremiah expressed succinctly this tension between God's Words and man's words, stating *"all the remnant of Judah...shall know whose words shall stand, mine, or theirs"* (Jer. 44:28).

Exegesis of vv. 6-7

The Hebrew grammar of the OT prepares for the exegesis Ps. 12:6-7. The serious student of Scripture must recognize the biblical phenomenon of feminine antecedent nouns taking masculine pronouns. Once this is recognized, then careful exegesis may be achieved.

The Biblical Phenomenon

It is important for the careful exegete of the Hebrew Scriptures to recognize the biblical phenomenon wherein the biblical writers employed masculine pronouns in reference to feminine antecedent nouns when those feminine nouns were synonyms for the Words of God (cf. Ps. 119). Since the words of Jehovah are an extension of this strong patriarchal

---

[262]The exaltation of the wicked parallels the vanishing of the godly in verse one.

God, the OT writers occasionally seemed to use masculine pronouns for the following synonyms. The Hebrew words Law (*torah* תּוֹרָה), Testimony (*`eduth* עֵדוּת), Commandment (*mitzwah* מִצְוָה), Statute (*chuqqah* חֻקָּה), and Word (*`imrah* אִמְרָה) are feminine in gender. The normal Hebrew grammatical pattern is that concordance occurs between the gender and number of the pronoun with its respective antecedent noun. For instance, a masculine singular (m.s.) noun would take a masculine singular pronoun, and a masculine plural (m.p.) noun would take a masculine plural pronoun. However, the biblical writers deviated from this 'grammatical norm' for theological purposes, emphasizing specific truths. The inspired Scripture is the only authority for the biblical languages (Hebrew, Aramaic, and Greek), including their respective vocabulary and grammar. There are examples in all three divisions of the *Tanak* illustrating this Scriptural Hebrew phenomenon of gender discordance for theological purposes.

The following are examples of the phenomenon:

Law (*torah*)

1. *"That thou mayest observe to do according to all the **law** (torah—f.s.)…turn not from **it** (mimmennu—*מִמֶּנּוּ* m.s.),"* (Josh. 1:7).

2. *"For he established a **testimony** (`eduth--f.s.) in Jacob, and appointed a **law** (torah—f.s.) in Israel, which he commanded our fathers, that they should make **them** (lehodiy`am—*לְהוֹדִיעָם* m.p. suffix) known to their children"*

(Ps. 78:5).

Testimony (`eduth)

1. Ps. 78:5 (see above)
2. *"Thy **testimonies** (`edoth—f.p.) have I taken as an heritage for ever: for **they** (hemmah—הֵמָּה m.p.) are the rejoicing of my heart"* (Ps. 119:111).
3. *"Thy **testimonies** (`edoth—f.p.) are wonderful: therefore doth my soul keep **them** (netzaratham—נְצָרָתַם m.p. suffix)"* (Ps. 119:129).
4. *"Concerning thy **testimonies** (`edoth), I have known of old that thou hast founded **them** (yesadtam—יְסַדְתָּם m.p. suffix) for ever"* (Ps. 119:152).
5. *"My soul hath kept thy **testimonies** (`edoth—f.p.), and I love **them** (wa'ohavem—וָאֹהֲבֵם m.p. suffix) exceedingly"* (Ps. 119:167).

Commandment (*mitzwah*)

1. *"Therefore shall ye keep my **commandments** (mitzwoth—f.p.), and do **them** ('otham—אֹתָם m.p.): I am the LORD"* (Lev. 22:31).
2. *"If ye walk in my **statutes** (chuqqoth—f.p.), and keep my **commandments** (mitzwoth—f.p.), and do **them** ('otham—אֹתָם m.p.)"* (Lev. 26:3).
3. *"And remember all the **commandments** (mitzwoth—f.p.) of the LORD, and do **them** ('otham—אֹתָם m.p.)"* (Num.

15:39).

4. *"If thou wilt walk in my **statutes** (chuqqoth—f.p.), and execute my judgments (mishpat—m.p.), and keep all my* **commandments** *(mitzwoth—f.p.) to walk in* **them** *(bahem—*בָּהֶם *m.p. suffix),"* (I Ki. 6:12).

Statute (*chuqqah*)

1. *"And you shall keep my **statutes** (chuqqoth—f.p.), and do* **them** *('otham—*אֹתָם *m.p.)"* (Lev. 20:8).

2. Lev. 26:3 (see above).

3. I Ki. 6:12 (see above).

4. *"For they have refused my judgments (mishpat—m.p.) and my **statutes** (chuqqoth—f.p.), they have not walked in* **them** *(bahem—*בָּהֶם *m.p. suffix)"* (Ezk. 5:6).

5. *"And hath kept all my **statutes** (chuqqoth—f.p.), and hath done* **them** *('otham—*אֹתָם *m.p.)"* (Ezk. 18:19).

6. *"They shall also walk in my judgments (mishpat—m.p.); and observe my **statutes** (chuqqoth—f.p.), and do* **them** *('otham—*אֹתָם *m.p.)"* (Ezk. 37:24).

Word (*'imrah*)

1. *"The **words** ('imroth—f.p.) of the LORD are pure **words** ('amaroth—f.p.) as silver tried in a furnace of earth, purified seven times. Thou shalt keep* **them** *(tishmerem—*תִּשְׁמְרֵם *m.p. suffix), O LORD, thou shalt preserve* **them** *(titztzerennu—*תִּצְּרֶנּוּ *m.p. suffix) from this generation for*

ever" (Ps. 12:6-7).

The Exegesis

The psalmist recognized the tangible help that God gives for the believer in the midst of the threats and claims of the wicked is His "Words" (*'imroth* אִמְרוֹת). He likened the pure "Words" (*'amaroth* אֲמָרוֹת]) of the Lord unto *"silver"* (*ceseph* כֶּסֶף). The verbs and pronominal suffixes of verse seven are critical. The LORD is addressed as the subject of the verbs *"thou shall keep them"* (*tishmerem* תִּשְׁמְרֵם) and *"thou shall preserve them"* (*titztzerennu* תִּצְּרֶנּוּ). The object of the first verb *"thou shall keep them"* must be its closest antecedent, which is *"words."* Although *"words"* is feminine plural and the suffix on the verb is masculine plural, this gender discordance is not unusual in other psalms dealing with God's Words (see above). For instance, in the great psalm on the Words of God, Ps. 119, [263] the psalmist deliberately masculinized the verbal extension of the patriarchal God of Scripture. As this phenomenon exists throughout the *Tanak*, the interpreter has been prepared for gender discordance in this psalm. Furthermore, the examples set forth in Ps. 119 preclude the exegete from moving prior to the closest antecedent for the sake of gender concordance. It would be ridiculous to seek gender concordance where this

---

[263] This is the *locus classicus* Psalm detailing the full panoply of the attributives for the complete and perfect Word of God.

phenomenon occurs in Ps. 119:111, for then the gender concordance would teach that the psalmist rejoiced in his heart for the masculine plural *"wicked"* (v. 110). Again in v. 129, applying the exclusive 'rule' of gender concordance, the psalmist promised to keep the Lord's masculine plural *"precepts"* (v. 128)—a synonym for *"testimonies"* which is the closest antecedent anyway. Observing v. 152, the psalmist recognized that the Lord had *"founded"* what *"forever"*—the feminine plural *"testimonies"* or masculine plural participle *"they that follow after mischief"*? Finally, what did the psalmist love *"exceedingly"* (v. 167)? Was it the feminine plural *"testimonies"* or the masculine plural participle *"they which love"* (v. 165)?

Throughout the Hebrew OT, pronouns usually correspond to their antecedent nouns in proximity and with gender/number concordance. However, a phenomenon exists, which fresh Hebrew exegesis observes,[264] that feminine synonyms for the Words of God are addressed by masculine pronouns for the apparent purpose of masculinzing the patriarchal Jehovah God.

The second verb *"thou shalt preserve them"* has the masculine singular pronominal suffix (*titztzerennu* תִּצְּרֶנּוּ) which refers to the individual Words. Since Hebrew does not have the neuter pronoun "it," the pronoun "him" (v. 7) refers

---

[264]It is a tragic day in so-called fundamental "scholarship" when capable Hebrew exegetes defer to the interpretations of four hundred years of conservative interpretation rather that applying prayer and true biblical study to texts such as Ps. 12:6-7.

to the individual item of *"them"* (v. 6).[265] The KJV has the marginal note "Heb. him: i.e., everyone of them," which of course would then refer to every individual word. The first verb refers to all the *"Words"* that the Lord preserved, and the second to the very individual *"Words"* He preserved (cf. Lk. 4:4). The Lord promised to preserve every one and all of His *"Words"* for every generation, because every generation will be judged by the canonical *"Words"* (i.e., OT and NT) of the Lord Jesus Christ. The Lord stated this very truth, *"He that rejecteth me, and receiveth not my words, hath one that judgeth him: the word that I have spoken, the same shall judge him in the last day"* (Jn. 12:48).

Conclusion

The structure, context and exegesis, both preparatory and immediate, of the Masoretic Hebrew text of Psalm 12 all argue forcefully and irrefragably for the promise of everlasting preservation of the perfect *"Words"* of the LORD. This is one of several clear passages in which the Lord promised to preserve His canonical *"Words"* for every generation. Man's pervasive words are lies and are temporal; God's ever-present *"Words"* are Truth and are everlasting. This is the tangible help that the righteous man has in every generation—the perfectly preserved *"Words"* of the LORD.

---

[265]That is, the masculine pronoun refers to every individual word, and NOT to every individual man (v. 5).

APPENDIX H

Quadricentennial of the KJV (1611-2011)[266]

Introduction

Until the publication of the NASV (1971) and the NIV (1973), most conservative (fundamental) Christians used the KJV, believing that it was the authoritative Scripture. Once the modern versions were published, several responses occurred within "fundamentalism." The faculty of BJU began to promote the NASV, and Peter Ruckman responded to BJU with his developed heresies of "inspired English words" and "advanced revelation" in the KJV. The battle developed over the doctrine of "inspiration" and how it related to the KJV. In another camp, Donald Waite began to defend manuscript evidence and to develop the doctrine of preservation. Most attacks made against the KJV were against Ruckman's unbiblical views, about which critics lumped together all defenders of the KJV. There was not much discussion concerning the doctrine of preservation until the publication of the book edited by Kent Brandenburg entitled *Thou Shalt Keep Them: A Biblical Theology of the Perfect Preservation of Scripture* (El Sobrante, CA: Pillar & Ground Publishing, 2003), 315 pp. Proponents of modern versions and the underlying Critical Greek Text (United Bible

---

[266] Dr. Thomas M. Strouse read this paper at the Crowne Plaza, Cromwell, CT on April 14, 2011 for the Bible Baptist Theological Seminary Spring Lecture Series.

Society Greek New Testament)[267] have consistently peppered the KJV advocates with extreme questioning (ministry of questioning [I Tim. 1:4]), while never presenting an overview of their alternative position. The following are some of the questions with brief answers:

1. **Are the *KJV* words inspired?** Both inspiration and preservation deal with the biblical language words of Hebrew, Aramaic, and Greek. God preserved the originally inspired words for all subsequent generations and made them available for accurate translations, such as the KJV. Inspiration and preservation extend to the original language words only.

2. **Where was the word of God before 1611?** It was in the received "Traditional" Old and New Testament texts behind the translations of the Waldensians (pre-Reformers), of Luther's German (1522), of Tyndale's NT (1525), Matthew's Bible (1537), of the Great Bible (1539), and of the Geneva Bible (1560).

3. **Which *Textus Receptus* is inspired?** All of the "*Textus Receptus*" editions (Erasmus, Stephens, Elzevir brothers, Beza, etc.), were based on the Traditional Text or Received Bible Movement, with minor differences primarily based on spelling or word order. By faith we accept as preserved and inspired the text behind the 1611 KJV, which ultimately is the Greek Text compilation by Scrivener (1894).

4. **How can the KJV be called "the word of God" if it is not perfectly flawless?** The Bible gives guidelines for accurate translations (e.g., Neh. 8:8) coming from the

---

[267]Kurt Aland, *The Greek New Testament* (NY: United Bible Societies, 1975).

preserved texts which the Lord expects church members to employ in making translations (Mt. 28:19-20). Accurate, faithful, and true translations in any language before or after 1611, coming from the Received Bible Movement, may be called "the words of God" in that respective language.

5. **If local churches are the pillar and ground of the truth, why weren't they involved in the early translations (i.e., 1611)?** The Lord's NT assemblies are indeed the pillar and ground of the truth and have indeed had very strong impact on both the canon and the words of Scripture. The Roman Catholic Church, the Greek Orthodox Church, and Protestantism have popularized and perpetuated the results of the NT process of the preservation of inspired OT and NT texts originally given to Christ's churches.

I. The Critical Text Alternative

The following are a composite of the propositions posited by proponents of the Critical Text of both the OT and NT and its subsequent modern versions including the ERV (1887), the ASV (1901), the RSV (1952), the NAS (1971), the NIV (1973), and the ESV (2001), as the alternative to the Received Text and KJV:

1. That God **did not promise** to preserve His words (but just his concepts [hence "word preservation"]. ***Contra*** *"The words of the LORD are pure words: as silver tried in a furnace of earth, purified seven times. Thou **shalt keep them**, O LORD, thou **shalt preserve them** from this generation for ever."* (Ps. 12:6-7).

2. That God **in fact did not preserve** His inspired

words. ***Contra*** *"But he answered and said, **It is written**, Man shall not live by bread alone, but by every word that proceedeth out of the mouth of God"* (Mt. 4:4).

3. That man's responsibility is not to receive by faith the Lord's preserved words, since they are in fact "not preserved," but **"to restore or reconstruct"** the non-preserved words of God to a close approximation of the originals. How one would know when and where the non-preserved words are finally "restored" is not known nor should be asked. ***Contra*** *"He that **rejecteth** me, and **receiveth not my words**, hath one that judgeth him: the word that I have spoken, the same shall judge him in the last day"* (Jn. 12:48).

4. That "Christian" scholars are to do this restoration or reconstruction process by using **the principles of secular Textual Criticism**, which include using the "oldest and best manuscripts" and the "hardest" readings, which must be closer to the originals and therefore more pristine, since early, pious scribes always improved the manuscripts by changes and/or additions. ***Contra*** *"For this cause also thank we God without ceasing, because, when ye received the word of God which ye heard of us, **ye received it not as the word of men**, but as it is in truth, the word of God, which effectually worketh also in you that believe"* (I Thes. 2:13).

5. That the **Holy Spirit is not involved** in revealing the words of Scripture, but instead the practice of Textual Criticism is the means that the best of Christian scholarship may employ to determine the right readings in manuscript evidence. ***Contra*** *"But the anointing which ye have received of him abideth in you, and ye need not that any man teach you:*

but as ***the same anointing teacheth you of all things***, *and is truth, and is no lie, and even as it hath taught you, ye shall abide in him"* (I Jn. 2:27).

6. That Christian scholars **may trust the textual research and interpretation of theological infidels and liberals** since they are unbiased critical scholars. ***Contra*** *"But unto **the wicked** God saith, **What hast thou to do to declare my statutes**, or that thou shouldest take my covenant in thy mouth?   Seeing thou hatest instruction, and castest my words behind thee"* (Ps. 50:16-17).

7. That NT church members **should not expect to hear the voice of the Lord** regarding His words since He works exclusively through Textual Critics and secular Textual Criticism. ***Contra "My sheep hear my voice***, *and I know them, and they follow me"* (Jn. 10:29).

8. That this **process of restoration will continue** as long as archaeologists continue to discover ancient manuscripts for Textual Critical scholars to continue to apply their secular principles. ***Contra*** *"For I testify unto every man that heareth the words of the prophecy of this book, **If any man shall add** unto these things, God shall add unto him the plagues that are written in this book: **And if any man shall take away** from the words of the book of this prophecy, God shall take away his part out of the book of life, and out of the holy city, and from the things which are written in this book"* (Rev. 22:18-19).

9. That all manuscripts are ***"good"*** and therefore must be considered in the manuscript pool, even though there are many doctrines affected in their voluminous differences. ***Contra*** *"Now the serpent was more subtil than any beast of*

*the field which the LORD God had made. And he said unto the woman, **Yea, hath God said**, Ye shall not eat of every tree of the garden?"* (Gen. 3:1).

10. That these manuscripts are *"good"* because there **was no known conspiracy** to change the text of Scripture. ***Contra** "And account that the longsuffering of our Lord is salvation; even as our beloved brother Paul also according to the wisdom given unto him hath written unto you; As also in all his epistles, speaking in them of these things; in which are some things hard to be understood, which **they that are unlearned and unstable wrest**, as they do also the other scriptures, unto their own destruction"* (II Pet. 3:15-16).

11. That para-church organizations and pseudo-church groups **have the exclusive privilege** to be the primary agencies involved in determining textual readings and changes. ***Contra** "But if I tarry long, that thou mayest know how thou oughtest to behave thyself in the house of God, which is the church of the living God, **the pillar and ground of the truth**"* (I Tim. 3:15)

12. That the Lord's churches and pastors **have no little or no stewardship responsibility** in bibliology, including receiving, recognizing, preserving and defending of the Scriptures, which are not preserved anyway. All responsibility and authority is left to the Textual Critics. ***Contra** "He that hath an ear, **let him hear what the Spirit saith unto the churches**"* (Rev. 2:6).

13. That Christians should expect to have the **underlying Greek and Hebrew texts in an unstable and evolving form** which will bring uncertainty and questioning to believers through the corresponding translations; but this is

normative. ***Contra*** *"Have not I written to thee excellent things in counsels and knowledge, That I might make thee **know the certainty of the words of truth**; that thou mightest answer the words of truth to them that send unto thee?"* (Ps. 22:20-21).

It should be apparent that the Critical Text Alternative to the TR is neither predicted in Scripture as a viable option nor based on any biblical principles. Therefore, it must be rejected as humanistic and diabolical, the subtle product of *"the doctrines of devils"* (I Tim. 4:1). It is a Gnostic-laced text fabricated and perpetuated by Bible critics and favored by cultists and theological liberalism. Its fruit is doubt and carnality within professing Christianity.

II. The *Received Bible Movement*

The *Received Bible Movement* looks to the Bible for its prediction and to history for its fulfillment. The following are biblical principles which find their fulfillment in the Received Texts of the OT and NT, and in translations built upon these Received Texts (Hebrew Masoretic and Greek Received Texts), such as the OT and NT of the 1611 KJV:

1. God's Words are preserved in Heaven.

a. *"For ever, O LORD, thy word is settled **in heaven**"* (Ps. 119:89).

b *"But **I will shew** thee that which is noted in **the scripture of truth**: and there is none that holdeth with me in these things, but Michael your prince"* (Dan. 10:21, 11:2 ff.).

c. *"The words of Amos, who was among the herdmen of Tekoa, which **he saw**…"* (Amos 1:1).

d. *"The word of the LORD that came to Micah the Morasthite in the days of Jotham, Ahaz, and Hezekiah, kings of Judah, which **he saw**…"* (Mic. 1:1).

e. *"The Revelation of Jesus Christ, which **God gave unto him**, to shew unto his servants things which must shortly come to pass; and he sent and signified it by his angel unto his servant John"* (Rev. 1:1).

2. God's Words were inspired perfectly in the *autographa.*

a. *"**All scripture is given by inspiration of God**, and is profitable for doctrine, for reproof, for correction, for instruction in righteousness"* (II Tim. 3:16-18).

b. *"For the prophecy came not in old time by the will of man: but **holy men of God spake** as they were moved by the Holy Ghost"* (II Pet. 1:21).

3. The Lord promised to preserve these inspired Words for each subsequent generation.

a. *"Thy word is true from the beginning: and every one of thy righteous judgments **endureth for ever**"* (Ps. 119:160).

b. *"Heaven and earth shall pass away, but **my words shall not pass away**"* (Mt. 24:35).

4. He used the Jews to preserve the OT Scriptures and the NT candlesticks to preserve the OT and NT Scriptures

a. *"Much every way: chiefly, because that unto them [Jews] were committed the oracles of God"* (Rom. 3:2)

b. *"Go ye therefore, and teach all nations, baptizing them in the name of the Father, and of the Son, and of the Holy Ghost: Teaching them to observe all things whatsoever I have commanded you: and, lo, I am with you alway, even unto the end of the world. Amen"* (Mt. 28:19-20).

5. These preserved inspired words were made available for each generation.

a. *"For this commandment which I command thee this day, it is not hidden from thee, neither is it far off...But the word is very nigh unto thee, in thy mouth, and in thy heart, that thou mayest do it"* (Dt. 30:11, 14).

b. *"And Jesus answered him, saying, It is written, That man shall not live by bread alone, but by every word of God"* (Lk. 4:4).

5. His NT churches have recognized, received and preserved the Lord's Words while rejecting wrested Words and forged canons offered by Satan.

a. *"For this cause also thank we God without ceasing, because, when ye received the word of God which ye heard of us, ye received it not as the word of men, but as it is in truth, the word of God, which effectually worketh also in you that believe"* (I Thess. 2:13).

b. *"As also in all his epistles, speaking in them of these things; in which are some things hard to be understood, which they that are unlearned and unstable wrest, as they do also the other scriptures, unto their own destruction"* (II Pet. 3:16).

c. *"That ye be not soon shaken in mind, or be troubled, neither by spirit, nor by word, nor by letter as from us, as that the day of Christ is at hand"* (II Thess. 2:2).

d. *"Now the serpent was more subtil than any beast of the field which the LORD God had made. And he said unto the woman, Yea, hath God said, Ye shall not eat of every tree of the garden?"* (Gen. 3:1).

6. These same churches were the basis for the *Received Bible Movement* begun by the Lord Jesus Christ, Who received canonical words from the Father and in turn gave them to His apostles who in turn received and inscripturated His words.

a. *"For I have given unto them the words which thou gavest me; and they **have received** them, and have known surely that I came out from thee, and they have believed that thou didst send me"* (Jn. 17:8).

b. *"Then they that **gladly received his word** were baptized: and the same day there were added unto them about three thousand souls"* (Acts 2:41),

c. *"Now when the apostles which were at Jerusalem heard that Samaria **had received the word of God**, they sent unto them Peter and John"* (Acts 8:14).

d. *"And the apostles and brethren that were in Judaea heard that the Gentiles had also **received the word of God**"* (Acts 11:1).

e. *"These were more noble than those in Thessalonica, in that they **received the word** with all readiness of mind, and searched the scriptures daily, whether those things were so"* (Acts 17:11).

f. *"For this cause also thank we God without ceasing, because, when ye **received the word of God** which ye heard of us, ye received it not as the word of men, but as it is in truth, the word of God, which effectually worketh also in you that believe"* (I Thes. 2:13).

6. The Lord has given His explicit words of revelation to man in order that man may be able to demonstrate his stewardship with all of God's words at his respective judgment.

a. *"He that rejecteth me, and receiveth not my words, hath one that judgeth him: the word that I have spoken, the same shall judge him in the last day"* (Jn. 12:48)

b. *"And I saw the dead, small and great, stand before God; and the books were opened: and another book was opened, which is the book of life: and the dead were judged out of those things which were written in the books, according to their works"* (Rev. 20:12).

7. The Lord Jesus Christ expects man to receive by faith His revelation and produce accurate translations based on the Received Bible movement which originated with Him.

a. *"Neither pray I for these alone, but for them also which shall believe on me through their word"* (Jn. 17:20).

b. *"Now to him that is of power to stablish you according to my gospel, and the preaching of Jesus Christ, according to the revelation of the mystery, which was kept secret since the world began, But now is made manifest, and by the scriptures of the prophets, according to the commandment of the everlasting God, made known to all nations for the obedience of faith"* (Rom. 16:25-26).

8. This *Received Bible Movement* was recognized and so named in 1633 (*textum...nunc ab omnibus receptum*)—the *Received Text* (TR) movement.

9. The Lord's NT immersionist assemblies have employed the TR and *KJV* texts in their Baptist confessions from the 17th to 21st centuries.

Conclusion

Does the Bible predict that God will not preserve His words and that man must restore them? Of course not! The need for Textual Criticism and its product, the Critical Text, is non-existent. Discerning Bible believers may rejoice that the Lord has not only promised to preserve His words but in fact did preserve them for accurate translations in the languages of the world. Furthermore, He revealed the divinely authorized institution to carry of the ministry of Scripture preservation—the NT immersionist assembly. The Lord Jesus Christ has preserved His words through His preserved churches to the glory of God!   One evident fruit of this truth is the Quadricentennial anniversary of the KJV (1611-2011).

BOOK REVIEWS

Book Review #1

James B. Williams, ed. *From the Mind of God to the Mind of Man* **(Greenville, SC: Ambassador-Emerald International, 1999), 231 pp.**

Introduction

This recent volume entitled *From the Mind of God to the Mind of Man* (Greenville, SC: Ambassador-Emerald International, 1999, 231 pp.)[268] is the product of James B. Williams and his eleven authors. These writers and their book appear to represent Bob Jones University and the Fundamental Baptist Fellowship. This inference is established by the connection of the authors to BJU and the endorsements by the leadership of the FBF. Williams states that his purpose is "to provide accurate, understandable information that will serve as a guide for laymen when selecting a translation" (p. 10). Although this may be a commendable goal and many may therefore read the book, it should be received with extreme caution for two reasons: first, it falls short of its stated goal; and second, it points toward a dangerous trend.

From the Mind of God to the Mind of Man should be received with extreme caution in the first place because the

---

[268]This article originally appeared in *Sound Words from New England* Volume 1, Issue 2, November - December 2000.

book falls short of the editor's stated task. It does so due to the following eight factors.

To begin with, it is of questionable literary quality. There are glaring spelling, grammatical, and format gaffes. For instance, Westcott is regularly misspelled (e.g., pp. 172-178). Typos and misquotes (e.g., p. 3) and noun-verb disagreement (e.g., p. 170, footnote 2) appear, and font sizes vary (e.g., pp. 2-3). It appears that the rush to publish jeopardized the literary quality of the book. While some may excuse literary errors as inconsequential, they do reflect on the arguments raised by the writers. Careless literary preparation may suggest careless scholarship as well. More significant, though, are the seven additional factors that cause the book to fail in the editor's purpose.

For instance, a substantial reason for the book's failure is its curious approval of apostasy. The cover of the book pictures a copy of the Revised Standard Version. Since its publication in 1952, this version has been identified with apostate liberalism (p. 198) through the National Council of Churches because of its anti-supernatural renderings of Isaiah 7:14 and II Timothy 3:16. Why would those purporting to advance fundamentalism use the liberal's version of the Bible on their cover? Furthermore, Williams accurately outlines the theological battles fundamentalists have had with liberals, neo-evangelicals and charismatics, yet the editor and authors, *in toto,* commend the textual works of liberals, neo-evangelicals and charismatics. They give absolutely no warning or condemnation about the men or their heresies (cf. footnote 5, p. 71). Is the uniting of fundamentalists with liberals in the text/translation issue a new way to glorify the

Lord Jesus Christ?

A third factor for the book's failure is its misstatement of fact. Several authors declare that the variants between the modern texts/translations and the *Textus Receptus (TR)* and the Authorized Version are so small ("less than one page of my entire Testament" p. 86) that *no concern* should be taken (pp. 97, 183). The fact of the matter is that the Critical Text of Westcott-Hort differs from the TR, mostly by deletions, in 9,970 words out of 140,521, giving a total of 7% difference. In the 480-page edition of the Trinitarian Bible Society *Textus Receptus* this would amount to almost 34 pages, the equivalent of the final two books of the New Testament, Jude and Revelation. This certainly does not sound like "no cause for concern."

Furthermore, no fundamentalist would deny that the 93% common text is the very inspired and preserved wording of the *autographa*. What one does with the remaining 7% is the crux of the issue. The substantial reason for the book's failure is its curious approval of apostasy. Does one *receive* the preserved words of God as found in the Received Bible, or does one attempt to *restore/ reconstruct* what God allegedly has not preserved?

Another misstatement of fact is that Textual Criticism is a pure, objective, and untainted discipline. Shaylor states, "textual criticism, not to be confused with other types of criticism, is not a negative attitude toward the inspiration of the Bible. It is in reality an effort to assure us that we have the inspired Word of God" (p. 24, cf. p. 61). This statement is insensitive to historical fact and oblivious to Biblical teaching. Historically, Biblical Criticism as a movement

(17-19th Century) and all its spawned criticisms (higher, lower [textual], form, literary, historical, etc.) are permeated with anti-supernatural, evolutionary rationalism. The tenets of Textual Criticism, such as the oldest is best and the shorter is probable, bespeak the evolutionary principle of simple to complex. The Received Text is not the product of evolution and conflation, whereas the Critical Text not only is the product of rationalism but also manifests textual "deflation." Man cannot restore what God allegedly has not chosen to preserve. Biblically, the Lord Jesus Christ promised to preserve all of His Words *(logoi,* Mt. 24:35*)* for every generation (Jn. 12:48). Assurance in God's having inspired and preserved His Words does not come through Textual Criticism but through "faith [which] cometh by hearing, and hearing by the word of God" (Rom. 10:17). This is the historical faith of those of whom Jesus declared, "My sheep hear my voice" (Jn. 10:27).

A fourth factor for the book's failure is the extreme defense of fallible mortals such as Westcott and Hort. Williams assures the readers that "these men are now with the Lord" (p. 4). This is a gratuitous assumption that cannot possibly be proved and shows the "hero-worship" mentality of the Critical Text proponents (pp. 6, 212). The proponents of the Received Text position do not, on their part, magnify the men involved. The originator of the Received Text is not Erasmus, Stephens, Beza, Burgon, Wilkinson, Hills, or Fuller, but the Lord Jesus Christ Himself. He it was Who promised to preserve all of His words perfectly and requires believers to receive them (Jn. 17:8, 20). He is the sovereign One alone worthy of exaltation, Who both promised verbal plenary preservation and used fallible men to do achieve it.

A fifth factor causing the failure of *From the Mind of God to the Mind of Man* to achieve its purposes is the unbiblical nature of the major premise of the Westcott-Hort position. The very title of the book suggests that God gave His concepts to man so man could translate His concepts into translations. Fundamentalists have rejected the liberal Conceptual Inspiration View of Scripture and presently defend Verbal Plenary Inspiration. It is very difficult to understand why fundamentalists resist the Biblical and theological teaching of the Verbal Plenary Preservation View and yet default to the dangerous Conceptual Preservation View. Westcott and Hort wanted to restore the 4th Century text, based on Catholic (B) and Egyptian (papyri) MSS, arguing that there was no textual tampering and utilizing inapplicable Genealogies, assumed Text-types, and the supposed Lucianic Rescension to dispose of the *Textus Receptus*. The goal of modern Textual Criticism is to restore or reconstruct the Biblical text (p. 106) that God apparently chose not to preserve. The liberals' humanistic approach seems obvious, but why do some fundamentalists fail to see that the Lord does not need man's help? It is strange indeed for fundamentalists to countenance liberal views, either deliberately or by default.

A sixth factor for failure is the book's acrimonious spirit not towards liberals, modernists, neo-evangelicals, or charismatics, but towards other fundamentalists. The very attitude Pickering denounces in his Preface runs rampant throughout the essays. He bemoans that some KJV proponents have practiced "vilification of character, personal attacks, and a generally unchristian spirit." He assures the reader that "the authors of this work have presented their information objectively and without attacks on the character of their opponents" (p. ix). But such is not the case. The author who betrays the most glaring example of an acrimonious spirit is Williams the editor. He deliberately lumps all that use the KJV into one of the five categories of King James Version Onlyism concocted by James White (who is no expert in the field of bibliology). Williams labels all of these who are lumped together (where do fundamentalists of his stripe fit in?) as extreme (pp. 2-3). Without any evident distinction, Williams attacks representatives from the various categories of the whole spectrum as "misguided" "mis-informers," whose heresies are a "cancerous sore" (p. 7). The book thus gives evidence of a double standard.

Hypocrisy is the seventh factor for the book's failure. Both Minnick and Gephart argue that the text/translation issue may be a "rabbit trail." They argue that no one should be beating their drums for or against the KJV but rather be preaching Christ. Gephart questions the worth of the issue, asking, "can we afford to spend so much time on this issue?" (p. 218; cf. 97-98). Is not their hypocrisy apparent that they can spend time and money writing this 231-page book, using twelve authors and the input of eight academicians, and yet the defenders of the KJV have no right to do the same? They evidently feel that the time spent to produce their book is well spent, but time spent by their opponents is ill spent. Such an attitude is partisan hypocrisy. It shows a Catholic-like lordliness of silencing the opposition and has no place among fundamental Baptists.

The eighth and final factor for the book's failure is the unscriptural call for unity at the expense of doctrine (pp. xii, 2, 98). Since verbal plenary preservation is a teaching of Scripture (Psm. 12:6,7; 119:111, 160; Lk. 21:33, *et al),* it is a doctrine. Those who hold to differing doctrinal views concerning preservation or any other doctrine cannot and should not unite. Paul taught the Thessalonians to separate from those who held to a different eschatological doctrine and its resultant practice (II Thess. 3:6, 14). Should not fundamentalists (and Bible believers) follow this Pauline principle with regard to all biblical doctrines? Theological compromise is far worse than the lack of unity.

This dangerous call to compromise for the sake of unity is the second reason that *From the Mind of God to the Mind of Man* should be received with extreme caution. Historically, Bible-believing people have not hesitated to part from those taking a differing view of biblical doctrine. Now, however, the reader is being told that this issue, doctrinally significant though it may be, is nothing to separate over. Unity is more important. This is certainly an alarming trend among those who would call themselves fundamentalists.

In contrast to the opinion of the book's contributors, God has revealed both His intention to preserve perfectly all of His words for every generation and His means of doing so through the local churches (Mt. 4:4; 5:17 and Mt. 28:20; I Tim. 3:15, respectively). Liberals hold to Dynamic Inspiration. This leads to Dynamic Preservation, as manifested in the Critical Text, translated with Dynamic Equivalence to produce the Modern Versions. Historic fundamentalists hold to Verbal Plenary Inspiration which demands Verbal Plenary Preservation, manifested in the *Textus Receptus,* and translated with Formal Equivalence to produce the KJV. Strangely and dangerously, neo-fundamentalists hold mixed views regarding Verbal Plenary Inspiration, Dynamic Preservation, the Critical Text, Dynamic Equivalence, and Modern Versions. This mixed and fluid position moves in only one direction: away from fundamentalism and into liberalism. For one to take the initial step into this moving stream, either deliberately or by default, may lead to drowning in the ocean of apostasy.

Conclusion

The Lord Jesus Christ has required believers of all ages to receive His preserved words (Jn. 17:8, 20; Acts 2:41; 8:14; 11:1; 17:11; I Thess. 1:6; 2:13). Since man cannot restore what God allegedly has not preserved, it is folly for fundamentalists to embrace any of the modern translations. Fundamentalists must return to the centuries-old confidence of God's people in the Traditional Text. They must not be swept away with the relatively recent, rationalistic theories of Westcott, Hort, and others. Fundamentalists must realize that we have the Lord's preserved words in the received texts of the Bible (Masoretic text and *Textus Receptus).* May Christians believe that *the WORDS OF GOD have been given to the HEART OF MAN.*

Book Review #2

James B. Williams, ed. *God's Word in Our Hands: The Bible Preserved for Us* **(Greenville, SC: Ambassador-Emerald International, 2003), 430 pp.**

Introduction

Books, but especially Christian theological works, are commentaries on the authors' biblical knowledge about and belief in divine revelation. *God's Word in Our Hands: The Bible Preserved for Us* (Greenville, SC: Ambassador Emerald-International, 2003), 430 pp. edited by James B. Williams is no exception. Although the title of this sequel to *From the Mind of God to the Mind of Man* (*MOGMOM*) promises great assurance to the reader about Bible preservation, the book is a commentary on the writers, academicians, professors, etc., who ultimately deny the Scriptural teaching of the preservation of God's Words. The basic "message" of the book is that God has promised to preserve His message but not His Words, and therefore there is no single Bible in the English language (certainly not the KJV) that can make the exclusive claim of being the Word of God. But this should be no concern for fundamentalists, the book alleges, because Satan's attack upon the Bible (Gen. 3:1 ff.) is not in the texts, translations or through Textual Criticism. However, it would not be "fair" for this reviewer to critique the authors' "message" without looking at their "words."

God's Word in Our Hands (*GWOH*) is "*deja vu* all over again." The thesis, arguments, and historical evidence are basically the same as *MOGMOM*, with the additional pages being attributed to several *ad hoc* explanations of preservation passages. Since this reviewer publicly critiqued the *MOGMOM* book in *Sound Words from New England,* Vol. 1, Issue 2, Nov.-Dec., 2000, many of his criticisms may be leveled at this sequel. At the outset, however, it is refreshing that this sequel has on its cover an artist's rendering of a Hebrew text, albeit un-pointed, instead of the liberal *RSV* (blurred in the 3rd and 4th editions) that graced the four editions of the *MOGMOM* book. This new cover does not mean, however, that the authors warn about the apostasy of many of the architects of their textual theory. In fact, the editor Williams is quick to acknowledge that many non-Fundamentalists find the book profitable (p. vi), presumably because of this silence. He does make a disclaimer about any blanket endorsement of the textual researchers, but it is difficult to comprehend how unregenerate Bible critics can "benefit or advance" the discussion of truth (p. xii). After all, the Lord asked of the wicked through Asaph, *"What hast thou to do to declare my statutes...?seeing thou hatest instruction, and castest my words behind thee"* (Ps. 50:16-17). The book, with two editors, five additional committee members and contributors, four more contributors, and ten academicians representing ten Bible schools and seminaries (International Baptist College, Central Baptist Theological Seminary, Calvary Baptist Theological Seminary, Pillsbury Baptist Bible College, Northland Baptist Bible College, Faith Baptist Bible College and Theological Seminary, Detroit Baptist Theological Seminary, Maranatha Baptist Bible College, Temple Baptist Seminary, and Bob Jones University), divides into three parts including The Faith of Our Fathers, The Transmission of the Word of God, and The Effect of Preservation on the Faith, to show that God preserved His message but not His words.

In a pastiche of articles such as this, it is expected that different literary style and skill will be noticed. However, just as its predecessor (*MOGMOM*), the quality of proofreading in *GWOH* has allowed several spelling, grammatical, and format gaffes to escape notice. Mis-spellings occur throughout (Wrestling for Wresting, p. 96; *ipsissama* for *ipsissima*, p. 193; Diety for Deity, p. 264; Athenasias for Athanasias, p. 395; steam for stream, p. 423), split infinitives intersperse the text (pp. xii, 208, 342, 370), grammatical errors appear (lets for let's, p. 269) and format gaffes happen ("Dr." in front of Paul W. Downey in the chapter title and no other author has this designation although several writers have earned doctorates, p. 365).

GWOH is the outworking of a chain of events in American fundamentalism. Davey discusses "the fracturing of Fundamentalism over preservation" but fails to mention the culprit behind the fracturing (p. 193-194). The "bastion of fundamentalism" in Christian education, Bob Jones University, has employed Greek professors who have had an affinity for the Critical Text (CT) since the school's inception. This affinity turned into a love affair with the completed NASV in 1971, as BJU was one of the educational institutions to assist the Lockman Foundation's publication of this modern translation. By the middle 70's, BJU promoted the

NASV as an alternative to the KJV. Through the years, BJU and many Bible schools influenced by them used the KJV in chapel and the classroom while denigrating the underlying Greek TR text. In the middle 90's, Pensacola Christian College exposed this "dirty little secret" of BJU in a series of videos, charging them with bringing the leaven of Textual Criticism into fundamentalism. This charge has brought a groundswell of concern on the part of fundamental Baptists pastors and parents as to where to send their "preacher boys" for theological education. The BJU-originated publications *MOGMOM*, *GWOH*, and Schneider and Tagiapietra's *Bible Preservation and the Providence of God* (*BPPG*) are efforts aimed at these rightfully concerned fundamental Baptists to say there is no difference between the NASV and the KJV and there is no concern for alarm. In fact, Williams implies that the preservation of the Scriptures is a non-essential (p. xix) even though he has edited two books about this doctrine. Hutcheson declares "some today are sidetracked from the proper battlefield and have busied themselves fighting their brethren over a particular translation" (p. 28). The coalition of ten schools wants to write voluminously about preservation but expects the KJV Only group to be quiet and non-disagreeable. This hypocrisy suggests the "academic agenda" that is elaborated on later in this review.

Concerns for Fundamentalists

Neo-Orthodoxy Tendencies

Neo-orthodoxy developed out of liberalism after World War I as apostates began to redefine Biblically orthodox terms. One major area of redefining was with regard to the Bible. Neo-Orthodox theologians referred to the Word of God but did not identify it with the Scriptures. *GWOH* gives a new and un-Biblical definition to the expression "the Word of God," coming strikingly close to the claims of the old Neo-Orthodoxy. Neo-Orthodoxy speaks of the Word of God as something other than the written Bible. One of the academicians, Samuel Schnaiter, has labored under cloud of the charge of Neo-Orthodoxy since 1983 when Charles Woodbridge labeled him thus. Although "Word of God" may mean the spoken or preached message of God, it ultimately refers to the inscripturated canonical Words of God, which definition *GWOH* rejects. The thesis of the *GWOH* is that God has preserved the Word of God, or "the message," in the totality of manuscripts (pp. xxi-xxii). Harding bemoans that "serious departures from the preserved *message* in Scripture are occurring..." (p. 335). This suggests two Neo-Orthodox affirmations: God's Word is the message and the message (God's Word) is in, but not identical to, the Scripture. Furthermore, Downey asserts "God's Word transcends written documents, even the physical universe, and will be completely and ultimately fulfilled if not one copy remains. The power and effectiveness and duration of the Word of God, and man's responsibility to obey it, do not demand the presence or even the existence of any physical copy" (p. 376).   These surmisings are not Biblical since the Lord identifies the inspired Word of God with the inscripturated canonical Words of God, stating, *"He that rejecteth me, and receiveth not my words (remata), hath one that judgeth him: the word (logos) that I have spoken, the same shall judge him in the last day"* (Jn. 12:48; cf. Rev. 20:12).   The writers emphasize that not all of Christ's Words or God's Words are written down (p. 367).   That is true.   But that for which the mankind will be responsible are the preserved, written canonical Words of God (Mt. 24:35). Christ wrote some unknown Words in the sand (Jn. 8:6, 8), but man will not be held responsible for them at the judgment. Christ presumably said things in His teachings that were not written down (Jn. 21:25) and man won't be accountable for those words.   Believers will now be accountable for *"it is more blessed to give than to receive"* (Acts 20:35) only because Paul preached and Luke recorded this *"agrapha"* of the Lord.   Man will not be held responsible for God's spoken revelation other than the perfectly preserved and inscripturated canonical Scriptures.

Man-Centered Anthropology

A strange and unhealthy anthropology permeates this volume. Biblical anthropology, or what the Scriptures say about man, teaches that all men are fallible and can contribute nothing to the truth without the Bible and the help of the Holy Spirit. Anthropology that focuses on the exaltation of man at the expense of truth is non-Biblical. This man-centered anthropology manifests itself in four examples. First, Williams continues his "hero worship" of the Anglican Bible critics Westcott and Hort. In *MOGMOM* he asserted they were in heaven, and in *GWOH* he denigrates those who criticize them as misrepresenting or misinterpreting their commentaries (p. xv). Williams' lack of discernment concerning these English Romanists is disconcerting, and to such an extent, that Minnick apparently wants to distance himself from Westcott-Hort when he affirms, "the Westcott-Hort Testament is not the text of modern translations" (p. 273). Downey evinces this lack of spiritual discernment by arguing for the genuineness of the salvation of the Roman Catholic patristics Athanasias, Origen, and Augustine (p. 395). From reading the Gnostic ramblings of Origen and the Romish dogmas of Augustine, can anyone seriously consider them saved men? Although Athanasias defended the deity of Christ, he nevertheless was part of the Roman Catholic Church leadership and complicit in their sacral society cacadoxy.

A second manifestation of strange anthropology is the incessant barrage of acrimonious vitriol upon fundamentalists, and fundamentalists only, who want to speak out against other translations including the NASV. It would seem that regular warnings against the apostasy of Metzger and Aland, who have gone on record advocating the possibility of reducing the NT canon, and against the drift of the Neo-Evangelicalism of Wallace, Carson and Erickson, would permeate *GWOH*. Instead, the authors seem to have difficulty constraining themselves as they charge fundamentalists with being vitriolic (p. 391). Williams chides, "Although there were those who had strong convictions about the matter, they did not convey the mean spiritedness and use the vitriolic language so often present today in discussions of translations" (p. xvii). Downey directs this verbal attack against fundamentalist Waite stating: "His outrage toward those who do not accept his theory of perfect preservation seems a bit overdone" (p. 393). Other examples may be observed throughout (cf. pp. 2, 28, 110, 272, 365, *et al*).

The third manifestation of faulty anthropology is the repeated plea for "healing" for "this needless division over translations" (p. xviii). Doctrine divides Christians, and when it does, those with Scriptural authority need to rebuke those who make errant statements about doctrine and expect forthcoming repentance (II Tim. 2:24-28). Professed Christians with doctrinal deviations do not need to be healed, they need to be rebuked with expected repentance or else marked and avoided (Rom. 16:17). This faulty anthropology as expressed in *GWOH* does not reflect the Biblical teaching of the fallibility of the believer, and therefore offers the invalid antidote of "healing."

The most predominate manifestation of un-Biblical anthropology is the exaltation of man and man's words. Two early sections in the book promote what man has to say about preservation. Hutcheson utilizes 34 pages and 68 footnotes, in his chapter "The Heritage of American Orthodoxy," to give what earlier and later fundamentalists have taught about preservation. He cites men from James Brooks to John Rice to demonstrate that fundamentalists have not countenanced the TR and Bible preservation view. For the historical record, Hutcheson overlooks men for his historic fundamentalist chart of comparison such as W. Aberhart, B. F. Dearmore, and B. M. Cedarholm as strong defenders of the preserved text position (p. 29-30). Conley's chapter entitled "The Voice of the Preachers" continues to exalt man's words about the Words of God. His inclusion of baptismal regenerationalist Augustine as one of the "great preachers," exacerbates his faulty anthropology through this lack of orthodox discernment, even though he makes a disclaimer about Augustine's sermons "advocating prayers for the dead" (p. 72). When will the committee members of *GWOH* recognize that "trusted voices" of men are secondary and therefore inferior authorities concerning revelation? The catenae of names the authors have used indicates that Protestant fundamentalism was both ignorant of and imprecise about the Biblical doctrine of preservation of the Words of God.

Williams echoes the committee members' fallacious anthropology by assuring his readership that "The translators of some of the most popular translations are reputed to be good, godly, and scholarly believers who would not purposely corrupt the Bible" (p. xvi). Hutcheson claims that R. A. Torrey's "credentials as a soulwinner are unimpeachable" (p. 25). The authors of *GWOH* would have Christians believe that the un-Biblical doctrine of good, godly scholars and soulwinners can be trusted absolutely whenever they speak about the Bible. The student of the Bible should consider that a few years after the good, godly, scholarly and soul-winning Apostle Peter won thousands to Christ (Acts 2:14-41), Paul rebuked him for his hypocrisy concerning the truth (Gal.

2:11-14). Even the NT Apostles were fallible except in their inscripturated canonical sermons and writings. Man's restatement of Scripture must be judged with Scripture to determine its accuracy (I Cor. 14:29; cf. Dt. 13:1-5). No man, not even a fundamentalist (living or dead), is infallible in his expression of Biblical truth, and such expressions must be scrutinized by the Bible (cf. Gal. 1:8; I Thess. 5:21). Paul's warning to Timothy should be seriously implemented by every Biblical fundamentalist: *"Take heed unto thyself, and unto the doctrine; continue in them: for in doing this thou shalt both save thyself, and them that hear thee"* (I Tim. 4:16).

The Buried Bible View

Shaylor initially states that God has preserved His written Word "in the totality" of manuscripts (p. xxi). But the authors contradict their major thesis throughout *GWOH,* suggesting they do not believe that which they cannot and have not proved. Minnick assures the reader that the significant variations between the TR and the CT (in 25% of the NT) are only 1.19% (p. 271), whereas Downey concedes that there is a 7% deviation between the TR and the Westcott-Hort texts (p. 388). Again, Shaylor declares that "we can hold it [God's Word] in our hands" (p. 401), even though he quotes favorably Harding's belief that "we do not currently possess a Hebrew manuscript with that reading ["thirty"]" in I Sam. 13:1 (p. 414; cf. 361). Shaylor continues by stating "Perhaps in God's own time we will be allowed to discover that manuscript. Our confidence in the perfection of the *autographa* is not shaken by incomplete understating of how and where its wording is preserved" (p. 414). Shades of Neo-Orthodoxy; they hold to the "non-preserved preservation" view! The committee's affirmation of their position culminates in their declaration concerning Mt. 5:18: "Neither does this passage guarantee that all the words will be always available at all times" (p. 106). Preservation demands availability or the doctrine of preservation is meaningless. Downey asserts that the word "word" has been lost in the Hebrew text of Dt. 8:3 but recovered by and therefore preserved in the *LXX* translation (pp. 374-375). Finally, Shaylor concludes by stating "confusion arises when Christians assume that they can have the exact words of God in their language" (p. 406).

GWOH teaches the "Buried Bible" position. In effect, the committee and authors argue that we have the Word of God, but we do not have the Words of God because some Words are lost and need to be discovered through archaeological finds and restored through Textual Criticism. The Message is preserved but the Words of the Message are different (from 1.19% to 7% in the two competing texts) and missing but that does not affect the Message. The Bible is out there, but we are not sure where it is and when we will have all of it, but our responsibility is to dig it up through the sciences of archaeology and Text Criticism. The Christian may have great assurance that God has preserved His Buried Bible somewhere although it might not be available. This message is not spiritually appealing to Biblical Christians who believe the Lord Who has assured that His canonical Words will be available to every generation (Mt. 24:35; Jn. 12:48).

Ad Hoc Exegesis

God's Word in Our Hands: The Bible Preserved for Us purports to be a book about the Biblical doctrine of preservation as the subtitle suggests. At least two chapter titles and contents continue this promising theme: "What the Bible Really Says," and "What the Preservation Issue Has Taught Us." Yet, the authors are not interested in what the Bible says as much as what others say about the Bible, which in turn influences what the authors think the Bible says. The committee of *GWOH* admits that there is "implicit teaching regarding the preservation of the Word of God" (p. 83) while Davey rightly condemns Glenny for refusing to argue for "an explicit verse" which teaches preservation (p. 207). Since the authors of *GWOH* base their doctrine only on implicit teaching of the Bible, and implicit means something not clearly stated, it follows that they are arguing dogmatically for an unclear teaching in the Bible. This unclear teaching is perpetuated by the scores of scholars who quote one another. In fact, *GWOH* is about what past and present Bible critics have said about the Bible, and the authors admit that their real thesis is not the explicit teaching of the Bible about Bible preservation. In this 430 page volume, the committee states: "Obviously there are dozens of other passages cited by various advocates of the King James Only position that we have not addressed. Space would not permit a thorough exegesis of all of them. Such an exhaustive treatment would require an independent volume on the subject" (p. 117). They have space to cite hundreds of quotations from commentators, scholars, critics, preachers and historical fundamentalists, who support their Buried Bible position, but purposely very little space for meaningful Hebrew and Greek exegesis, and then that exegesis being *ad hoc*.

Only two sections in *GWOH* give extensive coverage of preservation passages (pp. 83-111 and 368-377). It appears that the authors scrambled to find commentators who were as imprecise and inaccurate as they in their exposition. The authors of *GWOH*, many who are capable of the exegesis of the Hebrew and Greek, give token explanations of significant passages. The chapter by the Editorial Committee entitled "What the Bible Really Says about Its Preservation" is extremely disappointing. First, 52 of the 63 endnotes in this chapter give the commentaries of others on passages such as Ps. 12:6-7; Ps. 119:89; Ps. 119:152; Isa. 40:8; I Pet. 1:23-25; and Mt. 5:18 (cf. pp. 111-117). The greatest problem with citing past and present scholars, including ex-member of the executive committee of the Dean Burgon Society Thomas Cassidy, is that they pass on what their predecessors taught *ad infinitum* so that no fresh exegesis is forthcoming. A case in point is Ps. 12:6-7. The committee, authors, and academicians are not aware that their token argument of the supposed gender discordance rule has been rejected by the fresh exegesis of Scripture itself. In trying to argue against the word "them" (masculine plural) having "words" (feminine plural) as the natural antecedent on the basis of gender discordance, the contributors have fallen into their own linguistic snare. It is common in Hebrew poetry for feminine nouns to take on masculine pronouns. The writer of Ps. 119, who deals with the Words of the Lord, accepted gender discordance as good Hebrew grammar with four outstanding examples in verses 111, 129, 152, and 167. Ps. 119:152 is one of the passages that *GWOH* rejects as teaching the preservation of the Lord's testimonies or "written words" forever (95). But according to the authors of *GWOH*, their Hebrew rule of good linguistics in Ps. 12:5-7, would not allow "them" (masculine plural) to refer to "testimonies" (feminine plural) in Ps. 119:152. Instead, the antecedent of "them" must go back to the nearest word that is masculine plural, which in this case would be those who *"follow after mischief"* (Ps. 119:150). This of course is ludicrous. The two linguistic obstacles *GWOH* has to overcome to make Ps. 12:6-7 refer to the preservation of the poor and needy are the proximity rule of nearest antecedent and the rule of accepted gender discordance. However, they have not and cannot overcome these linguistic obstacles which guard the truth, and so the exegetical interpretation of Ps. 12:6-7 stands that God has promised the perfect preservation of His Words for every generation from the time of their inscripturation forward.

The authors seek to explain away the doctrine of the preservation of the Words of God in the other aforementioned preservation passages. This hermeneutic practice is based on sophomoric exegesis girded up with straw men arguments and ad hoc explanations. In explaining Mt. 4:4, Downey calls a "theory" the orthodox expression: "God's justice demands complete availability of every word for which mankind is accountable" (p. 374), in spite of the teaching of Mt. 4:4 and Jn. 12:48. Never once does Downey refer to the perfect tense verb "it is written" Γέγραπται which demands that Moses' book of Deuteronomy, along with the rest of the Torah, had been and still was written in Christ's day. He bolsters his rejection of the Lord's bibliology with the straw man argument of denying that Christ was "promising the perpetuity of a manuscript" (p. 375). The advocates for the TR/KJV position defend the preservation of His Words, not manuscripts. He argues that the Hebrew word for "word" was lost but recovered in the LXX, undermining what the Lord said about the preservation of every consonant (jot) and vowel (tittle) of every Hebrew word of Scripture (Mt. 5:18). Although Davey understands the truth that the Bible must have the last say about itself by stating "all arguments about Scripture and which concern Scripture must—in some respect—rest on exegetical and theological data" (p. 208), *GWOH* for the most part ignores the application of this Biblical necessity.

Unproved Assumptions

The authors of *GWOH* are guilty of perpetuating several unproved assumptions as fact. These include the fallacious assumption that Christ and the Apostles used the *LXX* (p. 342, 360, 414), that Textual Criticism is a beneficial tool, and that different words in different Greek texts do not affect doctrine. The New Testament teaches explicitly that the Lord Jesus Christ used only the preserved Hebrew text, and that He and His apostles never had the Biblical, theological, or practical necessity to use the *LXX* for evangelizing the Gentiles. The lines of Biblical argument which are normally ignored include the Lord's usage of Γέγραπται for the Hebrew text (Mt. 4:4; Lk. 4:4), His reference to Hebrew Jots and Tittles (Mt. 5:18), and His reference to the three-fold division of the Hebrew *Tanak* (Torah, Prophets, and Writings) in several passages (Lk. 11:50-51; 24:27, 44). Alleged quotes by the Lord and the Apostles from the OT are usually not *verbatim*, and history cannot prove that there was a pre-Christian *LXX* nor disprove a post-Christian LXX. The Lord gave inspired Targums, or explanatory commentary, on the OT Scripture, producing inspired elaboration on OT texts (cf. Lk. 4:17-19). As far as the Gentile evangelism necessity, the Lord Jesus utilized the Hebrew OT for Jews (e.g., Mt. 5-7) and His authoritative Greek words for Gentiles (Mt. 15:21 ff.). Likewise, the Apostles used the Hebrew OT in evangelizing the Jews, and Greek NT words for the Gentiles (cf. Acts 13-21). On the day of Pentecost, the Lord used tongues to evangelize various people groups (Acts 2:1 ff.).

Gephart expresses the committee's unproved assumption for "The Need for Textual Criticism" (p. 165-166). He declares that "text criticism is mandated" but he does not give a Biblical authority. Somehow, Timothy ministered at Ephesus without a Pauline course in Text Criticism (cf. I Tim. 6:3-5). Instead, textual critics (p. 164-165) and historical evidence mandate the use of Textual Criticism. Since Textual Criticism works for secular literature, "reverent textual criticism" must work "to recover the exact form of words and phrases used in the original" (p. 166). Gephart fails to define historically Textual Criticism and uses it anachronistically for Erasmus and the KJV translators. In contrast to this unproved assumption for the need of Textual Criticism, the Lord promised to preserve all of His Words for every generation to recognize and receive by faith. (Ps. 12:6-7; Jn. 12:48; 17:8, 20). Textual Criticism will never recover what the Lord supposedly chose not to preserve, and has thus far manifested this lack of recovery, and if Textual Critics would ever claim the final restoration of the Lord's text, how would anyone know authoritatively?

A third unproved assumption is that different words in texts and translations do not mean different doctrine. Minnick's chapter on "How Much Difference Do the Differences Make?" (pp. 229-277) is a blatant example. After a series of charts and analysis, Minnick confidently maintains that even though "only a small percentage of variants affect understanding significantly" (p. 270), "not a single variant in any way alters what Christians believe and practice" (p. 271). Yet, how does he know, since the Bible warns about changes through textual and canonical tampering which began to occur in the first century (II Pet. 3:16; II Thess. 2:2; cf. also Dt. 12:32; 13:1-5; Rev. 22:18-19). To prove the worthlessness of his whole chapter, all this reviewer would have to do is add or subtract two words, "no" and "not," to Minnick's concluding arguments on pages 271-272, and thereby change his position to say exactly the opposite of what he wants to say (2 words out of 497 words or .004 difference!).

Uncertain "Certainty"

Williams bemoans the fact "that such large numbers of Americans have lost that confidence in the Bible as the inerrant Word of God" (p. xi). He fails to give the primary reason for this loss of confidence among Americans, which is the multiplication of translations, including the NASV. When options occur and there is no absolute authority, uncertainty arises. *GWOH* argues that the final authority for the best translation American fundamental Christians should use should be fundamentalist leaders and their "totality of manuscripts" view. Harding presents this position of "certainty" (p. 336 ff.) based on the totality of manuscripts view (p. 343), which leads to uncertainty since no one knows which words are the final absolute authority. This uncertain "certainty" position of Harding and company is in contrast with what Solomon told his understudy: *"Have not I written to thee excellent things in counsels and knowledge, That I might make thee know the **certainty of the words of truth;** that thou mightest answer the words of truth to them that send unto thee? "* (Prov. 22:20-21).

Academic Agenda

Since this book represents at least ten Bible colleges and seminaries (p. iv), there seems to be an academic agenda behind *GWOH*. All of these schools would claim to be in the mainstream of historic fundamentalism and consequently need the support of fundamental churches and parents to send their fundamental "preacher boys" to them for theological education. This of course puts the contributors of *GWOH* in an awkward and unenviable position. Most fundamental churches in America, especially independent Baptist churches, still believe in and preach and teach from the KJV. This coalition of ten schools must convince these pastors and parents that the NASV is a viable option to the KJV, that their professors are orthodox even if they teach from the NASV, that there is really no difference between the NASV and the KJV, that they should not listen to the KJV Only "nay-sayers," and that their preacher boys will be indoctrinated in "the science of textual criticism" and ultimately reject their respective pastors' and parents' KJV Only "mentality."

While dealing with academia, this reviewer noticed several unusual expressions. There seems to be an inference that some of the writers have a loose understanding of what inspired means or to what it refers (p. 3). The terms "balanced" and "orthodox" permeate this volume and are defined from their perspective as referring to *GWOH*'s unproved view of preservation (p. 3). Furthermore, the committee asserts that the "third heaven" is "the eternal abode of God" (p. 92) but Solomon states *"the heaven and heaven of heavens cannot contain thee [God]"* (I Kings 8:27).

Denial of the Means of Preservation

The contributors of *GWOH* perpetuate the mantra that God has not revealed "how" He would preserve His Words (p. xix). The Bible is clear that Israel was the means for preserving the OT (Rom. 3:2) and the NT churches were the means for preserving the OT and NT (Mt. 28:19-20). The authors of *GWOH* have a faulty bibliology because they have a faulty ecclesiology. They hold to the Protestant universal church reforming the Roman Catholic Church (pp. xiii-xiv) which was a "good movement gone bad." They maintain that the Church, "the body of believers called 'the church'" (p.

xiii), must restore (through scholars using Textual Criticism) the Word of God. Their Platonic catholicity (p. 376) in ecclesiology drives their neo-catholic rationalism so that they must have historical proof to believe the doctrine of verbal preservation (cf. Jn. 20:29). Paul Downey chides the KJV Only advocates saying, "The Christian faith has never been a blind fideism, but has always relied on both the revelation of God and empirical evidence" (p. 393). But another Paul says *"(For we walk by faith, not by sight:)"* (II Cor. 5:7).

The Bible teaches that the local, NT immersionist (Baptist) churches must receive and preserve the Words of God. With all deference to lifetime missionary J. B. Williams, the reviewer is amazed that Williams does not understand "the main purpose for the church's existence" (p. xiv; cf. p. 40); he thinks it is merely soul winning. All four Gospels and Acts give the purpose of the Lord's churches and that is the Great Commission which includes evangelism, baptizing, and instructing to observe or "preserve" the Lord's commandments (Mt. 28:19-20). The church, the one with bishops and deacons, and which immerses converts, is the pillar and ground of the truth (I Tim. 3:15). It is the exclusive role of the Lord's candlesticks to work with Him to preserve His Words for future generations (Rev. 22:7-10; cf. also Dan. 12:4, 9). Those outside the Lord's churches have no privilege and no authority to be involved in preserving God's Words (cf. Rev. 2:1 ff.). In understanding and perpetuating "all the counsel of God" (Acts 20:27), scholars who do not have NT church authority are no match for the shepherds of the Lord's flocks and for His sheep (I Jn. 2:20, 27), who hear the Lord's voice (Jn. 10:27).

Conclusion

What the Bible Teaches

The Bible teaches the following truths which *GWOH* mainly rejects, ignores or distorts:

1. God's Words are preserved in Heaven (cf. Ps. 119:89; Dan. 10:21, 11:2 ff.; Amos 1:1; Micah 1:1; Jn. 17:8; Rev. 1:1).
2. God's Words were inspired perfectly in the autographs (II Tim. 3:16-18; II Pet. 1:21).
3. The Lord promised to preserve these inspired Words for each subsequent generation (Ps. 12:6-7; Mt. 24:35).
4. He used the Jews to preserve the OT Scriptures (Rom. 3:2) and the NT candlesticks to preserve the OT and NT Scriptures (Mt. 28:19-20; Rev. 22:7-10).
5. NT churches are to recognize, receive and preserve the Lord's Words (Jn. 17:8, 20; I Thess. 2:13) while rejecting wrested Words (II Pet. 3:16) and forged canons (II Thess. 2:2) offered by Satan (Gen. 3:1 ff.; cf. Dt. 13:1-5). These same churches have recognized the KJV as the Words of God in the English language and have rejected at the same time modern versions, including the NASV, as embracing Gnostic laced readings in both text and translation.
6. The Lord has given His explicit Words of revelation to man in order that man may be able to demonstrate his stewardship with all of God's Words at his respective judgment (Jn. 12:48; Rev. 20:12).
7. The Lord Jesus Christ expects man to receive by faith His revelation and produce accurate translations based on the

Received Bible movement which originated with Him (Jn. 17:8, 20; Rom. 16:25-26; cf. Neh. 8:8).

Final Thoughts

1.   It is apparent that the Biblical doctrine of the preservation of the Words of the Lord Jesus Christ has not been enunciated or elucidated Biblically by many Christian theologians of the past whose writings are extant.

2. Twentieth century historical fundamentalism, for the most part, has failed to study the Scriptures for Christ-honoring bibliology. It is apparent that historic fundamentalism, in doctrine and/or practice, is not necessarily the same as Biblical NT Christianity.

3. In spite of this recent spate of books purporting to espouse "Bible preservation," great confusion has arisen, and therefore fundamental Baptist pastors and parents who uphold the KJV need to study the Scriptures for their defense of the TR and KJV.

4. These same pastors and parents are the target of Critical Text Bible schools who want to change their individual and collective position on Bible texts and translations. The next generation of "preacher boys" is at stake.

5.   The Bible says Christians should have all of the Words of God available in their own hands. *GWOH* says the Bible does not say this and that Christians should not expect to have God's Words in their hands or to think that this really matters anyway.

6. The Christian in his local NT church with the Words of God and the indwelling Holy Spirit has all authority, privilege and

responsibility to reject the best of man's reasoning (e.g., *GWOH*) and receive all of the Lord's Words.

7. The Lord has inspired His *autographa* (II Tim. 3:16-17), promised to preserve all of His Words (Ps. 12:6-7), and commanded believers to make accurate translations (Mt. 28:19-20) based on the Received Bible mindset (Jn. 17:8, 20), which movement He began (cf. Acts 2:41, 8:14, 11:1, 17:11; I Thess. 2:13). The fulfillment of these truths in the English language is the King James Version.

BIBLIOGRAPHY

Kurt Aland, *The Greek New Testament.* NY: United Bible Societies, 1975.

___________ and Barbara Aland, *The Text of the New Testament.* Grand Rapids: Wm. B. Eerdmans Publ. Co., 1987.

Ankerberg, John. "Which English Translation of the Bible is Best for Christian to Use Today?" *The John Ankerberg Show Transcript.* Chattanooga, TN: The Ankerberg Theological Research Institute, 1995.

Archer, Gleason L. *A Survey of Old Testament Introduction* Chicago: Moody Press, 1994.

___________. *Encyclopedia of Bible Difficulties.* Grand Rapids: Zondervan Publ. House, 1982.

___________ and Gregory Chirichigno, *Old Testament Quotations in the New Testament.* Chicago: Moody Press, 1983.

Bainton, Roland. *Here I Stand.* NY: Abingdon Press, 1950.

Barclay, William. *And He Had Compassion.* Valley Forge: Judson Press, 1975.

Barker, Kenneth. *Accuracy Defined and Illustrated.* Colorado Springs: International Bible Society, 1995.

Barr, James. *Fundamentalism.* Philadelphia: The Westminster Press, 1978.

Bauer, Walter, William Arndt and F. Wilbur Gingrich, *A Greek-English Lexicon of the New Testament and Other Early Christian Literature.* Chicago: The University of Chicago Press, 1957.

Beacham, Roy E. and Kevin T. Bauder, eds. *One Bible Only? Examining Exclusive Claims for the King James Bible.* Grand Rapids: Kregel Book Co., 2001.

Bishop, George Sayles. "The Inspiration of the Hebrew Letters and Vowel-Points." *Plains Baptist Challenger* L (July 1991).

Blass, F., and A. Debrunner, *A Greek Grammar of the New Testament and Other Early Christian Literature,* transl. and rev. R. W. Funk. Chicago: University of Chicago Press, 1961.

Brandenburg, Kent, ed. *Thou Shalt Keep Them: A Biblical Theology of the Perfect Preservation of Scripture.* El Sobrante, CA: Pillar & Ground Publ., 2003.

Brooks, Ken. "Seven Fatal Flaws of Fundamentalism." *Emmanuel Baptist Theological Journal* 2, no. 2 (Fall/Winter, 2006).

Brown, Colin, ed. *The New International Dictionary of New Testament Theology,* 3 Vols. Grand Rapids: Zondervan Publ. House, 1979.

Brown, Francis, S. R. Driver and Charles A. Briggs, *The New Brown-Driver-Briggs-Gesenius Hebrew and English Lexicon.* Peabody, MA: Hendrickson Publishers, 1979.

Bryson, Bill. *The Mother Tongue: English & How It Got That Way.* NY: Avon Books, 1993.

Bullinger, E. W. *Figures of Speech used in the Bible. Explained and Illustrated.* Grand Rapids: Baker Book House, 1968 rpt. of 1898 ed.

Burgon, John W. *The Last Twelve Verses of the Gospel According to S. Mark Vindicated Against Recent*

Critical Objectors and Established. London: James Parker and Co., 1871.

__________. *The Revision Revised.* Fort Worth: A. G. Hobbs Publ., 1983 rpt.

Burnett, Stephen G. *From Christian Hebraism to Jewish Studies Johannes Buxtorf (1564-1629) and Hebrew Learning in the Seventeenth Century.* NY: E. J. Brill, 1996.

Buxtorf, John, Jr. *Tractatus de Punctorum Vocalium, et Accentuum, in Libris Veteris Testamenti Hebraicis, Origine, Antiquitata, & Authoritate: opposites Arcano Punctationis Revelato, Ludovici Capeli.* Basil: Martini Wagneri, 1648.

Calvin, John. *Institutes of the Christian Religion*, Vol. I. Grand Rapids: Wm. B. Eerdmans Publ. Co., 1975.

Carson, D. A. *Exegetical Fallacies.* Grand Rapids: Baker Book House, 1984.

__________. *The King James Version Debate: A Plea for Realism.* Grand Rapids: Baker Book House, 1979.

Cheynell, Francis. *The Divine Triunity of the Father, Son, and Holy Spirit: Or, the Blessed Doctrine of the Three Coessentiall Subsistents in the Eternall Godhead Without any Confusion or Division of the Distinct Subsistences, Or Multiplication of the Most Single and Entir.* London: T.R. and E.M., 1650.

Clark, Gordon H. *Logical Criticisms of Textual Criticism.* Jefferson, MD: The Trinity Foundation, 1986.

Clark, Samuel. *The Divine Authority of the Holy Scriptures Asserted in Two Discourses.* London: St. Paul's Church-yard, 1699.

Cloud, David. *Dynamic Equivalency: Death Knell of Pure Scripture*. Oak Harbor, WA: Way of Life Literature, 1990.

__________. *Things Hard to be Understood*: A Handbook of Biblical Difficulties. Port Huron, MI: Way of Life Literature, 2001.

Collett, Sidney. *All About the Bible: Its Origin—Its Language—Its Translation—Its Canon—Its Symbols—Its Inspiration—Its Alleged Errors and Contradictions—Its Plan—Its Science—Its Rivals.* Westwood, NJ: Fleming H. Revell, 1964.

Colwell, E. C. *What is the Best New Testament?* Chicago: University of Chicago Press, 1952.

Combs, William. "The Preservation of Scripture," *Detroit Baptist Seminary Journal* 5 (2000).

Coy, George H. *The Inside Story of the Anglo-American Revised New Testament.* Dallas, OR: Itemizer-Observer, 1973.

Custer, Stewart. *Witness to Christ, A Commentary on Acts.* Greenville: BJU Press, 2000.

Dana, H. E. *The New Testament World.* Nashville: Broadman Press, 1937.

Davis, John. *A Short Translation to the Hebrew Tongue, Being a translation of the Learned John Buxtorfius' epitomi of his Hebrew Grammar: that those which are ignorant of the Latin tongue, may attaine by this English introduction to the knowledge and apprehension of the originall Text of Scripture.* London: Roger Daniel, 1655.

Davis, John J. *Biblical Numerology: A Basic Study of the*

Use of Numbers in the Bible. Grand Rapids: Baker Book House, 1968.

__________. *Paradise to Prison: Studies in Genesis.* Grand Rapids: Baker Book House, 1975.

Driver, S. R. *Notes on the Hebrew Text and Typology of the Books of Samuel.* Oxford: At the Clarendon Press, 1913.

Evans, Craig A. *New International Biblical Commentary, Luke.* Peabody, MA: Hendrickson Publ., 1990.

Evans, R. L. and I. M. Berent. *Fundamentalism: Hazards and Heartbreaks.* La Salle, IL: Open Court, 1988.

Ewert, David. *From Ancient Tablets to Modern Translations.* Grand Rapids: Zondervan Publ. House, 1983.

Ferre, Nels. *The Extreme Center.* Waco, TX: Word Books, Publ. 1973.

Fluegel, Felix, eds. Im. Schmidt and G. Tanger Brunswick. *A Dictionary of the English and German Languages for Home and School.* Brunswick: George Westermann, n.d.

Fowler, E. W. *Evaluating Versions of the New Testament.* Watertown, WI: Maranatha Baptist Press, 1981.

France, R. T., *The Gospel According to Matthew: An Introduction and Commentary.* Grand Rapids: Wm. B. Eerdmans Publ. Co., 1985.

Geldenhuys, Norval *The New International Commentary on the New Testament, The Gospel of Luke.* Grand Rapids: Wm. B. Eerdmans Publ. Co., 1979.

Geisler, N. and W. Nix. *A General Introduction to the Bible.* Chicago: Moody Press, 1986.

Gill, John. *A Dissertation Concerning the Antiquity of the*

Hebrew Language, Letters, Vowel-Points, and Accents. London: G. Keith, 1767.

Govett, Robert. *English Derived from Hebrew; with Glances at Greek and Latin.* London: S. W. Partridge and Co., 1869.

Grisanti, Michael A., ed. *The Bible Version Debate: The Perspective of Central Baptist Theological Seminary.* Plymouth, MN: Central Baptist Theological Seminary, 1997.

Gromacki, Robert. *New Testament Survey.* Grand Rapids: Baker Book House, 1974.

Haik-Vantoura, Suzanne. *The Music of the Bible Revealed.* Berkeley: Bibal Press and King David's Harp, Inc. 1991.

Haley, John W. *Alleged Discrepancies.* Springdale, PA: Whitaker House, n. d.

Harrison, R. K. *Biblical Criticism: Historical, Literary and Textual.* Grand Rapids: Zondervan Publ. House, 1979.

Henry, Matthew. *Commentary on the Whole Bible*, Vol. II. NY: Fleming Revell Co., n.d.

Hills, E. F. *The King James Version Defended!* Des Moines: The Christian Research Press, 1973.

House, Wayne. "Biblical Inspiration in II Tim. 3:16," *Bibliotheca Sacra* 137 (Jan. - Mar., 1980).

Hoskier, H. C. *Codex B and Its Allies: A Study and an Indictment.* London: Bernard Quaritch, 1914.

Huey, F. B. and Bruce Corley. *A Student's Dictionary for Biblical and Theological Studies.* Grand Rapids: Zondervan Publ. House, 1983.

Hunter, A. M. *Introducing New Testament Theology.* Philadelphia: The Westminster Press, 1957.

Jenkens, C. A. *Baptist Doctrines.* Watertown, WI: Baptist Heritage Press, 1989 rpt.

Kaiser, Jr., Walter C., Peter H. Davids, F. F. Bruce, and Manfred T. Brauch. *Hard Sayings of the Bible.* Downers Grove, IL: InterVarsity Press, 1996.

Kautzsch E. and A. E. Cowley, editors. *Gesenius' Hebrew Grammar.* Oxford: At the Clarendon Press, 1970.

Kelly, J. N. D. *Early Christian Doctrines.* London: Adam and Charles Black, 1972.

Kidner, Derek. *Proverbs, An Introduction and Commentary* Downers Grove: InterVarsity Press, 1976.

Kittel, Gerhard, and Gerhard Friedrich, eds. *Theological Dictionary of the New Testament.* Translated and edited by Geoffrey W. Bromiley, 10 Vols. Grand Rapids: Wm. B. Eerdmans Publ. House, 1993.

Kleinknecht, H. "Theos," *Theological Dictionary of the New Testament.* Grand Rapids: Wm. B. Eerdmans Publ. Co., 1985.

Kulus, Chester W. *One Tittle Shall in No Wise Pass: Destroying the Scholarly Myth That God Did Not Inspire the Vowels of the Old Testament.* Newington, CT: Emmanuel Baptist Theological Press, 2009.

__________. *Those So-Called Errors: Debunking the Liberal, New Evangelical, and Fundamentalist Myth that You Should Not Hear, Receive, and Believe All the Numbers of Scripture.* Newington, CT: Emmanuel Baptist Theological Press, 2003.

Lange, Peter. *Commentary on the Holy Scriptures, Matthew.*

Grand Rapids: Zondervan Publ. House, n.d.

Lawlor, G. L. *Almah...Virgin or Young Woman?* Des Plaines, IL: Regular Baptist Press, 1973.

Lenski, R. C. H. *The Interpretation of The Epistle to the Hebrews and The Epistle of James.* Minneapolis: Augsburg Publ. House, 1966.

Levita, Elias. *The Massoreth ha-Massoreth of Elias Levita, Being an Exposition of the Massoretic Notes on the Hebrew Bible, or the Ancient Critical Apparatus of the Old Testament in Hebrew, with an English Translation, and Critical and Explanatory Notes, by Christian D. Ginsburg.* NY: KTAV Publ. House, Inc. 1968.

Lindsell, Harold. *The Battle for the Bible.* Grand Rapids: Zondervan Publ. House, 1979.

Lumpkin, W. L. *Baptist Confessions of Faith.* Valley Forge: Judson Press, 1969.

Luther, Martin. *Werke,* Weimar edition, 34.1, p. 356.

Masterman, E. W. G. "Mustard," *The International Standard Bible Encyclopaedia,* Vol. III. Grand Rapids: Wm. B, Eerdmans Publ. Co., 1939.

Manson, William. *The Moffatt New Testament Commentary, The Gospel of Luke.* London: Hodder and Stoughton, Ltd., 1955.

Maynard, Michael. *A History of the Debate over I John 5:7-8: A Tracing of the Longevity of the Comma Johanneum.* Tempe, AZ: Comma Publ. 1995.

McClintock, John and James Strong, eds. *Cyclopedia of Biblical, Theological, and Ecclesiastical Literature,* 12 Volumes. NY: Harper & Brothers, 1891.

M'Intosh, Hugh. *Is Christ Infallible and the Bible True?*

Minneapolis: Klock & Klock, 1981 rpt.

Merwe (van der), Christo H. J., Jackie A. Naude, and Jan H. Kroeze, *A Biblical Hebrew Reference Grammar.* Sheffield, England: Sheffield Academic Press, 2002.

Metzger, B. M. *A Textual Commentary on the Greek New Testament.* London: United Bible Societies, 1975.

Mickelsen, A. B. *Interpreting the Bible.* Grand Rapids: Wm. B. Eerdmans Publ. Co., 1963.

Miller, Edward. *A Guide to the Textual Criticism of the New Testament.* Collingswood, NJ: Dean Burgon Society, Inc., 1979.

Moncrieff, John. *An Essay on the Antiquity and Utility of the Hebrew Vowel-Points.* London: Whittaker, Treacher, and Arnot, 1833.

Morris, Henry and John Whitcomb. *The Genesis Flood: The Biblical Record and its Scientific Implications.* Philadelphia: The Presbyterian and Reformed Publ. Co., 1961.

Morris, Leon. "Hebrews," *The Expositor's Bible Commentary.* Grand Rapids: Zondervan Publ. House, 1981.

Mounce, William D. *Basics of Biblical Greek: Grammar.* Grand Rapids: Zondervan Publ. House, 1993.

Mozeson, Isaac E. *The Origin of Speeches: Intelligent Design in Language.* Springdale, AR: Lightcatcher Books, 2005.

Nicole, R. "The Nature of Inerrancy," *Inerrancy and Common Sense.* Grand Rapids: Baker Book House, 1980.

Nolan, Frederick. *An Inquiry into the Integrity of the Greek Vulgate or Received Text of the New Testament.* N.P.,

1815.

Norton, Mark. "Manuscripts of the Old Testament," *The Origin of the Bible*, ed. Phillip Comfort. Cambridge: Tyndale House Publ., 1992.

Oehler, Gustave F. *Theology of the Old Testament.* Grand Rapids: Zondervan Publ. House, n.d.

Owen, John. *Biblical Theology. The Nature, Origin, Development, and Study of Theological Truth, in Six Books* Morgan, PA: Soli Deo Gloria Publications, 1996 rpt. of the 1661 ed.

Payne, J. Barton. *The Theology of the Older Testament.* Grand Rapids: Zondervan Publ. House, 1962.

Pickering, Wilbur N. *The Identity of the New Testament Text.* Nashville: Thomas Nelson Publ., 1980.

Pinnock, Clark. "The Evangelical Struggle to Understand the Creation Texts," *The Best in Theology*, Vol. 4. Carol Stream, IL: Christianity Today, Inc., 1990.

Pratico Gary D. and Miles V. Van Pelt. *Basics of Biblical Hebrew Grammar.* Grand Rapids: Zondervan Publ. House, 2001.

Ramm, Bernard. *Protestant Biblical Interpretation.* Grand Rapids: Baker Book House, 1970.

Ramsay, W. M. *Was Christ Born at Bethlehem?* Grand Rapids: Baker Book House, 1979 rpt.

Reeves, Caswell A. *The Doctrine of Heaven's Music.* Endicott, NY: Heritage Baptist Publ., 2013.

Roberts, A. and J. Donaldson. *The Ante-Nicene Fathers*, Vol. III. Grand Rapids: Wm. B. Eerdmans Publ. Co., 1980 rpt.

Robertson, A. T. *Word Pictures in the New Testament*, Vol. I.

Grand Rapids: Baker Book House, 1930.

Rogerson, J. W. and J. W. McKay, *The Cambridge Bible Commentary on the New English Bible, Psalms 1-50.* Cambridge: Cambridge University Press, 1977.

Ruckman, Peter. *The Monarch of Books.* Pensacola, FL: Pensacola Bible Institute, 1973.

Ryrie, C. C. *Biblical Theology of the New Testament.* Chicago: Moody Press, 1973.

Sailhamer, John H. *Genesis, The Expositor's Bible Commentary*, Vol. 2. Grand Rapids: Zondervan Publ. House, 1990.

Schmidt, W. H. *Old Testament Introduction.*   NY: Crossroad Publ. Co., 1984.

Schnaiter, Sam and Ron Tagliapietra. *Bible Preservation and the Providence of God.* Philadelphia: Xlibris Corp., 2002.

Scrivener, Frederick H. A. *A Plain Introduction to the Criticism of the New Testament.*   4th ed.   Edited by E. Miller.   2 Vols.   London: George Bell and Sons, 1894.

__________. *Scrivener's Annotated Greek New Testament: Being the Exact Greek Textus Receptus that Underlies the King James Bible.* Collingswood, NJ: Dean Burgon Society Press, 1999.

Smith, Miles. "The Translators to the Reader," *The Holy Bible, 1611 Edition, King James Version.* Nashville: Thomas Nelson Publ., 1982.

Spong, J. S. *Rescuing the Bible from Fundamentalism.*   NY: Harper Collins Publ., 1991.

Sproul, Michael D. *God's Word Preserved: A Defense of*

Historic Separatist Definitions and Beliefs. Tempe, AZ: Whetstone Precepts Press, 2007.

Spurgeon, C. H. *The Metropolitan Tabernacle Pulpit*, Vol. 35. Pasadena, TX: Pilgrim Publ., 1972.

Stein, Robert H. *The New American Commentary, Luke*. Nashville, Broadman Press, 1992.

Stibbs, A. *The First Epistle General of Peter*. Grand Rapids: Wm. B. Eerdmans Publ. Co., 1978.

Strong, Augustus. H. *Systematic Theology*. Valley Forge, PA: Judson Press, 1907.

Strouse, Thomas M. *An Exegesis of Psalms 1-41*. Newington, CT: Emmanuel Baptist Theological Press, 2006.

__________. *An Exegesis of Psalm 119*. Newington, CT: Emmanuel Baptist Publ., 2008.

__________. *But Daniel Purposed in His Heart. An Exegetical Commentary on Daniel*. Cromwell, CT: Bible Baptist Theological Press, 2013 revised.

__________. *But God Meant it for Good: An Exegetical Commentary on Genesis*. Cromwell, CT: Bible Baptist Theological Seminary, 2012 revised.

__________. *Christ Also Suffered for Us. The Theology of the Petrine Epistles*. Cromwell, CT: Bible Baptist Theological Press, 2013.

__________. "Christ's Use of Targums." *Emmanuel Baptist Theological Journal* 3, no. 1 (Spring 2007).

__________. *En Epheso. An Exegetical Commentary on the Epistle to the Ephesians*. Newington, CT: Emmanuel Baptist Publ., 2009.

__________. "Geocentricity: A Case Study in Bibliology." *Emmanuel Baptist Theological Journal* 2, no. 2

(Fall/Winter 2006).

__________. *Having then Gifts. A Practical Guide to Spiritual Gifts.* Cromwell, CT: Bible Baptist Theological Press, 2015 revised.

__________. *He Maketh His Sun To Rise. A Look at Biblical Geocentricity.* Cromwell, CT: Bible Baptist Theological Seminary, 2010.

__________. *I Will Build My Church. The Doctrine and History of Baptists.* Cromwell, CT: Bible Baptist Theological Seminary, 2013 revised.

__________. "Luke 16:17—One Tittle," *Emmanuel Baptist Theological Journal* 2, no. 1 (Spring 2006).

__________ and Jeffrey Khoo. *Reviews of the book From the Mind of God to the Mind of Man.* Pensacola: Pensacola Theological Seminary, 2001.

__________. "Scholarly Myths Perpetuated on Rejecting the Masoretic Text of the Old Testament," *Emmanuel Baptist Theological Journal* 1, no. 1 (Spring 2005).

__________. "Should Fundamentalists Use the NASV? *Sound Words from New England* 2:1 (July-August, 2001).

__________. *Sound Doctrine. The Theology of I and II Timothy.* Cromwell, CT: Bible Baptist Theological Press, 2014 revised.

__________. "The Permanent Preservation of God's Words, Psalm 12:6-7," Kent Brandenburg, ed. *Thou Shalt Keep Them. A Biblical Theology of the Perfect Preservation of Scripture.* El Sobrante, CA: Pillar & Ground Publ., 2003.

__________. *To the Seven Churches: A Commentary on the*

Apocalypse of Jesus Christ. Cromwell, CT: Bible Baptist Theological Seminary, 2013.

__________. *To Wait for His Son From Heaven. A Commentary on I and II Thessalonians.* Cromwell, CT: Bible Baptist Theological Press, 2014 revision.

__________. "Who is this Deity named Yahweh?" *The Biblical Astronomer* 15 (Winter 2005).

__________. "Ye are the Body of Christ," *Emmanuel Baptist Theological Journal* 2 (Fall 2005).

__________. "Ye Hold the Tradition of Men," *Emmanuel Baptist Theological Journal* 2, no. 1 (Spring: 2006).

Strouse, W. Aaron. "A Critique of Historical Fundamentalism." *Emmanuel Baptist Theological Journal* 2, no. 2 (Fall/Winter 2006).

Surrett, Charles L. *Which Greek Text? The Debate among Fundamentalists.* Kings Mountain, NC: Surrett Family Publ., 1999.

Teachout, Robert. *Wine, The Biblical Imperative: Total Abstinence.* Allen Park, MI: Robt. Teachout, 1986.

Thackeray, H. S. J., "Septuagint," *The International Standard Bible Encyclopaedia*, Volume IV. Grand Rapids: Wm. B. Eerdmans Publ., 1939.

Thayer, J. H. *Greek-English Lexicon of the New Testament.* Grand Rapids: Zondervan Publ. House, 1970.

Thiessen, H. *Lectures in Systematic Theology.* Grand Rapids: Wm. B. Eerdmans Publ. Co., 1983.

Tillich, Paul. *Systematic Theology.* Digswell, England: James Nisbet and Co., Ltd., 1968.

Toussaint, S. D. *Behold the King.* Portland, OR: Multnomah Press, 1980.

Unger, Merrill. *Archeology and the Old Testament.* Grand Rapids: Zondervan Publ. House, 1973.

__________. *Introductory Guide to the Old Testament.* Grand Rapids: Zondervan Publ. House, 1951.

__________. *Unger's Bible Dictionary* (Chicago: Moody Press, 1972.

Van Bruggen. Jakob. *The Ancient Text of the New Testament.* Winnipeg, Canada: Premier, 1976.

Vance, Laurence M. *Archaic Words and the Authorized Version.* Pensacola: Vance Publications, 1999.

Waite, D. A. *Defending the King James Version.* Collingswood, NJ: The Bible for Today Press, 1992.

Wallace, Daniel B. *The Basics of New Testament Syntax: An Intermediate Greek Grammar.* Grand Rapids: Zondervan Publ. House, 2000.

Waltke, Bruce K. and M. O'Connor. *An Introduction to Biblical Hebrew Syntax.* Winona Lake, IN: Eisenbraus, 1990.

__________. "The Textual Criticism of the Old Testament," *The Gaebelein Bible Commentary,* Vol. I. Grand Rapids: Zondervan Publ. House, 1987.

Weemes, John. *The Christian Synagogue: Wherein is contained the diverse Reading, The right Pointing, Translation, and Collation of Scripture with Scripture.* London: T. and B. Gates, 1630.

White, James R. *The King James Only Controversy: Can You Trust the Modern Versions?* Minneapolis: Bethany House Publ., 1995.

Whitfield, Peter. *A dissertation on the Hebrew vowel-points. Shewing that they are an original and essential part of the language.*   Liverpoole: Peter Whitfield, 1748.

Wight, Fred H.   *Manners and Customs of the Bible Lands.*   Chicago: Moody Press, 1953.

Williams, James B., ed.   *From the Mind of God to the Mind of Man: A Layman's Guide to How We Got Our Bible.*   Greenville, SC: Ambassador-Emerald International, 1999.

__________ and Randolph Shaylor, eds.   *God's Word in Our Hands: The Bible Preserved for Us* Greenville, SC: Ambassador-Emerald International, 2003.

Wilson, Robert Dick.   *A Scientific Investigation of the Old Testament.*   Revised by Edward J. Young.   Chicago: Moody Press, 1959.

Wood, John Turtle.   *Modern Discoveries on the Site of Ancient Ephesus.*   Charleston, SC: Nabu Press, 2010 rpt. of 1923 ed.

Wood, Leon.   *Distressing Days of the Judges.*   Grand Rapids: Zondervan Publ. House, 1976.

Wurthwein, E.   *The Text of the Old Testament.*   Grand Rapids: Wm. B. Eerdmans Publ. Co., 1981.

Yates, Kyle M. *The Essentials of Biblical Hebrew.* NY: Harper and Row, Publ. 1938.

Finis